I0811987

STUDIES IN IMPERIALISM

General editor: Andrew S. Thompson

Founding editor: John M. MacKenzie

When the 'Studies in Imperialism' series was founded by Professor John M. MacKenzie more than thirty years ago, emphasis was laid upon the conviction that 'imperialism as a cultural phenomenon had as significant an effect on the dominant as on the subordinate societies'. With well over a hundred titles now published, this remains the prime concern of the series. Cross-disciplinary work has indeed appeared covering the full spectrum of cultural phenomena, as well as examining aspects of gender and sex, frontiers and law, science and the environment, language and literature, migration and patriotic societies, and much else. Moreover, the series has always wished to present comparative work on European and American imperialism, and particularly welcomes the submission of books in these areas. The fascination with imperialism, in all its aspects, shows no sign of abating, and this series will continue to lead the way in encouraging the widest possible range of studies in the field. 'Studies in Imperialism' is fully organic in its development, always seeking to be at the cutting edge, responding to the latest interests of scholars and the needs of this ever-expanding area of scholarship.

Imperium of the soul

MANCHESTER
1824
Manchester University Press

SELECTED TITLES AVAILABLE IN THE SERIES

WRITING IMPERIAL HISTORIES
ed. Andrew S. Thompson

EMPIRE OF SCHOLARS
Tamson Pietsch

HISTORY, HERITAGE AND COLONIALISM
Kynan Gentry

COUNTRY HOUSES AND THE BRITISH EMPIRE
Stephanie Barczewski

THE RELIC STATE
Pamila Gupta

WE ARE NO LONGER IN FRANCE
Allison Drew

THE SUPPRESSION OF THE ATLANTIC SLAVE TRADE
ed. Robert Burroughs and Richard Huzzey

HEROIC IMPERIALISTS IN AFRICA
Berny Sèbe

Imperium of the soul

THE POLITICAL AND AESTHETIC IMAGINATION OF EDWARDIAN IMPERIALISTS

Norman Etherington

MANCHESTER UNIVERSITY PRESS

Published by Manchester University Press
Altrincham Street, Manchester M1 7JA
www.manchesteruniversitypress.co.uk

British Library Cataloguing-in-Publication Data
A catalogue record for this book is available from the British Library

Library of Congress Cataloging-in-Publication Data applied for

ISBN 978 1 5261 0605 6 hardback

First published 2017

ISBN 978 1 5261 0606 3 paperback

First published 2018

Typeset by Out of House Publishing
Printed and bound by
CPI Group (UK) Ltd, Croydon, CR0 4YY

CONTENTS

FIGURES

PREFACE AND ACKNOWLEDGEMENTS

Research I undertook years ago into the South African career of the novelist H. Rider Haggard convinced me that his most significant literary work could not be separated from his conservative, imperialist convictions. Most of his twentieth-century admirers denied this necessary connection because his political views had fallen out of favour. On my reckoning it was precisely the connection he made between personal and imperial politics that lifted his novels above the level of pedestrian conservative apologetics. A plethora of evidence attests that Haggard viewed the depths of his own psyche as a tumultuous cauldron of savage desires that needed to be kept under control at all costs. His faultless external presentation as the epitome of an English country gentleman sustained the illusion that he had succeeded; the content of his fiction proved he had not. His novels and stories lead gentlemen adventurers like himself into undiscovered lands, lost worlds and underground cities, where destructive passions, sexual deviance, murderous sibling rivalries and cannibalism erupt on an epic scale. Unsettled by a world turned upside down, Haggard's heroes very nearly succumb to strange desires and savage bloodlust. After desperate battles, order is restored and gentlemen return exhilarated, but unscathed, to their estates, their fortunes and their London clubs.

Haggard's imperial politics evoked an analogous struggle to impose order and civilisation on disruptive, deeply fascinating savages. Broadly speaking, this was not a novel view. Themistius, a Roman philosopher in the service of the Emperor Valens, remarked eighteen hundred years ago, 'there is in each of us a barbarian tribe extremely overbearing and intractable – I mean temper and those insatiable desires which stand opposed to rationality as Scythians and Germans do to the Romans'.[1] However, the ancient concept of the duality of man was given a powerful new twist by developments in the nineteenth century. Darwin's theory of evolution challenged both the Roman concept that stern self-discipline could efface the disordered internal savage and the Christian notion that the parental rod could beat the devil out of the wayward child. As part of a primate genus shaped over millions of years, it seemed highly unlikely that the barbarian within us could be purged. Disciplined suppression was the most that could be hoped for.

Born in 1856, Haggard belonged to the first generation of educated Europeans to grow up taking the truth of Darwin's theory for granted.

So did Sigmund Freud, born just a few weeks earlier. His theory of the psyche divided vertically into superego, ego and id was elaborated in far more intricate detail, but in its general outlines it corresponded to Haggard's model. Freud's id, buried deep in the subconscious mind, was the fount of the polymorphously perverse impulses and desires that so powerfully stirred the novelist's imagination. It was not, therefore, remarkable that Haggard's fiction should in turn have stimulated Freud, working its way into the psychologist's dreams as well as the advice he gave to patients on his famous couch. My explanation for the aesthetic force of Haggard's best-selling fiction – the factor that enabled it to rise above the limitations of his often pedestrian prose style – is the dynamic tension he created between the civilised imperative to put down savage customs and the countervailing desire to dive into the world of savagery. This gave his imperialism a psychological poetics. It could not simply be an affair of dispossessing or exterminating lesser beings. The imperial subject was no more capable of elimination than the wild man within. Each possessed a powerful transgressive potential that fascinated even as it repelled.

When I published my thoughts on Haggard in *Victorian Studies* in 1978, scholarly literature on the novelist was meagre. Since then it has expanded enormously, as a tributary of an ever-swelling river of publications on the relations between arts, culture and imperialism. During those thirty years we have passed through a number of revolutions in historiography and critical theory, in the course of which other writers found their own ways to some of my insights. To clearly indicate my starting point, I reprint my original essay in Chapter 1 exactly as it was written, apart from some additional notes. Readers can thus form their own opinions about where my work sits in the larger trajectory of imperial and literary studies.

Encouraged by the favourable reception accorded to that first article I set out to expand the scope of my research by finding others of the same generation whose aesthetic achievements might have been similarly linked to their conservative imperialist political views. John Buchan seemed a good follow-up case. A conservative politician who rose to be governor-general of Canada, he began to write novels of imperial adventure about the time Freud emerged as a celebrity psychologist on the world stage. If my surmise was correct, he was bound at some point to notice Freud in his fiction. And so it proved to be. Although I presented my paper to the incredibly stimulating seminar on Southern African Studies then presided over by Shula Marks at the Institute of Commonwealth Studies, I chose not to revise it for publication to a wider audience. By that time I had grown so fond of my investigation that I decided to refrain from publishing that or any of my subsequent essays until they could form linked chapters in a completed book. It has been some time in coming. Other projects got in the way, notably nine other books between 1978 and 2008. As invitations to write multiplied, I tended for better or worse to choose the bird in the hand with a guaranteed publisher and inflexible deadline over the elusive peacock lurking in the bushland of my imagination.

Selection of further artists for study proved no easy task. To fit the bill they needed to belong to the generation born between Freud and Buchan, to have been imperialist and conservative in their political opinions, to have been recognised for significant aesthetic achievements and to have dealt with my major theme: the invocation of the imperial vs savage metaphor in relation to the psyche. Captain Marryat (1792–1848), R. M. Ballantyne (1825–94) and G. A. Henty (1832–1902), who dealt with imperial themes and rivalled Haggard in the popularity of their books for boys, were born too early and are seldom praised for their artistic quality. Moreover, their fiction lacks the dramatic contrasts between the outer and inner existences of major characters that distinguished the works that resonated with Freudian theory. Henty's colonial settings operate as tests of character in which the inborn, unwavering gentlemanly virtues of his young heroes emerge under fire. Greater literary figures of the previous generation with strong links to imperial politics and patriotism such as Edward Bulwer Lytton (1803–73), Benjamin Disraeli (1804–81) and Lord Tennyson (1809–92) seldom took their characters into colonial settings and were likewise outside my time frame, though their legacy of romantic conservatism left its traces on the work of several of the artists who did make my list. Among visual artists, Frederic Leighton (1830–96), though considerably older than Haggard, drew my attention by the techniques he used to subject exotic themes to an overriding order in the design of his London studio, as well as by his Liberal Unionist politics and fascination with the Roman Empire.[2] It is difficult, however, to find in any of his academic paintings the dynamic tension between imperial overrule and barbarian insurgence that I wished to explore. Insofar as he operated to domesticate the exotic for refined British audiences, his work resembled that of his contemporary, Lockwood Kipling (1837–1911), who so spectacularly incorporated an Indian-themed Durbar Room into Osborne House, Queen Victoria's Italianate mansion on the Isle of Wight.[3] A former colleague, D. R. Hainsworth, called my attention to two other visual artists who might satisfy my criteria. It would have been satisfying to add the war and history painter, Elizabeth Thompson, Lady Butler (1846–1933), to my collection, not least because so few Victorian women possessed her aesthetic, political and imperial qualifications. However, it proved difficult to find in any of her work much if any engagement with the enemy or the savage.[4] For example, her *Defence of Rorke's Drift* took her deep into Haggard's Zululand. Yet in her depiction of the battle, a shaft of sunlight brilliantly illuminates the embattled British defenders, while leaving the Zulu foes barely discernible in the surrounding gloom. Hainsworth's other suggestion, architect Edwin Lutyens (1869–1944), came very close to meeting my needs. The right age, unquestionably a talent of the first rank and an ardent imperialist, he married a daughter of Edward Robert Bulwer-Lytton, viceroy of India, and went on to design the viceregal palace in New Delhi. His transition from Arts and Crafts, period house design to fervent, inventive classicism paralleled his professional involvement with the Empire. The trouble was that, apart from the viceroy's residence, which includes some highly stylised and abstract forms drawn from Indian architecture, Lutyens' later work does not engage the Empire's subject peoples, as it might have done by subordinating indigenous or primitive elements within his classical frame. It is all imperial overrule without a countervailing insurgency. That I would eventually find in Herbert Baker (1862–1946), his collaborator in the planning of the capital at New Delhi – which brings me at length to those who did make my list.

Like Haggard and Buchan, Baker got his first taste of imperial adventure in South Africa, when he was abruptly catapulted to celebrity as the architect chosen in 1893 by mining magnate Cecil Rhodes to remodel his Cape Town mansion at Groote Schuur. Baker's personal reserve, amounting sometimes to an awkward, tongue-tied silence, and his unwillingness to speak at all of his inner being set him apart from the impish, extroverted Lutyens. He threw himself enthusiastically into the cause of empire as one of the brilliant young men around High Commissioner Alfred Milner, who restructured the political and physical landscape of South Africa in the wake of the Boer War. As the oldest of 'Milner's Kindergarten', Baker came to know John Buchan, who captured the can-do atmosphere of their circle so perfectly in his novel of political ideas, *A Lodge in the Wilderness*. On first inspection Baker's great imperial commissions – Rhodes Memorial, Pretoria's Union Buildings and the Secretariat Buildings in New Delhi – did not present the aesthetic I was looking for. Their classicism overpowers the appropriated indigenous elements that Baker used to signal the comprehensive triumph of a new imperial order. It was only when I began to pay attention to their siting that I found my theme. Inspired by my teacher in architectural history at Yale, Vincent Scully, who first opened my eyes to the interplay between Greek temples and their surroundings, I began to see how Baker learned to project imperial power through theatrical positioning that pitted his buildings against the whole vastness of Africa. The landscape itself supplied the insurgent forces that Baker's classical order strove to command. This in turn suggested an answer to the question of why he so spectacularly fell out with Lutyens when they collaborated in the planning of New Delhi.[5]

Constructing an historical argument from visual evidence poses special difficulties. An invitation from Ian Phimister to reside as a visiting scholar at the University of Cape Town in the early 1990s helped me surmount some of these by giving me access to the records of Baker's architectural practice in the Centre for African Studies. Far more challenging was the employment of musical material in the study of Edward Elgar, who was first suggested to me by Professor Hal Bolitho of Harvard. Elgar ought to have been obvious. Just a year younger than Haggard and Freud, no figure in the history of music is so comprehensively identified with the British Empire, for which his 'Pomp and Circumstance March No. 1' has long served as an unofficial anthem. Precisely because the non-musical evidence for Elgar's political conservatism and imperialism is so overwhelming, his twentieth-century admirers – notably the film-maker, Ken Russell – went to extraordinary lengths to deny that his opinions were more than incidental to his musical opus. Elgar spoke of his aspiration to write a symphony that would invoke the career of General Charles George Gordon, whose death at the hands of Mahdist insurgents at Khartoum in 1885 ranked with the defence of Rorke's Drift and the Relief of Mafeking as a defining icon for late-Victorian British imperial sentiment. For a Roman Catholic composer, the vision of Gordon devoting his nighttime hours in Khartoum to annotating Cardinal Newman's religious poem, *The Dream of Gerontius*, presented tremendous possibilities. Although most musicologists assert that Elgar never accomplished his intention, what a symphony it would have been to illustrate my central theme: the square-jawed imperial hero simultaneously fending off external Mahdists and interior demons. One Elgar scholar, David Cox, has ventured a guess that the Symphony No. 1, which received its premier in 1908, realised some of what might have gone into a Gordon symphony.[6] Chapter 5 argues that the first symphony does indeed fit my imperial political and psychological paradigm. The method employed here is to use motifs Elgar used in compositions with words in order to propose an interpretation of a wordless symphony – one that the composer insisted had no programme apart from 'a wide experience of human life with a great charity (love) and a massive hope in the future'.[7] I place this chapter late in the book in the hope that by that point I may have won readers' assent to the broader argument, which would incline them to be more receptive to a case that rests mainly on musical evidence.

An entirely different set of problems arose when I turned my attention to Joseph Conrad and Rudyard Kipling, writers who had been on my agenda from the outset. A mountain of work had already been published; even as I read my way into it, new work kept rolling off the presses. Historians labour under a self-imposed masochistic professional code that requires us to read everything previously written on the subject, including unpublished dissertations. One beneficial consequence of struggling to keep up was getting in touch with the sharp critical minds drawn to these major figures within the field of English literature. Reassessments inspired by Edward Said's *Orientalism* and the development of postcolonialism from its original narrow base in Commonwealth literary studies expanded my mind without, so far as I am aware, replicating my argument. An ongoing challenge has been the continued mainstream assumption – based primarily on the novella *Heart of Darkness* – that Conrad was an anti-imperialist – which means he does not belong in this book. The growing minority who take the opposite point of view have benefited hugely from new biographical work exposing the process by which the aristocratic Jozef Korzeniowski turned himself into plain Captain Joseph Conrad.[8] This enables *Heart of Darkness* to be read as an Oedipal assault on the liberal idealism of his revolutionary father. In contrast, new work on Kipling's fiction and poetry has brought to light his underlying scepticism about the prospects for the imperialism he so enthusiastically embraced in public life. Faced with such an embarrassment of riches, I wrote far too much. The chapters on Conrad and Kipling that appear in this volume represent the distilled essence of many trials over a period of twenty years.

In addition to debts already acknowledged, I owe a great deal to my mentor in British Empire history, the late Robin Winks, who introduced me to John Buchan; to Robert Grant Irving, who generously shared his research on Herbert Baker; to the late Jeff Guy, Professor of History at the University of KwaZulu-Natal, who rekindled my interest in Rider Haggard during our joint explorations of Zululand; to Walter Reed of Emory University, whose conversations on psychoanalysis and literature enlivened my early researches; to Bruce Mazlish of MIT and Martin Green at Tufts, who encouraged me to push on when doubts assailed me. Most of all I thank all those friends who endlessly scolded me for not getting on with the book: Robert Dare, David Dolan, Margaret Lalchere, Nelson Luria and my wife Peggy. I am especially grateful that my sons Nathan and Ben reached maturity quickly enough in their respective architectural, musical and literary careers to offer sound professional advice to the old man.

Notes

1 Peter Heather, 'The barbarian in late antiquity: image, reality, and transformation', in Richard Miles (ed.), *Constructing Identities in Late Antiquity* (London: Routledge, 1999), p. 236.

2 Furthermore, the Islamic art Leighton installed was itself the result of imperial plunder; see John M. MacKenzie, *Orientalism: History, Theory and the Arts* (Manchester: Manchester University Press, 1995), p. 82.

3 Other candidates were suggested by Thomas Metcalf's brilliant exploration of Indo-Saracenic buildings in *An Imperial Vision: Indian Architecture and Britain's Raj* (Berkeley: University of California Press, 1989), pp. 55–90, but none quite fit my mould.

4 Her neglect of the savage foe is odd, considering that the sympathies of her general officer husband, W. F. Butler, were said by fellow soldiers to be generally 'with the other side'. See the discussion of husband and wife by J. O. Springhall, ' "Up guards and at them!": British imperialism and popular art, 1880–1914', in J. M. MacKenzie (ed.), *Imperialism and Popular Culture* (Manchester: Manchester University Press, 1986), pp. 63–8.

5 The controversy is delightfully set out by my old friend, Robert Grant Irving, in *Indian Summer: Lutyens, Baker, and Imperial Delhi* (New Haven, CT: Yale University Press, 1981).

6 David Cox, 'Edward Elgar', in Robert Simpson (ed.) *The Symphony, Vol. II: Mahler to the Present Day* (London: David & Charles, 1970), pp. 15–28.

7 Percy Young, *Letters of E. Elgar and Other Writings* (London: Geoffrey Bles, 1956), p. xvii.

8 Especially Zdzislaw Najder, *Joseph Conrad: A Chronicle* (New Brunswick, NJ: Rutgers University Press, 1983).

Introduction

Let me begin by summarising the argument of this book in one paragraph. The first generation of European intellectuals to encounter Darwin's *The Origin of Species* grew up with a radically altered view of human nature. Accepting the animal basis of existence carried the implication that inner urges to rage, fight, pillage and rape were not the snares of the devil but biologically inescapable attributes of the human condition born of the age-old struggle for existence. One of that generation, Sigmund Freud, built a new model of the psyche and society on that premise. On his reckoning civilisation itself depended on the effective repression of the wild and potentially destructive impulses of the inner self. Others born about the same time saw parallels between the mission of imperialism to subdue savage peoples and the civilised individual's need to keep a lid on the savage urges welling up from within. A number of conservative imperialists active in the creative arts exploited that parallel in works whose aesthetic power arises from the contest between the order they upheld in their politics and the countervailing forces of savagery: a contest whose outcome is always in doubt until the last moment, partly because the agents of rebellion and disorder exercise such a weirdly compelling attraction. Joseph Conrad would term this 'the fascination of the abomination'. A subsidiary argument is that the exaggerated conservatism in politics and dress affected by these artists betrayed an outsized anxiety about succumbing to the disruptive, disorderly forces harboured deep within their being. A recurring theme in the creative work of the Edwardian imperialists is the white man with the ability to enter so completely into the inner world of subject peoples that he becomes one with them. When they encountered a real-life war hero, T. E. Lawrence, who appeared to have lived out that fantasy, they sought him out and hailed him as the saviour of empire. His refusal to play the role expected of him exposed the fallacy in the analogy they had drawn between the practice of imperialism and the individual superego's struggle to command the unruly id that lurked within the psyche.

While this study necessarily ranges across the subject matter of several disciplines, I approach my subject matter primarily as a historian of ideas, economics and politics, paying little attention to the rules that govern professional writing for literary scholars, musicologists, psychoanalysts or architects. Literary critics may well reproach me for flirting with what they call the intentional fallacy in my treatment of fiction; the musicologists and architects, for departing from the canons of formal analysis; and the psychoanalysts, for treating Freudian theory as an historical artefact rather than a demonstrable body of knowledge. My defence is that I do not aim to make substantive contributions to any of those disciplines.

Scholars of the new field of masculinity studies may find the book useful because of the very masculine character of the Edwardian imperialists and their creative works.[1] Significantly, no woman figures as the central subject of any work by these men; when women do appear they figure as objects of desire, matrons or creatures requiring protection. Even the architect Herbert Baker took scant notice of women or their domestic sphere in his buildings. On the other hand, the masculine pursuits of hunting, fishing, fighting, ruling, sailing and exploring are prominent themes. There is, moreover, no female counterpart to the late-Victorian and Edwardian literature of exotic adventure for reasons that have yet to be adequately explicated.

It should be emphasised that the book makes no claim to explain everything about the work of the artists selected for study. Its modest and limited aim is to point out that at the turn of the twentieth century the idea of imperialism resonated with the new concept of the divided psyche that Freud did so much to popularise. This gave some members of Freud's generation extra-political motivations to explore the ramifications of imperialism in creative work. The best of that work operates at a different level from the straightforward political tract. That does not, however, mean that these creations had nothing to do with the culture of imperialism. Otherwise they would not have been so popular. That they outshone simpler invocations of imperial patriotism demonstrates that the culture of imperialism was itself a complex affair. The disturbing, yet oddly thrilling idea that ordinary Americans and Europeans harboured secret, subversive inner selves that required repression akin to that inflicted on far-flung subject peoples undermined the pseudo-scientific doctrines that trumpeted the superiority of a pure white race. As Lionel Trilling put it, Freud had discovered that man contained 'a kind of hell within him from which rise everlastingly the impulses which threaten his civilization'.[2] Imagining that a dark racial stranger seething with animal passions lurked in a hidden corner of one's own being must unsettle the most outwardly self-assured white supremacist. Adolf Hitler admitted as much when he asked his table talk circle if it had ever occurred to them that the Nazi project extended to killing the Jew within themselves.

It was, of course, possible for artists to take dramatically different attitudes to imperialism as a metaphor for the suppression of a turbulent inner self. Instead of agreeing with Freud that civilisation required repression of the id, an artist might be inclined instead to forget civilisation and let the inner savage out. This proposition operates as a key marker of modernism in early-twentieth-century art. Picasso sought out the primitive in the form of African masks and fitted them to the faces of his *Demoiselles d'Avignon*. He portrayed himself as a bull and a goat. James Joyce tried to render without moral judgement the soundless stream of disconnected thoughts and words that ran through the minds of characters in his *Ulysses*. Stravinsky unleashed torrents of frenzied rhythm in *Rite of Spring*. Darius Milhaud used the jazz idioms born in Chicago, New Orleans and Harlem to invoke *La Creation du Monde*. Conservatives and imperialists did not supply much of the audience for such experiments (unlike Fascists, who conducted some well-known flirtations with modernism). Modernist tastes in art more commonly ran alongside support for internationalism and sympathy for colonised peoples.

The subjects of this book personally set their faces against modernism. That does not mean they were uninterested in innovation and experimentation. Various critics have called attention to modernist elements in the work of Conrad, Baker, Kipling and Elgar. The men themselves, however, all proclaimed in various ways their hostility to modernism. Buchan found 'the rebels and experimentalists for the most part left me cold'.[3] When Conrad beheld the collection of impressionist and post-impressionist paintings hanging in the apartment of Van Gogh's friend, Paul Gachet, he thought them the products of a lunatic asylum.[4] Elgar showed no interest in Stravinsky; he turned down invitations to meet Schoenberg and Ravel.[5] Having found classicism, Herbert Baker sought no further revelations and, as a result, found himself scorned as a vandal and a man of the past by architectural historian, Nikolaus Pevsner, Britain's self-appointed champion of modernism. This shared antipathy to the avant-garde was a matter of temperament rather than age. The post-impressionists were their contemporaries. Frank Lloyd Wright was only five years Baker's junior and came out of the same Arts and Crafts movement, yet struck out in dramatic new directions after 1900. Leoš Janáček, three years older than Elgar, emerged from the chrysalis of Czech musical nationalism as a modernist butterfly.

This raises the question of personality as a possible common thread linking their approach to imperialism, politics and creative work. Friends and acquaintances universally remarked on their reserved and undemonstrative demeanour. And while it is no surprise to find them photographed in the fashions of their time, they all incline towards an excessive gentlemanly punctiliousness in dress. All acquired country properties where they appeared to live like landed gentry (although only Haggard went in for practical agriculture). Conrad revelled in his Elizabethan residence, where he 'could feel like a country squire, master of his small manor house'.[6] Sculptor Jacob Epstein objected to depictions of Conrad as 'an open-necked, romantic, out-of-door type of person': 'In appearance Conrad was the very opposite. His clothes were immaculately conventional, and his collar enclosed his neck like an Iron Maiden's vice or garrotter's grip. He was worried if his hair and beard were not trim and neat as became a sea captain. There was nothing shaggy or Bohemian about him.'[7] Elgar flummoxed young Arnold Bax on their first meeting: 'Hatless, dressed in rough tweeds and riding boots, his appearance was rather that of a retired army officer turned gentleman farmer than an eminent and almost morbidly highly strung artist. One almost expected him to sling a gun from his back and drop a brace of pheasants on the ground.'[8] None affected the artistic manner. No capes, berets or patriarchal beards. No divorces or public liaisons. They steered clear of literary and artistic circles. Only Buchan and Kipling ventured into autobiography in their own lifetimes – under very unrevealing titles. Kipling offered *Something of Myself*; Buchan chose *Memory Hold-the-Door*, implying that much was concealed. Haggard left the sealed manuscript of *The Days of My Life* with instructions that it not be published until after his death. The closest Baker came to self-revelation was a book on his patron: *Cecil Rhodes, by His Architect*. Elgar found no difficulty resisting the publisher who pestered him for an autobiography.[9]

Admirers of their work marvelled at the mismatch between the public personae and the character of their creations. Henry Miller put his finger on the 'duality in Rider Haggard ... An earthbound individual, conventional in his ways, orthodox in his beliefs ... this man who is reticent and reserved, English to the core, one might say, reveals through his "romances" a hidden nature, a hidden being, a hidden lore which is amazing'.[10] Perceptive critics could see beneath Elgar's glacial reserve 'a man of nerves. As he raises the baton, which he holds between his thumb and first two fingers, as one might take hold of a pen, he seems to quiver with excitement ... As one might expect from these manifestations of a febrile temperament, his orchestral renderings are marked by waves of emotion.'[11] Ernest Newman remarked of his violin concerto that 'human feeling so nervous and subtle as this had never before spoken in English orchestral music'.[12] Angus Wilson saw that behind the apparently unselfconscious jingoism of Kipling's patriotism lay the ability to evoke 'the most powerful nightmares of the precariousness of a ruling group'.[13] Michael Keath, who made a most insightful study of Herbert Baker's South African architectural practice, found 'his private life almost impenetrable ... and a full biographical picture of Baker, the man, almost impossible to depict'.[14] A young Scot who had read his way into Buchan's fiction was moved to ask, after hearing that prim, reserved lecturer speak in public: 'Is this wonderful pagan of *The Grove of Ashtaroth*, the man who revels in travel and enterprise? And where, between the adventurer and the man of affairs, does the elder of St Columba's[15] fit in? Who is this person who wears so many masks, and under which mask may he himself be found?'[16] If others could so readily imagine a hidden self beneath the disguises, the tortured souls within must often have risen to confront them as they stood before their shaving mirrors. All are known to have suffered moods of bleak despondency. Five are known to have come close to serious mental breakdowns. Elgar's first flush of late-blooming success – the period of his *Pomp and Circumstance* marches – coincided with a period of inner blackness, when, according to his wife, he often spoke of suicide.[17] Haggard entered the slough of despond following the unexpected death of his son, Jock, a tribulation he attributed to divine retribution for his carnal sins. 'Then in truth I descended into Hell.'[18] John Buchan, after the death of his brothers, fell prey to depression and an assortment of ailments that caused him at length to consult a psychoanalyst.[19] Kipling, however deeply he may have been affected by the death of his daughter from whooping cough at age seven and his son who went missing in action on the Western Front in 1915, was in fact a lifelong melancholic. Well before he married, he suffered some sort of mental crisis that became a matter of public knowledge when papers announced that 'Mr. Rudyard Kipling has broken down from overwork.'[20] Conrad's breakdown in 1910 took him to the edge of madness, engaging in audible conversations with the imaginary characters of his novel *Under Western Eyes*.[21]

Such an arresting and literal case of the author in his work rarely comes along. It was enough to inspire Bernard Meyer to attempt a psychoanalytic biography of Conrad.[22] Others have tried a similar approach to the works of Kipling, Buchan and Haggard. Repressed homosexuality has been suggested as a motivating force in all of them. Looking for the troubling and conflicted content of their subconscious minds is tempting but ultimately fruitless. We have too little to go on. Unable to put them on the analyst's couch, we can only guess at the causes of their inner turbulence. Their childhood experiences and relations with their parents were diverse. Haggard and Elgar had mothers with literary aspirations, whom they idolised, and fathers with whom their relations were more distant. Buchan and Kipling seem to have doted on both their parents. Conrad lost an adored mother when he was a child and sat by the bedside of the dying father who had provided the whole of his education up to age eleven. Oedipal themes aplenty figure prominently in the lives and work of these artists, but they play out in different ways. Angus Wilson was right in one respect, when he wrote in regard to Kipling that 'Freudianism is too easy ... He was a gentle-violent man, a man of depressions and hilarity, holding his despairs in with an almost superhuman stoicism. Manic-depressive does no more than repeat this in big words.'[23] Albert Guerard hit on another kind of psychological significance when he asked, 'Was Conrad a psychoanalytic novelist *sans le savoir*?', adding, perceptively, that 'His distaste for Freud proves no more than his distaste for Dostoievski.'[24] This goes for all the subjects of this book. They call Freud to mind less because they are suitable subjects for treatment than because they shared his fundamental assumptions about the psyche and society. They endorsed Freud's contention that repression is necessary for civilisation and extended it to the mission of empire.

Without forming a self-conscious group like the Pre-Raphaelites or the Vienna Secession, they found each other, touching each other's lives in a variety of ways. Close friends who maintained a decades-long friendship, Haggard and Kipling collaborated on the plot for his novel *The Ghost Kings*, 'writing down our ideas in alternate sentences upon the same sheet of foolscap'.[25] Elgar finally fulfilled a long-cherished hope in the midst of the First World War with his patriotic setting for Kipling's *Fringes of the Fleet*. Young John Buchan marvelled at the 'savage glory' of Haggard's *King Solomon's Mines*.[26] Thanks to their joint patron, Cecil Rhodes, Herbert Baker began his association with Kipling when the poet was in residence at Cecil Rhodes' Cape Town estate, where the magnate had put Woolsack Cottage (another Baker design) at the poet's disposal for the rest of his life. Later they corresponded about concepts for Rhodes Memorial. Baker renewed his acquaintance with Buchan at Elsfield, his mansion near Oxford, where the architect designed memorials for a much-loved family servant. They would also have met on many occasions at Rhodes House, Oxford, which Baker designed for the Rhodes Trust. Whether Conrad knew or cared about Baker or Elgar is doubtful, but he certainly kept up with fellow authors.

He pointedly refused, when invited, to disparage Kipling and knew his work well enough to complain in 1899 that young John Buchan's short story, 'The Far Islands', looked like a rehash of Kipling's much earlier 'Finest Story in the World'.[27] Later, Kipling and Conrad are known to have corresponded, though none of the letters appear to have survived.[28]

Individual chapters in this book explore in depth the relationship of these artists with conservatism and imperialism, movements that defy easy generalisations in this period. It might have seemed true enough in 1882, as a character declaims in Gilbert and Sullivan's *Iolanthe*, that

> Nature always does contrive – Fal, lal, la
> That every boy and every gal
> That's born into the world alive
> Is either a little Liberal
> Or else a little Conservative.

However, the presumptions about party affiliations that governed British politics during the long rivalry between William Gladstone and Benjamin Disraeli were about to shatter. Gladstone won the general election of 1880, having promised an end to overseas imperial adventures. Two years later his government invaded Egypt to ensure control of the Suez Canal – the start of an occupation that would last long into the twentieth century. By 1886 his Liberal party had split over another imperial issue, Home Rule for Ireland. The dissident Liberal Unionists comprised a most unlikely group of political bedfellows, ranging from bigoted anti-Catholics to radicals like the fiery former Mayor of Birmingham, Joseph Chamberlain. At the same time serious socialism raised its head for the first time in British politics. The 1880s saw the formation of a Marxist party, H. M. Hyndman's Social Democratic Federation, and the middle-class Fabian Society, as well as the entry into parliament of socialist Robert Cunninghame Graham, who contested the general election of 1886 for the Scottish Labour Party. For a time both the Liberal and Conservative parties courted radical support in an effort to win working-class votes. Imperialists were also to be found on all sides of politics.

The vicissitudes of public life for imperialists of this era are well illustrated in the career of Alfred Milner, whose figure became something of a rallying point for most of the characters in this book during the first two decades of the twentieth century.[29] Born in 1854 to a physician of modest means, he won a scholarship to Oxford, where he shone as a brilliant student, attracting the attention of Benjamin Jowett and T. H. Green, who were reformulating the intellectual and moral foundations of liberalism. Next he joined forces with the social and educational reformer, Arnold Toynbee. Milner would maintain a lifelong association with Toynbee Hall in Whitechapel, which carried on his friend's work. He also developed a strong interest in socialism, giving lectures on the subject. Within a few years he had drifted into journalism, working for W. T. Stead's crusading *Pall Mall Gazette*. This led in turn to an unsuccessful bid to be elected to parliament as a Liberal in the general election of 1885. Indignation at the failure to save General Gordon at Khartoum and opposition to Gladstone's Irish Home Rule Bill led Milner to join the Liberal Unionists in the historic split of 1886. Through the patronage of Unionist G. J. Goschen, he secured a post as Director General of Accounts in Egypt. From there he went on to a series of important public service appointments. Meanwhile his political philosophy had undergone further development, under the influence of Benjamin Kidd's *Social Evolution* (1894), which argued that nations, races and empires now competed for survival in the same way that individuals and species had done in ages past. About the same time Milner met Cecil Rhodes and some of his key associates, beginning an association with African affairs that culminated in his appointment as High Commissioner for South Africa in 1897. Here his autocratic tendencies came increasingly to the fore as he pushed inexorably for extinction of the independence of the Transvaal Republic. When negotiations failed, Milner sent British soldiers marching to Pretoria. Long before hostilities ended, he installed himself as virtual dictator of the conquered territory. Realising he had little chance of recruiting experienced men to his staff, he decided to go for youth and brains. After reading an article by John Buchan in the *Spectator*, he invited him to come to South Africa as his private secretary.[30] Just before leaving Cape Town, Milner visited Herbert Baker, encouraging him to come up to Johannesburg because 'the new colonies wanted architectural advice'.[31] A few years later he read with viceregal satisfaction Kipling's defence of his work in 'The Pro-Consuls (Lord Milner)'.

Back in England Milner persevered with the perverse mix of contrary tendencies that had marked his previous career. He was for a time numbered among the salon of so-called Coefficients whom the Fabian socialists Beatrice and Sidney Webb had gathered to discuss contemporary questions of empire and international military rivalry. Others in the company included Bertrand Russell and W. Pember Reeves, the New Zealand prime minister famed for his government's experiments in social welfare and state ownership. When Elinor Glyn published her book *Three Weeks*, which featured an adulterous affair consummated on a tiger skin, Milner sent the novelist a real tiger skin as a token of his appreciation.[32] While serving as master of the Anglo-Colonial Masonic Lodge, he maintained his links to north-east Africa as chairman of the

Bank of Egypt, even as he meddled in Spanish copper mines through the Rio Tinto Company. When the prospect of Home Rule for Ireland loomed again in 1912, Milner went to the barricades for the Ulster Unionists. In 1914 he issued a manifesto at the head of 'twenty distinguished men' who pledged to 'take or support any action that may be effective to prevent' Home Rule from being implemented. Among his first twenty were Rudyard Kipling and, surprisingly, Edward Elgar, whose imperialism overrode his Catholicism where Irish affairs were concerned. During the First World War Milner joined Lloyd George's government as minister without portfolio, charged with responsibility for home security, including the secret service and propaganda branches, where his old subordinate John Buchan performed so well. He also took a leading role in supporting Zionist dreams of a national home for Jews in Palestine; his was the hand that drafted the Balfour Declaration that laid the foundation for the future state of Israel. After the war he continued, until his death in 1925, to involve himself in imperial affairs as one of the Rhodes trustees, as the author of a scheme for granting limited independence to Egypt and as a prominent supporter of the *Round Table* journal founded by his old South African subalterns Leo Amery and Lionel Curtis.

A century on, Milner's causes appear confused and contradictory. But such was the nature of the conservatism and imperialism that won the hearts and minds of his near contemporaries, the subjects of this book. Like today's neo-conservatives, Milner retained from his early radical days a belief that the world could be permanently changed for the better. Great Britain would be the vehicle for that change, provided it could hold off the challenge of rival empires. He also knew very well the intellectual strength of the doctrines that stood in the way of his dream: nationalism, internationalism and revolutionary socialism. Milner's imperial politics thus resembled the best creative work done by his artist acolytes – marked by an increasingly desperate struggle to save the Empire from insurgent forces whose power he understood all too well because of his own fascination with them.

The subjects of this book will generally be found standing with Milner at every important political juncture, beginning with the British political crises of 1885–86. On hearing the results of the general election of 1885, which kept Gladstone in power and increased the vote of the Irish Nationalists, Conrad despaired at what he imagined was the triumph of the radicals. 'Where's the man to stop the rush of social-democratic ideas? The opportunity and the day have come and are gone! Believe me: gone for ever! For the sun is set and the last barrier removed. England was the only barrier to the pressure of infernal doctrines born in continental back-slums. Now, there is nothing!'[33]

Kipling, who had grown to hate Gladstone for the sins of his government in India, shared with Elgar the feeling that the preventable death of Gordon at Khartoum betrayed every ideal the British Empire ought to stand for.[34] Haggard commented on the election of 1886 in his draft manuscript for *She*, casting handsome young Leo Vincey as 'a red hot conservative' and proposing, as the awesome Ayesha's plan to solve the Irish problem, mass murder of all the Irish.[35] For Haggard, the betrayal of Gordon revived bitter memories of Gladstone's earlier sacrifice of Theophilus Shepstone, on whose staff he had served during the short-lived British annexation of the Transvaal in South Africa.[36] During the Boer War Buchan, Baker and Kipling were all deeply involved with Milner in South Africa, while Haggard and Elgar fretted at home that the humiliations of the 1880s were about to be revisited.[37] Elgar correctly read Kipling's poem 'Recessional', which he hoped to set to music in 1900, as a warning against complacency in the face of Boer duplicity and foreign rivals.[38] Anti-imperialists who had expected the author of *Heart of Darkness* to condemn the war were disappointed with Conrad, who feared a British defeat would encourage German ambitions. He regarded the conflict 'not so much a war against the Transvaal as a struggle against the doings of German influence'. Besides, he had little sympathy for the Boers, whom he described as an 'essentially despotic people'.[39]

Not only did Elgar and Kipling join Milner's group of 'twenty eminent men' pledged to stand by Protestant Ulster, even if it meant defying the British government, but they also took positions on the Executive Committee of the British Covenanters, the organisation Milner founded to bolster the Ulster cause.[40] Buchan did not go to those extremes, but continued passionately to oppose Home Rule for Ireland, as did Haggard. Herbert Baker was hard at work on the New Delhi capital during the Ulster crisis of 1914, but he wrote after war broke out to express his disappointment that Milner had not been included in the National Government war cabinet. Conrad pointedly refused to join an appeal for clemency on behalf of Roger Casement, who was caught smuggling German arms to Irish rebels, even though he had known and admired Casement in the Congo. The Easter Rebellion of 1916 Conrad regarded as a cowardly stab in the back when Britain was fighting for its very existence.[41] After the world war Haggard threw himself impetuously into the National Propaganda and the Liberty League – organisations dedicated to arousing public opinion against the Bolshevik menace. Kipling, Buchan and Baker continued their association with Milner and his ideals through work for the Round Table and the Rhodes Trust. Elgar continued to write occasional pieces for imperial occasions, but took no further active part in politics.

On the subject of where ultimate authority should reside within the Empire, the opinions of these men were diverse. Their commitment to democracy as a political system could at best be described as shaky. Milner maintained a barely concealed disdain for parliamentary politics, and never sought elected office after his failure in 1885 – though he was touted as a potential prime minister after the Great War. Haggard made two unsuccessful attempts to be elected and Elgar once or twice expressed regret that he had never stood for election as a Conservative candidate. John Buchan alone managed to win a parliamentary seat, though he never reached a cabinet position before bowing out to become governor-general of Canada as the newly created Baron Tweedsmuir. Baker, whose greatest success came as the favoured architect of wealthy and politically powerful patrons, took no part in electoral politics. On the eve of his departure for India to build the capitol at New Delhi, he marvelled at what could be done by imperial command: 'Hurrah for despotism' was the comment he scrawled in a letter to Lutyens. Kipling, famed for championing the common soldier and excoriated by the elite for pandering to the vulgar jingoism of the masses, seems to have nonetheless had little faith that democracy would deliver the right result. Conrad never lost his disdain for the behaviour of 'newly enfranchised idiots' in Western political systems.

For all of his haughty self-belief, Milner shared one other important personality trait with these artists: a sense of himself as an outsider. This was not in any twenty-first-century sense a matter of social class. He had been conceived out of wedlock five months before his father's marriage to the daughter of a British major general, the widow, Marie Ierne Cromie, who had been living for several years in Germany. Alfred received most of his schooling in that country prior to winning his university scholarship, experiences that set him apart from his Oxford contemporaries. Elgar also married the daughter of a major general, but nourished a neurotic sense of himself as permanently disadvantaged by his Roman Catholicism, his lack of a university education and his father's occupation as a piano tuner and music shop proprietor in a provincial city.[42] Son of a poor minister of the unfashionable Free Church of Scotland, John Buchan went on to win scholarships to the universities of Glasgow and Oxford, desperately relieved to escape the claustrophobic atmosphere of the puritanical parental home. None of the subsequent honours heaped upon him ever seemed quite enough to eclipse the obscurity of his beginnings, not even the glittering betrothal party – attended by Lord Milner – celebrating his engagement to Susan Grosvenor, cousin to the Duke of Westminster. Rudyard Kipling, whose establishment credentials seem impeccable – son of Queen Victoria's interior decorator, nephew of a famous painter and cousin of a future Tory prime minister – also saw himself as an outsider. Desperately unhappy after his parents sent him home from India to be schooled in England, he misremembered the rest of his childhood as something akin to Dickens's Oliver Twist. He fell in readily with his father's suggestion that he forgo the expenses of a university education and seek a career as a journalist in India. Even after returning to England triumphantly as the boy-wonder author of *Plain Tales from the Hills*, he nurtured the idea that a brighter, happier life awaited him some place overseas. Rider Haggard conceived of himself as a disinherited son of country gentry. Denied the university education given to his elder brothers and sent to South Africa at the age of seventeen, he used the wealth he earned from his fiction to buy back the ancestral manor. Herbert Baker also reclaimed the family estate, 'Owlets' in Kent, though his early apprenticeship in architecture followed a fairly conventional path. Notwithstanding his success in South Africa and India, he felt he would be denied the highest honours of his profession unless he left the colonies and established a practice in the metropolis. Joseph Conrad, of course, did not have to imagine himself an outsider. His affiliations with Polish nobility meant little in England, but he need not have gone to the lengths he did to distance himself from his origins, cultivating his reputation as a simple man of the sea married to an uneducated Englishwoman of humble origins.

If Alfred Milner best represented the complex and contradictory meanings of imperial patriotism for these political artists, then the man who captured their hearts and seemed likely to realise their aspirations for the future of the Empire was T. E. Lawrence – Lawrence of Arabia. Another outsider, born out of wedlock to an Anglo-Irish landowner, Lawrence made his way to Oxford on his academic ability, learned Arabic and fell in love with the Middle East as an archaeologist. This experience secured his attachment to the intelligence department of the British Expeditionary Force in Cairo shortly after war broke out in 1914. His role in encouraging an Arab revolt against the Turks came to the attention of a wider public when John Buchan, then working at the Ministry of Information, suggested to the American journalist, Lowell Thomas, that he cover Lawrence's spectacular operations at Aqabah on the Red Sea.[43] After two evenings of intense conversation in 1918, Rudyard Kipling convinced Lawrence to write his own account of the campaign.[44] When Herbert Baker met the war hero for the first time in the New College Common Room at Oxford, 'it was love at first sight; he radiated some magnetic influence, such as long ago I experienced in the presence of Cecil Rhodes. I felt I would have followed him, had I been younger, in any adventurous quest.' Installed on a cot in the attic of Baker's London architectural office, Lawrence wrote much of his epic *Seven Pillars of Wisdom*.[45] Further assistance came through a fellowship from All Souls College, Oxford, where Lawrence formed close friendships with Leo Amery, Lionel Curtis and other former members of Milner's South African 'Kindergarten'. All Souls seemed to many of its intimates to be 'an unofficial committee for running ... the destinies of the British Empire'.[46] On weekends Lawrence would, from time to time, be seen at Buchan's country home outside Oxford in serious conversations with groups that included not only Round Table men but also heads of government departments, history lecturers and leading Fabian socialists.[47] In 1920, Lawrence first met Conrad and 'probed him on the methods of his craft'.[48] The admiration was clearly mutual, for Conrad went to some lengths to provide Lawrence with a special edition of his memoirs.[49] As far as Lawrence was concerned, Conrad was 'absolutely the most haunting in prose that ever was ... He's as much a giant of the subjective as Kipling is of the objective.'[50] Elgar did not meet Lawrence until near the end of his life, but when he did, the same spark of sympathy was kindled. The younger man wrote, 'your 2nd Symphony hits me between wind and water. It is exactly the mode that I most desire, and so it moves me more than anything else – of music – that I have ever heard.'[51]

The final chapter in this book explores the reasons why Lawrence did not – could not – perform the role in which his elder admirers cast him, as creative artist and master statesman of Empire. Certainly, as many of his biographers argue, Lawrence's deeply conflicted psyche drove him to flee the limelight, give up his commission and enlist under an assumed name in the humble ranks of the British military. (Ever helpful, Buchan assisted in securing his transfer from the tank corps to the Royal Air Force.) It is reasonable to ask, however, whether he or any other man could truly have accomplished the mission on which Haggard sent the fictional Sir Henry Curtis into Africa, that Kipling set in India for Kim, that Buchan set for Sandy Arbuthnot in Asia Minor: to enter completely into the life of a subject people, make their cause one's own and win them for the Empire. At the climax of *King Solomon's Mines*, Curtis has discarded his European clothes and dressed himself in feathers and leopard skins to fight alongside Ignosi on behalf of the oppressed Kukuanas. In Elgar's oratorio the British warrior king Caractacus thanks his Roman conquerors, singing 'Grace from the Roman! Peace and rest are ours.' The Anglo-Irish boy hero of Kipling's *Kim* goes through semi-magical rituals to achieve the disguises that enable him to pass unnoticed among all the peoples of India, saving them at last from the Franco-Russian menace. In Buchan's *Greenmantle*, Sandy Arbuthnot, a Scot 'adept at getting under another's skin', adopts a disguise so perfect that he is able to ride undetected into

Constantinople at the head of Islamic horsemen bent on taking Turkey out of the war. Like Conrad's Lord Jim, Lawrence tried living out the whole adventure. He would dress like Bedouins, live like Bedouins, stir them into revolt against the Turks and secure their freedom under British sponsorship. His ambition, as he expressed it in a letter to Lord Curzon, was 'that the Arabs should be our first brown dominion, and not our last brown colony'.[52] By that he meant that they should eventually stand on the same footing within the Empire as Australia, Canada, New Zealand and South Africa. 'Arabs', he continued, 'react against you if you try to drive them, and they are as tenacious as Jews: but you can lead them without force anywhere, if nominally arm in arm. The future of Mesopotamia [Iraq] is so immense that if it is cordially ours we can swing the whole Middle East with it.' His literary account of the revolt, *The Seven Pillars of Wisdom*, recapitulates the romantic hero's journey through privation, prison and defilement in many episodes that critics point out could not have happened – so that it might appear that he had shared the lives of his Arab insurgents even unto the most repugnant details.

As Conrad presciently argued in *Lord Jim* (one of Lawrence's pre-war favourites), the full imperial romance could not be lived. One could not be simultaneously master and subject, conqueror and liberator. Dreams of heroic accomplishment could never deliver the results achieved through rules and discipline. It was exciting to imagine allying one's inner savage self with real-life barbarians to achieve justice and freedom within an empire of freely associated equals. But it was nonetheless a fantasy. The imagined savage within was as unreal as the colonial subject conjured up by Orientalists. Having seen his Middle Eastern dream founder on the facts of ethnic rivalries and international diplomacy, Lawrence froze like Conrad's Jim in the face of 'Gentleman Brown's' desperadoes. The conqueror of Aqabah sat by his mother's side, sometimes 'the entire morning between breakfast and lunch in the same position, without moving, and with the same expression on his face'.[53] Despite the repeated urgings of his influential friends he vowed never again to accept any position of command. Nor did he return to the Middle East or nationalist politics.

Fantasy or no, the idea has proved artistically energising over a long period. The subjects of this study played on the analogical association they drew between the struggle to repress the irrepressible inner self and the imperial project of ruling subject peoples. Their best works rose to significant heights of achievement by exploring the ramifications of the metaphor. Whether those works achieved greatness is a separate question. Historians seldom venture aesthetic judgements these days. Reflecting the influence of post-structural and postcolonial theory, the same can be said of most scholars of art, music and literature. Yet the argument of this book demands that the aesthetic question be squarely faced.

Edward Said has not been the only critic to rank Conrad and Kipling among the authentic geniuses of English literature, but his opinions carry a special authority by dint of his lifelong struggle against the culture and politics of imperialism.[54] If the votes of consumers are any measure of quality, the ongoing popularity of these artists suggests their output was built to last. Novels by Buchan, Haggard, Kipling and Conrad continue to find film-makers eager to make new versions. Herbert Baker remains South Africa's most admired architect. Elgar's symphonies are enshrined in the standard orchestral repertoire and his first *Pomp and Circumstance* march still wraps up London's 'Last Night of the Proms'. From a philosophical perspective it is more difficult to pinpoint the nature of their achievements. Measured against Aristotle's criterion that great art holds a mirror to nature, none of the protagonists' creations would qualify. They certainly did not strive for beauty, classical proportions, eternal harmonies or depictions of lived reality. The most compelling of them belong to the category that the eighteenth-century philosophers Edmund Burke and Immanuel Kant called the sublime. Their works plunge readers into unexplored and dangerous territories where the landscape – a character in its own right – frequently oppresses, overawes, even terrifies the senses. According to Burke's aesthetic theory the sublime moves us by mingling power with terror. Tracing power 'through its several gradations unto the highest of all, where our imagination is finally lost … we find terror, quite throughout the progress, its inseparable companion, and growing along with it, as far as we can possibly trace them'.[55] While comparable in its power to arouse our emotions, the sublime is in most respects the antithesis of the beautiful:

> sublime objects are vast in their dimensions, beautiful ones comparatively small: beauty should be smooth and polished; the great, rugged and negligent; beauty should shun the right line, yet deviate from it insensibly; the great in many cases loves the right line, and when it deviates it often makes a strong deviation: beauty should not be obscure; the great ought to be dark and gloomy; beauty should be light and delicate; the great ought to be solid, and even massive.[56]

Empire, conquest and the struggle for subjugation are quintessentially big themes more calculated to evoke the sublime than the beautiful. As they are everywhere accompanied by their opposites – freedom, liberation and resistance – they contain an inexhaustible creative potential. Strange to say, the *Aesthetic Theory* of the Marxist philosopher

Theodor Adorno offers more insights into the achievements of this clutch of conservative imperialists than do their ardent conservative admirers. Using the example of the composer Anton Bruckner, Adorno argued that even when an artist consciously sought to revivify a bygone Catholic spirituality, he could not avoid making something strikingly new by appropriating 'the harmonic and instrumental discoveries' of his own time.[57] Similarly, the work of the politically conservative Haggard, Kipling, Conrad and Elgar made audiences sit up with a start. Here was something new. In this sense they concur with Adorno's contention that 'all artworks, even the affirmative, are a priori polemical. The idea of a conservative artwork is inherently absurd.' Contemporary critics found 'horrible', 'shocking' and 'foolish' aspects to deplore, as they would in frankly modernist works. Again, as Adorno points out, it was only 'during World War I and prior to Stalin' that 'artistic and politically advanced thought went in tandem; whoever came of age in those years took art to be what it in no way historically had been: a priori politically on the left'.[58] The ungainly, horrific and misshapen contents that many deplored in the work of the imperialist artists conforms to Adorno's dictum that:

> The divergence of the constructive and the mimetic, which no artwork can resolve and which is virtually the original sin of aesthetic spirit, has its correlative in that element of the ridiculous and clownish that even the most significant works bear and that, unconcealed, is inextricable from their significance. The inadequacy of classicism of any persuasion originates in its repression of this element; a repression that art must mistrust.[59]

Even as Herbert Baker heaped praise on architectural classicism, he loaded his buildings with tacky plaques, faked antique patinas and mismatched historical styles. Time and again Elgar inserted bad jokes, political satire and stylistic pastiche into his music without apparent embarrassment. Passed over as Poet Laureate because of the alleged vulgarity in his work, Kipling did not repent but flung more of the same into his genteel critics' faces.

From a psychological point of view, the imperialist artists paradoxically conform to the personality type Adorno singles out as least likely to respond to innovation:

> Empirically it has been confirmed that inhibited, conventional, and aggressive-reactionary individuals tend to reject 'intraception' – self-awareness – in any form, and along with it expression as such, as being all too human. They are the ones who, in a context of general estrangement from art, declare themselves with particular resentment against modernism.[60]

And yet, in these particular creators, something insistent and contradictory kept peeping out of their buttoned-up quotidian personae. To reiterate, the argument of this book is that the fount of their creative imagination was precisely their inability to hold a lid on the inner 'savage' self that stood opposed to all their fervently expressed support for order and discipline – which so closely mimicked the appealing but hopeless mission of imperialism in world affairs. Their best works rose to impressive heights as the result of the almost unbearable tension and contradiction at their heart. That is what enables them to generate the 'shudder' that Adorno identifies as the hallmark of genuine artworks since the time of Poe and Baudelaire. Whatever the expressed intentions of their makers, their art 'always desired dissonance'. With them it is pre-eminently true that 'What crackles in artworks is the sound of the friction of the antagonistic elements that the artwork seeks to unify.'[61] In the hierarchy of creative genius, 'the rank of an artwork is defined essentially by whether it exposes itself to, or withdraws from, the irreconcilable ... Those works are deep that neither mask the divergent or antagonistic nor leave it unreconciled.'[62]

From this perspective the imperialist artists share more with their modernist contemporaries than they or posterity have generally acknowledged. It is a mistake to pit them against each other – one faction clinging to the past, the other hurrying towards the future. Both were authentic products of their age. If, 'after the fall of formal beauty, the sublime was the only aesthetic idea left to modernism', so it was the moving spirit of their differently constituted creative agenda.[63] The real champions of the past were salon painters of the Royal Academy such as Alma Tadema and Leighton, establishment critics like Ruskin, professors of music and architects trapped in the conceits of the Gothic revival. As Adorno expressed it, 'academic works are bad because the elements their logicality should synthesize engender no counter-impulses and in fact do not exist. The work undertaken by their unity is superfluous, tautological, and, insofar as it appears as the unity of something, inconsistent.'[64] Although avowed supporters of the constituted political order, the imperialist artists set their face against the established verities, regulations and pattern books of their own fields. At a gut level imperialism appealed to them as the creed of their times that echoed all the dissonant and contrary impulses they felt in their inmost selves. Their age spoke through them because:

> The historical moment is constitutive of artworks; authentic works are those that surrender themselves to the historical substance of their age without reservation and without the presumption of being superior to

> it. They are the self-unconscious historiography of their epoch; this, not least of all, establishes their relation to knowledge.[65]

Doubtless a time will come when the works of the imperialist artists cease to arouse, thrill, horrify or delight audiences. Judging from books in print, adaptations for stage and screen, concert performances, academic studies and the critical admiration of today's practitioners of art and architecture, that day is not yet come. Though we may no longer be gripped by the mixture of fear and fascination that early-twentieth-century readers felt when first looking into Freud, imperialism lives – fraught as ever with misguided idealism, impossible ambitions and frightful retributions. Its power to inspire artistic imaginations of all political complexions remains undimmed.

Notes

1 Historical works on masculinity have begun to accumulate on library shelves previously populated by feminism and women's studies. R. W. Connell's *Masculinities* (Berkeley: University of California Press, 2005) helped to set the theoretical parameters of the field. A landmark in African history was a 1998 issue of the *Journal of Southern African Studies* devoted to the subject of various historical forms of masculinity; 24 (1998).

2 Cited by Dorothy Ross in 'American modernities, past and present', *American Historical Review* 116 (2011), 707. From L. Trilling, *Beyond Culture* (New York: Viking, 1965), p. 103.

3 John Buchan, *Memory Hold-the-Door* (London: Hodder & Stoughton, 1940), p. 202.

4 Letter to Marguerite Poradowska, 2 July 1891, in F. R. Karl and L. Davies (eds), *The Collected Letters of Joseph Conrad, Vol. I: 1861–1897* (Cambridge: Cambridge University Press, 1983), pp. 84–5. The incident is further discussed in Eloise Knapp Hay, 'Joseph Conrad and impressionism', *The Journal of Aesthetics and Art Criticism* 34 (1975), 139. Gene Moore has argued that what Conrad saw was Dr Gachet's consulting rooms in Paris, filled with paraphernalia associated with the treatment of madness rather than the paintings that filled his home at suburban Auvers; that leaves unexplained the question of why his relative should be temporarily living in the consulting rooms. See 'Conrad, Dr Gachet, and the "school of Charenton"', *Conradiana* 25 (1993), 163–77.

5 Hugh Wood, 'The hopes and glories of Edward Elgar', *Times Literary Supplement*, 19 March 2008.

6 Zdzislaw Najder, *Joseph Conrad: A Chronicle* (New Brunswick, NJ: Rutgers University Press, 1983), p. 365.

7 Jacob Epstein, *Epstein: An Autobiography* (London: Hulton Press, 1955), p. 74.

8 Arnold Bax, *Farewell, My Youth* (London: Longmans Green, 1943), pp. 29–31.

9 Percy Young, *Elgar, O.M.: A Study of a Musician*, 2nd edn (London: White Lion, 1973), pp. 251–2.

10 Henry Miller, *The Books in My Life* (London: P. Owens, 1952), p. 93.

11 Jerrold Northrup Moore, *Edward Elgar: A Creative Life* (Oxford: Oxford University Press, 1984), p. 556.

12 Quoted in Diana McVeagh, *Elgar the Music Maker* (Woodbridge, Suffolk: Boydell, 2007), p. 135.

13 Angus Wilson, *The Strange Ride of Rudyard Kipling* (New York: Viking, 1977), p. 72.

14 Michael Keath, *Herbert Baker: Architecture and Idealism 1892–1913, The South African Years* (Gibraltar: Ashanti, 1992), p. viii.

15 The Church of Scotland congregation in London, of which Buchan was a leading member.

16 Quoted in Janet Adam Smith, *John Buchan and His World* (London: Thames & Hudson, 1979), p. 85.

17 Moore, *Edward Elgar*, p. 358.

18 H. Rider Haggard, *The Days of My Life*, ed. by C. J. Longman, 2 vols (London: Longmans, 1926), 2:43.

19 Buchan's biographers invariably report this along with the psychoanalyst's opinion that he was entirely free of neuroses. This does not mean that he had not suffered a serious breakdown.

20 Wilson, *Strange Ride*, p. 159.

21 Najder, *Joseph Conrad*, pp. 357–8.

22 *Joseph Conrad: A Psychoanalytic Biography* (Princeton, NJ: Princeton University Press, 1967).

23 Wilson, *Strange Ride*, p. 342.

24 Albert Guerard, Jr, *Joseph Conrad* (New York: New Directions, 1947), p. 30.

25 Haggard, *The Days of My Life*, 2:124.

26 Janet Adam Smith, *John Buchan* (London: Rupert Hart-Davis, 1965), p. 142.

27 Najder, *Joseph Conrad*, p. 205.

28 Frederick R. Karl, *Joseph Conrad: The Three Lives* (New York: Farrar, Straus and Giroux, 1979), p. 472. See also Wilson, *Strange Ride*, p. 325, which records an incident in which Kipling discussed Conrad's work with a Polish diplomat.

29 There have been many biographies and studies of Milner, but for a superb thumbnail sketch of his career, see Colin Newbury, 'Milner, Alfred, Viscount Milner (1854–1925)', *Oxford Dictionary of National Biography* (Oxford University Press, 2004); online edn, October 2008 (www.oxforddnb.com/view/article/35037, accessed 12 July 2016).

30 Buchan, *Memory Hold-the-Door*, pp. 95–103.

31 Keath, *Herbert Baker*, p. 84.

32 So did Lord Curzon, former Viceroy of India; Anthony Glyn, *Elinor Glyn: A Biography* (London: Hutchinson, 1955), p. 126.

33 Conrad to Spiridion Kliszczewki, 19 December 1885, in Karl and Davies, *The Collected Letters of Joseph Conrad, Vol. I: 1861–1897*, pp. 15–17. Conrad was not to know that Joseph Chamberlain, whom he blamed for stirring up the 'newly enfranchised idiots' of the working class, would strike out on the Unionist path in the crisis of the following year.

34 Wilson, *Strange Ride*, p. 151.

35 Norman Etherington (ed.), *The Annotated She* (Bloomington: Indiana University Press, 1991), p. xx. Haggard removed these passages before publication.

36 Haggard, *Days of My Life*, 1:80.

37 Haggard, *Days of My Life*, 2:79.

38 Moore, *Edward Elgar*, p. 338.

39 Najder, *Joseph Conrad*, p. 161.

40 A. M. Gollin, *Proconsul in Politics: A Study of Lord Milner in Opposition and in Power* (London: Anthony Blond, 1964), p. 212. Kipling also contributed the immense sum of £30,000 to the Covenanters; John Evelyn Wrench, *Alfred Lord Milner: The Man of No Illusions, 1854–1925* (London: Eyre & Spottiswoode, 1958), p. 287.

41 Najder, *Joseph Conrad*, p. 414.

42 David Cannadine has skilfully deconstructed Elgar's self-image in 'Orchestrating his own life: Sir Edward Elgar as an historical personality', in Nicholas Kenyon (ed.), *Elgar: An Anniversary Portrait* (London: Continuum, 2007), pp. 1–35.

43 Lawrence James, 'Lawrence, Thomas Edward [Lawrence of Arabia] (1888–1935)', *Oxford Dictionary of National Biography* (Oxford: Oxford University Press, 2004); online edn, January 2008, www.oxforddnb.com/view/article/34440 (accessed 25 August 2008).

44 David Gilmour, *The Long Recessional: The Imperial Life of Rudyard Kipling* (New York: Farrar, Straus and Giroux, 2002), pp. 285–6.

45 Herbert Baker, in A. W. Lawrence, *T. E. Lawrence by His Friends* (London: Jonathan Cape, 1937), pp. 248–9.
46 Walter Nimocks, *Milner's Young Men: The 'Kindergarten' in Edwardian Imperial Affairs* (London: Hodder & Stoughton, 1970), p. 53.
47 F. Madden and D. K. Fieldhouse (eds), *Oxford and the Idea of Commonwealth* (London: Croom Helm, 1982), p. 17.
48 Herbert Baker, in Lawrence, *T. E. Lawrence by His Friends*, p. 250.
49 T. Hoenselaars and G. M. Moore, 'Joseph Conrad and T. E. Lawrence', *Conradiana* 27 (1995), 3.
50 David Garnett (ed.), *The Letters of T. E. Lawrence* (London: Jonathan Cape, 1938), pp. 301–2.
51 T. E. Shaw [Lawrence] to Elgar, 12 October 1932, in J. N. Moore (ed.), *Edward Elgar: Letters of a Lifetime* (Oxford: Clarendon Press, 1990), p. 456.
52 Lawrence to Curzon, 27 September 1919, in Garnett, *Letters of T. E. Lawrence*, pp. 291–2.
53 Related to Edward Garnett by Lawrence's mother, in ibid., p. 294.
54 Edward Said, *Culture and Imperialism* (London: Vintage, 1994), pp. 32, 181.
55 Edmund Burke, *On Taste, On the Sublime and Beautiful, Reflections on the French Revolution, A Letter to a Noble Lord* (New York: P. F. Collier, 1909), p. 55.
56 Ibid., p. 106.
57 Theodor W. Adorno, *Aesthetic Theory*, ed. by Gretel Adorn and Rolf Tiedemann, transl. by Robert Hullot-Kentor (London: The Athlone Press, 1997), p. 192.
58 Ibid., p. 254.
59 Ibid., pp. 118–19.
60 Ibid., p. 115.
61 Ibid., pp. 20, 110, 177.
62 Ibid., p. 190.
63 Ibid., p. 197.
64 Ibid., p. 188.
65 Ibid., p. 182.

CHAPTER ONE

Rider Haggard, imperialism and the layered personality[1]

At some time between July 1897 and September 1899, Sigmund Freud dreamed about H. Rider Haggard's novels. Freud habitually summoned writers to his aid when interpreting dreams but rarely surprised them in his bedchamber. How did the author of *King Solomon's Mines* get in? Freud himself insisted that nothing in dreams should be dismissed as trivial or fortuitous, so the question is worth pursuing. This was Freud's dream: he found himself in the laboratory engaged in the gruesome work of dissecting his own pelvis and legs. The scene changed to a perilous journey through a wild landscape peopled by savages ('Red Indians or gipsies'). At the end of the journey he had to cross a chasm on narrow planks. He awoke in a 'mental fright'.[2]

Despite the rich sexual imagery of the dream, Freud's interpretation stressed its intellectual content. Self-dissection he identified with his daring and traumatic self-analysis that was in progress at the time. The Indians came from Haggard's *Heart of the World* (1895) and the wild landscape from *She* (1887). Both novels were on Freud's mind because of a recent conversation with a patient:

> 'Lend me something to read', she said. I offered her Rider Haggard's *She*. 'A strange book, but full of hidden meaning', and began to explain to her: 'the eternal feminine, the immortality of our emotions ...' Here she interrupted me: 'I know it already. Have you nothing of your own?' – 'No, my own immortal works have not yet been written.' 'Well, when are we to expect these so-called ultimate explanations of yours which you've promised even we shall find readable?' she asked, with a touch of sarcasm.[3]

The production of his own 'immortal works' suggested to Freud the content of *She*, which 'describes an adventurous road that had scarcely ever been trodden before, leading into an undiscovered region'. At the same time Freud feared that the fate of Haggard's heroine might be his own – that death rather than immortality lurked at the end of the adventure.

Haggard's intrusion into Freud's dream world at a critical point in the development of psychoanalytic theory suggests an approach to the novels of imperial adventure that diverges considerably from that normally taken by historians and critics. Historians generally treat Haggard as a cause or consequence of late-Victorian grabbing for colonies. G. N. Sanderson puts Haggard and *The Boy's Own Paper* in charge of the extracurricular indoctrination of schoolboy imperialists.[4] Brian Street makes him a popular spokesman for poisonous doctrines of race developed by the budding science of anthropology.[5] Academic literary critics have also dismissed Haggard as a 'defender of the flag' without the saving graces of Rudyard Kipling. He was a 'tiresome success' who 'mechanically manufactured imitations'; the important thing about ideas to him 'was not whether they were true but whether they were marketable'; 'there is nothing of the first rank in Haggard's literary legacy'; 'the fact that a number of these ill-written books are still in print is no doubt an interesting sociological fact'.[6] There is a great deal of this sort of criticism.

Haggard has fared somewhat better with fellow writers. Apart from C. S. Lewis, who condemned him as insufferably shallow, and George Orwell, who could barely bring himself to include *She* in a list of 'good bad books', Haggard has won some impressive admirers.[7] Henry Miller is fascinated by the hidden meanings that Freud noticed in the novels:

> There is a duality in Rider Haggard which intrigues me enormously. An earthbound individual, conventional in his ways, orthodox in his beliefs ... this man who is reticent and reserved, English to the core, one might say, reveals through his 'romances' a hidden nature, a hidden being, a hidden lore which is amazing. His method of writing these romances – at full speed, hardly stopping to think, so to speak – enabled him to tap his unconscious with freedom and depth.[8]

Graham Greene likewise praises Haggard for conveying in a direct and vital way the central problems of identity and duality in the human personality: 'There are thousands of names for it, King Solomon's Mines, the "heart of darkness" if one is romantically inclined, or more simply as Herr Heuser puts it in his African novel "The Inner Journey", one's place in time, based on a knowledge not only of one's present but of the past from which one has emerged.'[9] Margaret Atwood sees exactly the same link between Haggard and Joseph Conrad: 'the journey into the unknown regions of the self, the unconscious, and the confrontation with whatever dangers and splendours lurk there.'[10]

Miller, Greene and Atwood are correct in ascribing the imaginative power of Haggard's romances to the metaphor of personality embodied in them. In the twilight of the Victorian era, new psychological models were emerging that conceptualised the self as a series of conscious and unconscious layers. Freud and C. G. Jung, it can be argued, took a particular interest in Haggard because they saw in his novels an implicit model of the self that corresponded closely to their own explicit models.

Read in this spirit, Haggard's works cannot be passed over as imperialist propaganda. In fact, it is remarkable how little imperialism creeps into the books that made him famous. Haggard divided his fiction into 'novels' and 'romances'. Apart from the anti-Boer *Jess*, the novels are all set in England and deal with country life. As an indoctrinator of nascent imperialists, Haggard's reputation rests on the romances published between 1885 and 1892, before his interests shifted to politics and agricultural reform. In these romances there is almost none of the imperialism that Haggard preached in the press or on the platform. The real-life Haggard eulogised Cecil Rhodes, apologised for the Jameson Raid and regarded the Matabele War as a very good thing. He scoffed at the idea that Africans could have built the impressive stone structures of Zimbabwe and doubted the ability of blacks to govern themselves.[11] In contrast, not one of the romances describes a colonial war or annexation. The reader does not go 'with Clive to India', 'with Kitchener to Khartoum', or upon any other imperial errand. Haggard's 'savages' are the best and cleverest since James Fennimore Cooper's Mohicans.

Consider, for example, *King Solomon's Mines* (1885), the first and still the most widely read of the romances. The book quite deliberately attempted to repeat the success of Robert Louis Stevenson's *Treasure Island* (1883). Written in six weeks, it was Haggard at his most automatic, fusing a highly imaginative narrative from bits and pieces of experiences, legends and stories that he had collected during the five years he spent in South Africa. Had he wished to write a romance in praise of British imperialism he could certainly have done so by drawing on his own experience as private secretary to Governor Bulwer of Natal, aide to Sir Theophilus Shepstone during the annexation of the Transvaal, and partner in an ostrich farming venture. Instead, part of the plot of someone else's failed novel of South African adventure, Karl Mauch's reports of the newly discovered Zimbabwe ruins, rumours of gold north of the Limpopo, a long-lost claimant to the Ndebele throne and highly coloured legends of the cruelty of Shaka the Zulu king were grafted onto Stevenson's device of the treasure map to produce a compelling story whose essential elements were to be reproduced in most of the later romances.[12]

A party of three whites – a wise old hunter, a handsome young aristocrat and an excessively English naval officer – set off in search of the nobleman's lost brother and fabled diamond mines sketched on a faded Portuguese parchment. They are accompanied by a highly intelligent, haughty and superbly muscled African. The party slaughters carloads of big game, crosses a scorching desert and passes along narrow defiles through spectacular mountain scenery until Kukuanaland sparkles gemlike before their feet. There the adventurers find a Zulu-speaking people whose neat, hygienic villages dot the countryside of a pastoral Elysium. Amid stone ruins testifying to the glories of a vanished civilisation, a tyrannical king rules the Kukuanas with the aid of his cruel son and a centuries-old shrivelled hag. At a savage ceremony the whites intervene to prevent the sacrifice of a beautiful maiden, thereby enraging the king and his retainers. Now the mysterious African who accompanied the whites reveals himself as the rightful king of the land and gathers supporters to challenge the tyrant. Thousands die in the ensuing battle in which the white men distinguish themselves in the service of their former guide. The victorious new king rewards his friends by forcing the old witch to lead them to a secret treasure cave where the diamonds are stored. While trapping the white party in the cave, the witch is herself killed by the beautiful maiden who has won the love of the naval officer. The party manages an escape through subterranean caverns, minus the maiden, and carries off enough diamonds to make the whole trip worthwhile. After the whites refuse an offer to make them lords in the land, the king announces his intention to seal off Kukuanaland against any future European incursions. The whites make their way back to England, happily saving the aristocrat's long-lost brother on the way.

Certainly there are elements of classical imperialism in this scenario. Big game and diamonds conjure up visions of boundless African wealth; the attribution of the ruins to vanished whites discounts African ability; the tyranny of the bad king is a caricature of savagery; and the death of the maiden conveniently removes the threat of miscegenation. Much more remarkable, however, are the features that do not accord with stereotypes of Victorian imperialism. The rightful king is no shuffling clown but a proud and intelligent aristocrat who will not conform to the subservient role that the old hunter Quatermain insists that he play. Daily life in Kukuanaland is healthy, tidy and chaste – soap, civilisation and missionaries are not wanted here. There is a real interracial love story, not mere concubinage; the naval officer swears after his return to Europe that no Englishwoman could hold a candle to the lost Foulata, 'either as regards her figure or the sweetness of her expression'.[13] The book ends on a strongly anti-imperialist note as the Kukuana king vows to keep Europeans out of his domain: 'No other white man shall cross the mountains ... I will see no traders with their guns and gin ... I will have no praying-men to put a fear of death into men's hearts, to stir them up against the law of the king, and make a path for the White folk who follow to run on.'[14] As imperialist indoctrination this is distinctly weak.[15]

Abandoning that line of analysis and taking up Atwood's suggestion that the trek into Africa is a trek from the known into the unconscious unknown self, a different message emerges from the events of the novel. Haggard's whites are all stock European types: hunter Allan Quatermain is a grizzled old colonial with colonial prejudices; Sir Henry Curtis is a gentleman of no African experience but willing to learn and inclined to treat Africans as equals; Captain Good of the Royal Navy is comically dedicated to maintaining English dress and manners regardless of climate or latitude. These three representatives of civilisation undergo a series of punishing tests. The tests are progressively severe and are marked by changes of terrain. First the party is tested in a straight contest with big game in which Good narrowly escapes being trampled by an elephant because of his 'passion for civilized dress', but he and the others prove themselves as brave sportsmen. Tests of desert heat, mountain cold and starvation follow. But the greatest tests are moral and take place in the special secluded landscape of Kukuanaland. The trio are confronted in rapid succession by a slaughter of accused witches (likened by Haggard to a Roman gladiatorial show and the execution of the nobility in revolutionary France), an orgiastic dance in which ravishingly beautiful women 'pirouette ... with a grace and vigour which would have put most ballet girls to shame', and an offer of free girls for the duration of their stay.[16]

Next there is an extraordinary trial by battle, a feature of which is the savagery of the whites and the civilisation of the blacks. Ignosi, the rightful king, is compared to a Roman emperor in charge of magnificently disciplined regiments. His order that no enemy wounded should be killed is obeyed without exception. 'Never before', remarks Quatermain, 'had I ever seen such an absolute devotion to the idea of duty.'[17] The three white men, on the other hand, all succumb to homicidal mania. Good longs for a Gatling gun with which to mow down the enemy. Quatermain, who previously professed an utter loathing for war, finds that in the heat of battle his blood, hitherto 'half-frozen with horror', pounds through his veins and he is possessed by 'a savage desire to kill and spare not'.[18] Even more spectacular is the conversion of Sir Henry Curtis, who goes out to fight clad in leopard skins and ostrich feathers – a replica of Ignosi. At the climax of the struggle, his Viking ancestry asserts itself and he kills for the sheer joy of killing:

> There he stood, the great Dane, for he was nothing else, his hands, his axe, and his armour all red with blood, and none could live before his stroke. Time after time I saw it sweeping down, as some great warrior ventured to give him battle, and as he struck he shouted 'O-hoy! O-hoy!' like his Berserkir forefathers, and the blow went crashing through shield and spear, through head dress, hair and skull.[19]

The last of Haggard's tests points up the moral challenges that preceded it. Gripped by mortal terror, the heroes listen as the ancient witch Gagool cackles materialistic philosophy at them:

> 'The old feel not, they love not, and, ha! ha! they laugh to see another go out into the dark; ha! ha! they laugh to see the evil that is done under the stars. All they love is life, the warm, warm sun, and the sweet, sweet air. They are afraid of the cold, afraid of the cold and the dark, ha! ha! ha!' and the old hag writhed in ghastly merriment on the ground.[20]

Haggard's characters have moved progressively through a symbolic landscape from physical tests to moral tests. The closer the adventurers come to the mines, the farther they are removed from the psychological and moral verities of their age. The severity of the moral tests is increased by Gagool's affirmation at the approach to the coveted mines that all is flux and matter; there is no God and no moral law.[21] The heart of Africa is in Haggard's romances just what Conrad said it was in Heart of Darkness – a special psychological terrain in which European man confronts and nearly succumbs to his deepest fears.

Haggard developed these themes in his next two romances. *Allan Quatermain* (1887) is another quest, this time for a lost white civilisation rumoured to exist in the centre of the African continent. The white trio of *King Solomon's Mines* is resuscitated and reinforced by Umslopogaas, the bravest Zulu of them all. Haggard prepares his audience with a soliloquy on civilisation and savagery. Quatermain has tired of prissy England and longs to go back to Africa 'where the wild game was, back to the land whereof none know the history, back to the savages, whom I love, although some of them are almost as merciless as Political Economy'.[22] He goes on to expound his own sociology and psychology:

> Ah! this civilization, what does it all come to? ... It is a depressing conclusion, but in all essentials the savage and the child of civilization are identical. I dare say that the highly civilized lady reading this will smile at an old fool of a hunter's simplicity when she thinks of her black head-bedecked sister ... And yet, my dear young lady, what are those pretty things round your own neck? ...

> This being so, supposing for the sake of argument we divide ourselves into twenty parts, nineteen savage and one civilized, we must look to the nineteen savage portions of our nature, if we would really understand ourselves, and not to the twentieth, which, though so insignificant in reality, is spread all over the other nineteen, making them appear quite different from what they really are, as the blacking does a boot, or the veneer a table.[23]

Haggard illustrates his theory by once again moving a white party through a progressively bizarre series of landscapes in which physical stamina and moral fibre are tested to the limits of endurance. Man-hunting supersedes big-game hunting very early when the heroic quartet, augmented by a preternaturally ferocious missionary, lays siege to a Masai encampment. The heroes snap necks 'like dry twigs' and unleash a murderous barrage of rifle fire. Sir Henry Curtis and Umslopogaas finish side by side swinging battle axes with deadly effect until both are 'red from head to foot – Sir Henry's armour might have been painted that colour', and the dead lie strewn about 'for all the world like the people on the grass in one of the London parks on a particularly hot Sunday in August'.[24]

After the fight, the party moves on through a subterranean river and a prodigious chasm to reach the lost white 'civilization'. Zu-Vendis, as the country is called, is a blend of Kukuanaland and feudal England. The inhabitants have no technology other than architecture and are for the most part peasant farmers. An aristocracy somewhat lighter in colour than the common people rules the land in conjunction with a superstitious and Jesuitical priesthood. In daily life the Zu-Vendi people are polygamous and inclined towards libertinism. A quarrel between sister queens over the love of Sir Henry Curtis precipitates a civil war that very nearly surpasses the sanguinary climax of *King Solomon's Mines*. At the end of the book Sir Henry elects to remain in Zu-Vendis to guard the kingdom against outside penetration:

> I am convinced of the sacred duty that rests upon me of preserving to this, on the whole, upright and generous-hearted people the blessings of comparative barbarism ... I have no fancy for handing over this beautiful country to be torn and fought for by speculators, tourists, politicians and teachers ... nor will I endow it with the greed, drunkenness, new diseases, gunpowder, and general demoralization which chiefly mark the progress of civilization amongst unsophisticated peoples.[25]

At this stage the parallel with *King Solomon's Mines* is so close that one wonders why Haggard painted the Zu-Vendis white and the Kukuanas black. In lifestyle and outlook they are nearly identical. Haggard even has his heroes use their Zulu titles among the Zu-Vendis. 'Are the

Zu-Vendi a civilized or a barbarous people?' Quatermain asks himself; 'Sometimes I think the one, sometimes the other.'[26] The real point of bringing colour and ancient ruins into the romance is not to make statements about race but to make statements about us, about our psychology, our past. In the Kukuanaland of *King Solomon's Mines*, white men discover their own interior savage selves – Sir Henry Curtis puts on skins and feathers and becomes a Viking. Ruins of vanished white civilisations remind us that the Africa that is our deepest self – the nineteen savage parts – is also our past. The real Africa that Haggard knew well, the Africa of disease, squalor and stinking corruption, was the last thing he wished to put into his romances. As a result, he could not write into his stories the brand of racism he casually espoused. His purpose was to use Africans to lay bare the inner core of European man, and he had, therefore, to emphasise similarities rather than differences.

In *She* (1887), Haggard exaggerated two minor features of *King Solomon's Mines*: challenges to Victorian sexual morality and speeches on behalf of Nietzschean morality. A two-thousand-year-old Persian priestess waits for the reincarnation of her ancient lover in the heart of Africa, where she rules a barbarous people among the ruins of a vanished race. The reincarnated lover, Cambridge-educated and accompanied by a grizzled don, makes his way towards his destiny with the aid of an inscribed potsherd. (In this story the identification of present European man with an African past is made explicit.) Along the way the travellers encounter not only the usual big animals and gruesome fights, but also a wide range of perversions and inversions of conventional mores. *She*'s people are handsome but sullen cannibals of indeterminate race ('whitish-yellow'). Local custom makes women the aggressors in sexual affairs. Marriages are sealed with a kiss and as easily dissolved. The wisest old man of the cannibals is a self-confessed necrophiliac who as a boy fell in love with one of the ancient mummies that litter the landscape:

> I learned to love that dead form ... I would creep up to her and kiss her cold face, and wonder ... who had loved and embraced her in the days that long have passed away ... till one day my mother ... followed me, and ... half in dread and half in anger ... set fire to her hair, and she burnt fiercely, even down to the feet ... Presently his face brightened, and with an exclamation he drew something forth ... and revealed to my astonished gaze a beautifully shaped and almost white woman's foot, looking as fresh and firm as though it had been placed there yesterday.[27]

Other flaming mummies illuminate nocturnal orgies. More than one man in the story tends to misogyny and flies into a jealous rage when a woman competes for the attention of his beloved male companion.

Presiding over the whole carnival of perversions is Ayesha (She), the masterwork of Haggard's imagination. In many ways Ayesha is Gagool tarted up to be sexually devastating, a Diana in jackboots who preaches materialism in philosophy and fascism in politics. Social Darwinism enables her to pursue her ends without regard to her means:

> Those who are weak must perish; the earth is to the strong, and the fruits thereof. For every tree that grows a score shall wither, that the strong one may take their share. We run to place and power over the dead bodies of those who fail and fall; ay, we win the food we eat from out the mouths of starving babes. It is the scheme of things.[28]

She amuses herself with chemistry and eugenics (her servants are specially bred deaf mutes and she boasts of having once 'reared a race of giants').[29] Her favourite ruling techniques are terror and torture. She despises democracy and hates Jews. She proposes to go off to England, overthrow Victoria and reign in tandem with her lover: 'In the end, I had little doubt, she would assume absolute rule over the British dominions, and probably over the whole earth and, though I was sure that she would speedily make ours the most glorious and prosperous empire that the world has ever seen, it must be at the cost of a terrible sacrifice of life.'[30] Here is imperialism in reverse – England to be invaded Dracula-like by an irresistible African conqueror. Haggard's heroes have no defence against such an onslaught. The Cambridge don throws himself shamelessly at her feet and the reincarnated Leo Vincey is seduced over the corpse of a former lover. Only an accident saves the British throne. When the naked Ayesha re-enters the sacred fire of immortality something goes wrong and she ages two thousand years in a few terrifying moments.

All of Haggard's basic themes and characters were developed in his first three romances; later books merely rearranged the parts. *Cleopatra* (1889) and *The World's Desire* (1890) replay the theme of beautiful, power-hungry women capable of seducing all men and perverting all established values. *Allan's Wife* takes hunter Quatermain to yet another unknown country strewn with ruins; there he is pitted in mortal combat against a white baboon lady who hates him for having won the love of her mistress: 'I am a woman as she is, and you are a man, and they say in the kraals that men love women better than women love women. But it is a lie.'[31] *Eric Brighteyes* (1891) and *Nada the Lily* (1892) make an instructive pair of novels inasmuch as one cast of characters is all white and Viking while the other is entirely black and Zulu. Except for skin colour, however, the books are almost interchangeable. A hero is raised from infancy in the company of the woman he loves; there is more than a hint of incest. A rejecting father figure then casts out the hero who is forced to make his fortune by murder and pillage. The hero is betrayed by a clever woman and acquires a male boon companion who hates women and vies with them for favours. Both books feature axe murderers prone to run amok: 'My axe hung on the wainscot. I snatched it thence, and of what befell I know this alone, that when the madness passed, eight men lay stretched out before me, and all the place was but a gore of blood.'[32] Paired in this way, the books also illustrate Haggard's consistent identification of the European past with the African present. His contemporaries regarded Africans as primitive, mired in a savage stage of development through which Europeans had passed long ago. Treating the hypothesis as fact, Haggard uses both European past and African present to provide examples of repressible but ineradicable human desires.

It is a question to what extent Rider Haggard was aware of the darker aspects of his romances. He once wrote that 'sexual passion is the most powerful lever with which to stir the mind of man, for it lies at the root of all things human'.[33] On the other hand, he would have winced at much of the analysis presented above. So sensitive was he to the moral reputation of his work that when it was suggested that his novel *Beatrice* encouraged adultery, he wrote an indignant disclaimer.[34] In a public lecture in 1899, Haggard denounced immorality in novels written for adolescents. He told his audience that he had been shocked to pick up a magazine 'and read in it what was known as a slum story, in which, in the course of eight or ten pages, was set out a synopsis of almost every vice that affected humanity. There was murder, there was treachery of the blackest kind, and there were other vices which he would not name.'[35] These were precisely what any modern reader would find in his own romances that he cheerfully commended to children. Neither Haggard nor most of his readers saw the hidden themes with conscious eyes, and in this lay part of the reason for his enormous popular success. In Africa or in ancient Iceland, the beasts that Victorians feared to encounter in themselves could be contemplated at a safe remove.

Whenever Haggard put aside romances and turned his hand to writing realistic novels for adults, the results were paradoxically much more innocent, much less challenging and sinister. All five of his serious novels published before 1892 concern star-crossed lovers thwarted by bad marriages brought about by jealous rivals, property considerations or plain rotten luck. The raw material for each of the stories Haggard drew consciously from his disastrous first love affair.[36] A preoccupation with the jejune themes of lifelong passion, lifelong despair and exquisitely plotted revenge makes the novels fail signally as portraits of life. They are nonetheless interesting because of their suppression of the elemental themes unleashed in Haggard's romances: *Dawn* (1884), *The Witch's Head* (1885) and *Beatrice* (1890) feature fierce sibling hostilities; the misogynist boon companion of the romances also appears in *The Witch's Head*; four of the novels pair opposed female characters – one powerful, immoral and intellectual, the other submissive, pure and intuitive. But none of the novels begins to approach the romances in bloodshed, horror or mental pathology. If all Haggard had done were to provide innocuous outlets for repressed desires, it would be easy to place him in a familiar category. Bram Stoker's vampires, whose horror derives from their supposed ability to force their victims into taking delicious delight in unnatural practices, the ghosts concocted by M. R. James and Henry James, and a legion of incubi and succubae belong to this genre. So do the good Indians and 'bad Injuns' in whose visages Romantics divined the features of the Dionysian and demoniac savages buried deep within European bosoms.[37]

What sets Haggard apart, what put him into Freud's dreams rather than onto his couch is the theory of personality that the romances embody. Haggard set the theory out in a rustic way in Quatermain's speech about the twenty parts of the self. 'If we would readily understand ourselves' we 'must look to the nineteen savage portions of our nature'. The theory is adumbrated more elegantly and intricately in the quests for lost civilisations and treasures. Like Freud, who conceptualised the self as a three-tiered structure of superego, ego and id, Haggard portrays three layers in the human personality. As the landscape changes in Haggard's quests, so do the personalities of his European characters. On the road to King Solomon's mines, Zu-Vendis, Kôr or wherever, the layers progressively fall away. First to go is the top 5 per cent of official civilisation. It is as unserviceable as Captain Good's immaculate clothing in the bushlands of the imagination. With the top layer off, the Englishman and African are equal, more fit to fight side by side than against one another. Leopard skins and ostrich feathers are appropriate dress for both. Beneath the layer of official civilisation brothers are always rivals, sisters are sworn enemies, sons are rejected by fathers whom they subsequently replace, homosexual love is as common and as passionate as the heterosexual variety. Still deeper, beneath the second layer of personality lurks a third, elemental and horrific, which is literally unconscious. In the heat of battle, Haggard's combatants, whether Zulu, Viking or English, succumb to bloodlust – go berserk – and kill without restraint until consciousness vanishes behind a sanguinary mist.

Jung conceived of personality in another way that also accords well with Haggard's implicit model. For Jung the personality comprises a layered structure but with a time dimension. Beneath a top layer of present consciousness (including awareness of the demands of official civilisation) lies a realm of historic past (including childhood) and a subterranean level of prehistoric or racial past (the collective unconscious). Haggard's adventurers proceed from present-day Europe towards an encounter with the past in Africa. The past they encounter is their own past. Centuries, even millennia, are stripped away in the course of each quest. Significantly, Haggard's Africa teems with the ruins of white civilisations, quite unlike real Africa, which, apart from the Nile Valley and Zimbabwe, is singularly bare of monumental ruins. Under Africa's spell, English gentlemen regress and become Vikings; Cambridge rowers become ancient Greeks.[38]

Freud and Jung follow Haggard in using metaphors of landscape to describe the discovery of new facets of the self. Haggard takes his reader through swamps, dense woods or desert to a mountainous landscape where caves or caverns must first be negotiated before the journey's goal is spectacularly revealed in a bird's-eye view.[39] Freud does the same thing in the theatrical opening to the vital third chapter of his *Interpretation of Dreams*: 'When, after passing through a narrow defile, we suddenly emerge upon a piece of high ground, where the path divides and the finest prospects open up on every side, we may pause for a moment and consider in which direction we shall first turn our steps.' In a letter to his friend Wilhelm Fliess, Freud sharpened and extended the metaphor:

> The whole thing [his book] is planned on the model of an imaginary walk. First comes the dark wood of the authorities ... where there is no clear view and it is easy to go astray. Then there is a cavernous defile through which I lead my readers ... and then, all at once, the high ground and the open prospect and the question: 'Which way do you want to go?'[40]

Dreams were for Freud the 'royal road to the unconscious'. The perilous path to his own 'immortal works' led through Haggard's landscape.

Jung in his turn spoke of Freud's 'passion for knowledge which was to lay open a dark continent to his gaze'.[41] Jung, with his concept of a 'collective unconsciousness', was much closer than Freud to Haggard's identification of the savage pasts of civilised men with the 'savages' of the other dark continent. L. F. A. Maury had speculated in 1878 that man reverts to 'the state of nature' when he dreams: Havelock Ellis thought that the study of dreams might reveal 'primitive stages in the evolution of mental life'.[42] Jung carried this line of speculation to extremes. Inspired writers might catch 'a glimpse of the psychic world that terrifies the primitive and is at the same time his greatest hope'.[43] The archetypes about which Jung wrote so confidently (and vaguely) he illustrated sometimes with references to our unknown ancestors, sometimes with references to living 'primitive men'.[44]

It did not occur to Jung that his admiration for Haggard arose from their common adherence to the theory of the layered personality. Jung treated Haggard's romances as raw psychological material that verified the truth of his own superior insight:

> In general, it is the non-psychological novel that offers the richest opportunities for psychological elucidation ... Good examples of such novels are those of Benoit, or English fiction after the manner of Rider Haggard ... An exciting narrative that is apparently quite devoid of psychological intentions is just what interests the psychologist most of all. Such a tale is constructed against a background of unspoken psychological assumptions, and the more unconscious the author is of them, the more the background reveals itself in unalloyed purity to the discerning eye.[45]

So *She* appears in a select list of works of art that reveal a world of 'primordial experiences' and 'primal beginnings' transcending the conscious intentions of their creators, a list that includes Dante's *Divine Comedy*, Goethe's *Faust* and Richard Wagner's *Ring*.

Without in any way denigrating the power of Haggard's imagination, it is possible to take another view of his achievement. Haggard's romances were immensely popular because they fed the imagination of a vast reading public that had already accepted the premises, but not the conclusions, of the looming Viennese psychology. As Ernest Jones has observed, the idea of an unconscious mind was casually expounded in many places in the last two decades of the nineteenth century; the shock of Freud lay in the content rather than the concept of the unconscious.[46] Rider Haggard would have been prepared for that shock despite his honest protestations of rectitude. He knew that the key to self-knowledge lay in 'the nineteen savage parts' and that 'sexual passion lies at the root of all things human'. Though he did not know to what extent he had written those notions into his novels, a Freud or Jung could see them at once. What they saw was not, however, a confirmation of their daring theories but a reflection of them.[47] Again and again Haggard marches virtuous men into the wilderness, where they reveal hidden savage impulses and confront the awesome mysteries of their deepest inner selves.

Finally, a word about imperialism. While there is no political or economic imperialism in Haggard's romances, the instinct that would place them among 'novels of empire' is not entirely mistaken. The imperial situation made a grand metaphorical stage for encounters and battles between different sections of the self. Conrad used it to play out the tragedy of civilised ego tempted and destroyed by savages within. His Kurtz went to the Congo to bear the white man's burden and finished by succumbing to the darkness in his own psyche, which responded all too readily to its external manifestation in the black African. Imperialism for Conrad is the price one pays for civilisation – the repression of savagery at home and abroad. This notion is closely related to Freud's view that without repression civilisation would dissolve.

Haggard wrote less self-consciously and consequently placed less emphasis on the role of the imperial ego. Command and rule are underplayed. Succumbing to and identifying with the savage are vital ingredients in the reiterated formula of his exotic tales. It may be that Haggard's own need for self-revelation led him to take this approach. As a child he was so self-contained that his parents thought him dull.[48] His early unsuccessful novels contain a few thinly disguised episodes from his painful early manhood, but his autobiography is distinctly unrevealing. The European characters of Haggard's romances do what he could not do. They dive deeply into African darkness and emerge shaken but refreshed. This different use of the imperial situation in his novels helps to explain the paradox that Haggard skirted imperialism in his romances and preached it on the platform while Conrad excoriated imperialism in politics and bowed down before the imperial idea in his books.

There are many other late-Victorian writers who found the imperial situation a wonderful arena for psychological drama. Henry Miller and Graham Greene attest in their different ways to its continuing utility in the twentieth century. The arresting metaphor rather than the scramble for colonies accounts for the popular vogue for literature of exotic adventure. This literature was neither a cause nor an effect of colonial expansion and deserves study quite apart from the problems of political and economic imperialism. At the same time there may have been influences emanating from novels of Africa that did subtly affect the men who ruled Africa. Conrad's sort of novel, with its heavy emphasis on the perils of 'going native', may have kept upper lips slightly stiffer. If going to Africa was perceived as a test of one's ability to repress subconscious savage impulses, then the men who chose to go may have been more than usually anxious to prove themselves on that count. Haggard's sort of novel, on the other hand, which emphasised the exhilaration of entering into the African's way of life and ended with disquisitions on the need to protect that way of life from European onslaughts, may have contributed something to the twentieth-century popularity of indirect rule among British colonial officials.[49]

Notes

1 For the reasons set out in the Preface to this book, this chapter repeats verbatim my article, 'Rider Haggard, imperialism, and the layered personality', which appeared in *Victorian Studies* 22 (1978), 71–88. In subsequent years scholarship on Haggard proliferated. My own views were further elaborated in *Rider Haggard* (Boston: Twayne, 1983). Not long after, D. E. Whatmore's *H. Rider Haggard: A Bibliography* (London: Mansell, 1987) provided a comprehensive survey of the author's works in print. Wendy Katz took up the formal literary analysis of Haggard's work in *Rider Haggard and the Fiction of Empire* (Cambridge: Cambridge University Press, 1987). Ann McClintock further explored the gendered nature of Haggard's imperial vistas in *Imperial Leather: Race, Gender and Sexuality in the Colonial Contest* (London: Routledge, 1995). In a similar vein, see Laura Chrisman, *Rereading the Imperial Romance* (Oxford: Oxford University Press, 2000). Haggard's treatment of African landscapes and the imperial frontier are explored in Lindy Stiebel, *Imagining Africa: Landscape in H. Rider Haggard's African Romances* (Westport, CT: Greenwood Press, 2001) and Gerald Monsman, *H. Rider Haggard on the Imperial Frontier: The Political and Literary Contexts of His African Romances* (Greensboro, NC: ELT Press, 2006). A notable contribution to scholarship on Haggard's *She* is Tania Zulli's edited collection, *She: Explorations into a Romance* (Rome: Aracne, 2009). Our knowledge of Haggard's life has been hugely enriched by the researches of Stephen Coan as well as Victoria Manthorpe's *Children of Empire: The Victorian Haggards* (London: Victor Gollanz, 1996).

2 Sigmund Freud, *The Interpretation of Dreams*, ed. by James Strachey (London: George Allen & Unwin, 1954), pp. 452–5. The English edition of H. Rider Haggard's novel *Heart of the World* appeared in 1896. Freud's self-analysis, mentioned in his account of the dream, began in 1897. *The Interpretation of Dreams* was finished in September 1899; Ernest Jones, *Sigmund Freud: Life and Work*, 3 vols (London: Hogarth Press, 1953), 1:391.

3 Freud, *Interpretation of Dreams*, p. 453.

4 G. N. Sanderson, 'The European partition of Africa: coincidence or conjuncture', *Journal of Imperial and Commonwealth History* 3 (October 1974), 43.

5 Brian V. Street, *The Savage in Literature* (London: Routledge & Kegan Paul, 1975), pp. 14, 182–4.

6 Susanne Howe, *Novels of Empire* (New York: Columbia University Press, 1949), p. 20; Malcolm Elwin, *Old Gods Falling* (New York: Macmillan and Co., 1939), pp. 256–61; *Times Literary Supplement*, 30 September 1960, p. 630; Christopher Hollis in *London Magazine*, n.s., 1 (1961), 87–8.

7 C. S. Lewis, *Rehabilitations and Other Essays* (London: Oxford University Press, 1939), pp. 100–2; Sonia Orwell and Ian Angus (eds), *The Collected Essays, Journalism and Letters of George Orwell*, 4 vols (London: Seeker and Warburg, 1968), 4:22.

8 Henry Miller, *The Books in My Life* (London: Peter Owen, 1952), p. 93.

9 Graham Greene, *Journey without Maps* (Harmondsworth: Penguin, 1946), pp. 19–20. See also his *The Lost Childhood and Other Essays* (Harmondsworth: Penguin, 1962), pp. 13–14.

10 Margaret Atwood, *Survival: A Thematic Guide to Canadian Literature* (Toronto: Anansi, 1972), p. 113.

11 H. Rider Haggard, 'Jameson's surrender', *The Times*, 14 March 1896, p. 10; *Saturday Review* 101 (1906), 693–4.

12 The resemblance of some elements in the story to *Ruined Cities of Zululand* by H. M. Walmsley (London: privately published, 1869) is marked. See N. Etherington, 'South African sources of Rider Haggard's early romances', *Notes and Queries*, n.s. 24 (1977), 436–8.

13 H. Rider Haggard, *King Solomon's Mines* (London: Cassell & Co., 1949), p. 355.

14 Ibid., p. 339.

15 From time to time, however, it has been argued that *King Solomon's Mines* is both racist and imperialist. See, for example, T. J. Couzens, 'Literature and ideology: the

Patterson embassy to Lobengula 1878 and *King Solomon's Mines*', *Collected Seminar Papers, Institute of Commonwealth Studies* 18 (1975), 16–27. In a similar vein Street argues that when the white party leaves, 'Kukuanaland has become in spirit, if not in fact, a colony of the British Empire' (*The Savage in Literature*, pp. 123–4). The contrary and, to me, more convincing case is put by Alan Sandison, who contends that 'in this book, as in every other he wrote on Africa, he repudiates without fuss the whole arrogant notion of the white man's burden'; *The Wheel of Empire* (London: Macmillan, 1967), p. 31. I am in complete agreement with Sandison's reasons for denying that Haggard used the imperial situation as anything more than a striking metaphor; my views on Haggard's use of that metaphor are different.

16 Haggard, *King Solomon's Mines*, p. 194.
17 Ibid., p. 239.
18 Ibid., p. 246.
19 Ibid., pp. 248–9.
20 Ibid., p. 278.
21 This points up the distance that separates Haggard's work from much late-Victorian philosophical imperialism. Materialism, the struggle for life and the survival of the fittest are the doctrines of Haggard's villains, not his heroes.
22 H. Rider Haggard, *Allan Quatermain* (London: Longmans, Green & Co., 1887), p. 7.
23 Ibid., pp. 4, 6.
24 Ibid., p. 86.
25 Ibid., pp. 276–7.
26 Ibid., p. 156.
27 H. Rider Haggard, *The Annotated She*, ed. by N. Etherington (Bloomington: Indiana University Press, 1991), p. 76.
28 Ibid., p. 136.
29 C. S. Lewis thought 'the shallowness and folly of the things put into the mouth of She herself and offered us for wisdom' to be the most glaring fault of the book (*Rehabilitations*, p. 101). Lewis mistakes the function of the character. Ayesha's philosophy is meant to frighten rather than enlighten.
30 Haggard, *She*, p. 170.
31 H. Rider Haggard, *Allan's Wife and Other Tales* (London: Spencer Blackett, 1889), p. 150.
32 H. Rider Haggard, *Eric Brighteyes* (London: Longmans, Green & Co., 1891), p. 73.
33 H. Rider Haggard, 'About fiction', *Contemporary Review* 2 (February 1887), 172–80.
34 H. Rider Haggard, *Beatrice* (London: Longmans, Green & Co., 1895), preface.
35 *Eastern Daily Press*, 22 June 1899. Later Haggard was to call himself a 'wowser', an Australian term signifying a moral puritan (*Sydney Morning Herald*, 21 April 1913). In the same speech Haggard revealed that he could see sinister tendencies in the work of others that he never discerned in his own. Speaking of romantic potboilers of his own day, he noticed that 'mostly these books were written by women, and there was a large sale for them. If the ladies who turned them out quite understood what they were doing they would "turn off the tap".'
36 Morton Cohen, *Rider Haggard* (London: Hutchinson, 1960), pp. 50–1.
37 Peter Thorslev, Jr, 'The Wild Man's revenge', in E. J. Dudley and M. E. Novak (eds), *The Wild Man Within* (Pittsburgh: University of Pittsburgh Press, 1972), especially pp. 284–5, 295–7 and 302. Thorslev specifically places Haggard in this tradition.
38 Haggard's use of Greeks in, for example, *She* and *The World's Desire* recalls Baudet's observation that elements of the eighteenth-century Indian savage were ascribed by nineteenth-century Romantics to ancient Greeks. See Henri Baudet, *Paradise on Earth* (New Haven, CT: Yale University Press, 1965), p. 50.
39 Peter Pierce has noted the importance of Haggard's aerial views in 'Rider Haggard' (B. Litt. thesis, Oxford University, 1975), pp. 13–21.
40 Freud, *Interpretation of Dreams*, p. 122.

41 C. G. Jung, 'In memory of Sigmund Freud', in *Collected Works of C. G. Jung*, 20 vols (London: Routledge & Kegan Paul, 1966), 13:148.
42 As cited in Freud, *Interpretation of Dreams*, pp. 60, 73.
43 Jung, *Collected Works*, 13:95–6.
44 For example, 'the archetype here is the *participation mystique* of primitive man with the soil on which he dwells, and which contains the spirits of his ancestors'; ibid., p. 82.
45 Ibid., pp. 87–93.
46 Jones, *Sigmund Freud*, 1:435–6.
47 A similar view is taken by Hayden White, who treats the concepts of Freud and the post-Freudians as a process of 'remythification' in which the ancient fiction of the Wild Man is interiorised and once again treated as fact; 'The forms of wildness: archaeology of an idea', in Dudley and Novak (eds), *The Wild Man Within*, pp. 6–8.
48 H. Rider Haggard, *The Days of My Life*, ed. by C. J. Longman, 2 vols (London: Longmans, Green & Co., 1926), 1:5.
49 In *Terrific Majesty: The Powers of Shaka Zulu and the Limits of Historical Invention* (Cambridge, MA: Harvard University Press, 1998), Carolyn Hamilton traces an intricate interplay of colonial policy-making and Zulu state-craft culminating in a view of the Zulu monarchy closely approximating that put forward by Haggard's novels.

CHAPTER TWO

Love and loathing: Rudyard Kipling's India

Rudyard Kipling returned repeatedly in fiction and memoir to the childhood trauma he suffered when his parents sent him to England for schooling while they remained in India. Scholarship has exposed some of his memories of persecution as inventions and discounted others as wild exaggerations. From an internal psychological perspective, however, the hurt was real. Although the adult Kipling derided psychoanalysis as the science of 'unclean deduction' peddled by 'torpedo-bearded' Central Europeans, it is not difficult to construct a Freudian reading of his misremembered persecution. Five years old at the time of his 'exile' to England, Rudyard had yet to enter the stage of 'latency' in which the infant's Oedipal feelings of rivalry with his father for his mother's affections are repressed. It was therefore not surprising that he perceived separation from his mother as the punishment his father inflicted on him for his guilty desires. He felt himself to be in every sense 'cut off'. Later on mechanisms of repression caused him to project responsibility for this punishment onto the relatively harmless people charged with his care and schooling in England. India stood imaginatively in his mind for a paradise lost of sensual delight – until, as will be seen, the dissonance between India remembered and India lived was thrown into almost unbearably sharp relief. Imperialism as a political creed recapitulated the exercise of repression required to suppress the unresolved Oedipal drama within. Writing imaginative literature about India as an imperialist enabled Kipling to explore a whole universe of perverse and forbidden pleasures without blowing the top off the volcano.

But only just. Not long after the publication of his *Plain Tales from the Hills*, he suffered a mental collapse from which he only slowly emerged. Over the next decade he painfully reworked his vision of British India into *Kim*, a novel that followed a boy's journey to manhood without reawakening the slumbering demons of his psyche. An orphan boy who is a 'little friend to all the world', who never knows the bitterness of exile and who is gradually inducted into a sort of order of imperial chivalry whose task is guarding India from enemies within and without. *Kim* accomplished the seemingly impossible task of winning critical praise from Indian nationalists and Western literary lions, while at the same time enjoying a reputation as a wholesome book for boys, fit to stand on the shelves alongside Haggard, Henty and Stevenson. It is all the more remarkable for the way it steered clear of Kipling's extensive catalogue of pet hates.

Kipling the hater

Kipling makes his own comment on books that made the Empire in his startling story, 'Mary Postgate'. A stolid, unimaginative English serving-woman stands in her garden burning the belongings of the dead soldier she had minded in his infancy – all the while ignoring the tormented cries of a dying German aviator who dangles from the treetops. Into the fire go the 'thumbed and used Hentys, Marryats, Levers, Stevensons, Baroness Orczys, Garvices, schoolbooks, and atlases'. Into the flames as well goes a trunkload of childhood memorabilia:

> piles of the *Motor Cyclist*, the *Light Car*, and catalogues of Olympia Exhibitions; the remnants of a fleet of sailing-ships from ninepenny cutters to a three-guinea yacht; a prep.-school dressing-gown; bats from three-and-sixpence to twenty-four shillings; cricket and tennis balls; disintegrated steam and clockwork locomotives with their twisted rails; a grey and red tin model of a submarine; a dumb gramophone and cracked records; golf-clubs that had to be broken across the knee, like his walking-sticks, and an assegai; photographs of private and public school cricket and football elevens, and his O.T.C. on the line of march.[1]

There is a strong temptation to read the passage as Kipling's own 'goodbye to all that' after his soldier son went forever missing in action in 1915. There must have been a similar conflagration behind the Kipling home at 'Bateman's'. And there is a tantalising hint of deeper regret in the line: 'Wynn's things were burning well in spite of the hissing wet, though now and again a book-back with a quite distinguishable title would be heaved up out of the mass.'[2] Whose books? His own? Rider Haggard's?

The temptation must be resisted. As the screams of the dying German attest, 'Mary Postgate' breathes the rank, implacable spirit of vengeance – of Lloyd George, Clemenceau and the Versailles peace settlement. Kipling's postwar politics were no different from his pre-war politics. If anything, his anguish for the lost sons of England hardened his old beliefs. If only Britain had armed herself better and earlier. If only she had turned a deafer ear to the pacifists, liberals and socialists. If only she had marshalled the forces of Empire to better effect. If only, he lamented in smouldering letters to Haggard, the West had not been traduced by Jewish speculators and revolutionaries.[3] Kipling's political hatreds inform all his writing and are unrepentantly spewed out in the autobiography that occupied his final days.

Understanding Kipling's imperialism requires reading his political beliefs in the round and in context. He would have been perplexed by the way that much late-twentieth-century scholarship tried to roll science, liberalism, militarism, racism, faith in progress and evangelical Christianity into a single juggernaut engine of Empire opposed to all the 'otherness' of Britain's subject peoples. In his thinking, these elements of late-Victorian thought were discrete entities. Some of them formed part of his credo, others were the creeds of his enemies. As Kipling was notoriously fond of lists, enumerating the things he hated may be as good a way as any of approaching his politics. There is no need to draw fine distinctions between the expression of these hatreds in fiction and in his other prose. The opinions do not vary. As John Bayley remarks, 'his convictions and prejudices are all on the surface; and he can be frenetic, almost hysterical in the way he airs and propounds them'.[4] Four particularly ferocious hatreds head the register.

1. Kipling loathed evangelical Christians – especially missionaries. His autobiography suggests the loathing arose first in the English boarding house to which he was sent as a child. It was, he wrote, 'run with the full vigour of the Evangelical as revealed to the Woman'.[5] In his story 'Baa Baa, Black Sheep', he embroiders childhood memory with Dickensian caricature.[6] Young Punch is punished for misbehaviour that 'could only be explained on the ground of possession by the Devil', wherefore he 'was not only most excellently beaten … but he was further prayed for at family prayers'.[7] Male and female versions of this loveless killjoy crop up throughout Kipling's work: the humourless aunt of 'Mrs Hauksbee Sits Out', who had 'missionary' written 'in every line o' that head';[8] Riley, the grasping, opinionated clerk of 'A Bank Fraud', who tortures his benefactors by reading from 'grim Methody tracts';[9] the treacherous Boer preacher in 'A Sahibs' War'; the miserable sisters of 'The House Surgeon', whose reason is deranged 'on the religious side';[10] the Anglican priest, Bennett, whose spiritual coldness compares so badly in *Kim* with the warmth of the Catholic, Father Victor. At times Kipling veers towards a condemnation of all organised religion. In 'The Finest Story in the World' he imagines the

sequence of events that might unfold after a discovery confirming the truth of reincarnation:

Preachers would found a fresh conduct of life upon it, swearing that it was new and that they had lifted the fear of death from all mankind. Every Orientalist in Europe would patronise it discursively with Sanskrit and Pali texts. Terrible women would invent unclean variants of the men's belief for the elevation of their sisters. Churches and religions would war over it ... I foresaw the scuffles that would arise among half a dozen denominations all professing 'the doctrine of the True Metempsychosis as applied to the world and the New Era'.[11]

2. Kipling hated Liberals and liberalism. Gladstone, the Liberal prime minister, is detested in general for 'calling down brimstone upon the British Dominions' and in particular for appointing another Liberal, Lord Ripon, to be viceroy of India. In *Something of Myself* Ripon is maligned for making it 'a matter of principle that Native Judges should try white women'.[12] (This is Kipling's misleading description of a bill that removed the right of Europeans to be tried by Europeans alone. As a court reporter, he would have known that it was extremely rare for a white woman to be tried for anything.) In the story 'The Head of the District', Ripon is caricatured as the Viceroy who, 'on principle', appointed a Bengali to be deputy commissioner in a frontier posting. Ripon's cherished 'principle' produces a rebellion among people incapable of respecting a bespectacled 'Babu'. Liberal principle, in Kipling's view, 'ends not seldom in bloodshed'.[13] Another hit at the Liberals appears as an irrelevant interlude in the love story, 'Without Benefit of Clergy'. A radical MP, 'wandering about India in pot-hat and frock-coat' and talking 'largely of the benefits of British rule', suggests 'as the one thing needful the establishment of a duly qualified electoral system and a general bestowal of the franchise'. This ghastly prospect is averted when the onset of a cholera epidemic scares the Member for Lower Tooting into taking 'his enlightened self out of India'.[14] Even the army is fatally touched by Liberal reform after the 1870s when new principles of territorial recruitment and short service make the raw English urbanite cannon fodder for the bloodthirsty Afghans. Armed with imperfect knowledge, cursed with the rudiments of an imagination, hampered by the intense selfishness of the lower classes and unsupported by any regimental associations, this young man is suddenly introduced to an enemy who in eastern lands is always ugly, generally tall and hairy, and frequently noisy.[15] The worst terrors of a hypothetical Liberal India are foreshadowed in the nightmare of Morrowbie Jukes who falls among outcast Indians and is fed on his own dead horse. 'Gunga Dass explained that horse was better than

crow, and "greatest good of greatest number is political maxim. We are now Republic, Mister Jukes, and you are entitled to a fair share of the beast. If you like, we will pass a vote of thanks. Shall I propose?" '[16]

3. Kipling despised most literary and artistic society. This is surprising, considering that his aunt married the painter Edward Burne-Jones, and he had spent the school holidays of his adolescence in houses where the shambling figure of William Morris was treated as a surrogate uncle and 'somewhere in the background were people called Jean Ingelow and Christina Rossetti'.[17] Hailed as the new Dickens after *Plain Tales from the Hills*, Kipling declined to settle among London's literary bohemians, choosing instead a busy side street off the Strand. Looking back on that period near the end of his life, he remembered mingling for a time with an artistic crowd

> whom I by no means loved. They were overly soft-spoken or blatant, and dealt in pernicious varieties of safe sedition. For the most part they seemed to be purveyors of luxuries to the Aristocracy, whose destruction by painful means they loudly professed to desire. They derided my poor little Gods of the East, and asserted that the British in India spent violent lives oppressing the Native
>
> The more subtle among them had plans, which they told me, for snatching away England's arms when she isn't looking – just like a naughty child – so that when she wants to fight she'll find she can't. (We have come far on that road since.) Meantime, their aim was peaceful, intellectual penetration and the formation of what today would be called cells in unventilated corners. Collaborating with these gentry was a mixed crowd of wide-minded, wide-mouthed Liberals.[18]

Plainly, it was politics rather than literature that alienated him from the artistic left. The discovery that his antipathy was cordially reciprocated reinforced his hatred: 'as soon as the first bloom had faded off my work, my normal output seemed to have the gift of arriding *per se* the very people I most disliked.'[19] In 'Dayspring Mishandled' Kipling paints another thoroughly unpleasant picture of similar characters – undisciplined, back-biting, plagued by drink and syphilis. He found a more sympathetic, better-dressed literary society at the Saville Club, along with Rider Haggard, Edmund Gosse, Andrew Lang and Thomas Hardy. His ideal editor was W. E. Henley, editor of the *Scots Observer*, who had an appealing 'organic loathing of Mr. Gladstone and all Liberalism'. It was thus to the *Observer* that Kipling sent *Barrack-Room Ballads* and verses denouncing Irish Home Rulers.[20]

4. It goes without saying that he despised pacifists of all stripes. He held them responsible for most British wars and deaths in battle, arguing

that military strength and the judicious use of force at the proper time prevented war by deterring aggressors. He offered no analysis of pacifism, but put the blame for that pernicious doctrine on the people he loved to hate: evangelical do-gooders, Liberals and revolutionaries. The evangelicals were simply hypocritical, denouncing army recruitment even as they talked of 'puttin' on th' whole armour o' righteousness, an' fightin the good fight o' faith'.[21] Liberals were penny wise and pound foolish, leaving the fighting forces perpetually undermanned and under-armed. He vaguely suggested that it was liberal thinking that generally prevented decisive action on the far-flung frontiers of the Empire, thereby wasting the money it sought to save. 'Thank Heaven', a clear-headed officer reflects in one story, 'the trouble came at once ... it is better to have a sharp, short outbreak than five years of impotent administration inside the Border. It costs less.'[22] It was failure to introduce conscription, not militarism and jingoism, that were to blame for 'the effortless, ordered drift towards Armageddon' in 1914.[23]

The Boer War leagued all his pacifist enemies together and generated wounding criticism of his own work – criticism that he answered in kind. In his opinion there would never have been a war if Gladstone had not foolishly granted independence to the Transvaal rebels in 1881. Misplaced kindness rather than cruelty explained the concentration camps where Boer women and children died. 'We charged ourselves step by step with the care and maintenance of all Boerdom – women and children included. Whence horrible tales of our atrocities in the concentration-camps.'[24] Refusing to use Indian regiments in the fighting on the grounds that black men should not be used against whites was another philanthropic mistake.[25] And the peace was a supreme folly.

> At long last, we were left apologizing to a deeply-indignant people, whom we had been nursing and doctoring for a year or two; and who now expected, and received, all manner of free gifts and appliances for the farming they had never practised. We put them in a position to uphold and expand their primitive lust for racial domination, and thanked God we were 'rid of a knave'.[26]

In Kipling's view, like it or not, England's safety depended on another kind of primitive lust, that shown by the trained killer, Stanley Ortheris, as he guns down an Indian deserter in the story 'On Greenhow Hill'.

> Ortheris suddenly rose to his knees, his rifle at his shoulder, and peered across the valley in the clear afternoon light. His chin cuddled the stock, and there was a twitching of the muscles of the right cheek as he sighted; Private Stanley Ortheris was engaged on his business. A speck of white crawled up the watercourse.

> 'See that beggar ... Got 'im.'
>
> Seven hundred yards away, and a full two hundred down the hillside, the deserter of the Aurangabadis pitched forward, rolled down a red rock, and lay very still, with his face in a clump of blue gentians, while a big raven flapped out of the pine wood to make investigation.
>
> 'That's a clean shot, little man,' said Mulvaney ... Ortheris did not reply. He was staring across the valley with the smile of the artist who looks on the completed work.

Kipling's admirers generally slide round his hatreds. It is harder to marvel at his stupendous craftsmanship when you think about some of the purposes to which it was put. However, Kipling's political passions are not incidental; they are fundamental to his artistic achievement. The best way to deal with them is to take the advice of the 'torpedo-bearded' psychiatrist in 'A Madonna of the Trenches': 'Suppose we face Bogey instead of giving him best every time.' Facing the bogey in this instance means confronting his views on race and empire head-on. In the process, it becomes possible to correct some common misreadings of his work.

On the first page of the first story in *Plain Tales from the Hills*, Kipling introduces the Himalayan hill woman, Lispeth, who reappears in the penultimate chapter of his masterwork, *Kim*. Raised from infancy on a mission station, she falls in love with an Englishman only to find her desire for marriage condemned on racial grounds by the very missionaries who had preached to her so fervently of the equality of all believers. Disillusioned, she rejects Christianity and returns to her own people:

> Look, you have cast out Love! What Gods are these
> You bid me please?
> The Three in One, the One in Three? Not so!
> To my own gods I go.
> It may be they shall give me greater ease
> Than your cold Christ and tangled Trinities

This story has been praised as a welcome deviation from the racial imperialism that affects so much of Kipling's work: 'it is Lispeth the hill girl the reader supports and not her English lover or the English missionaries who try to educate her into civilization.'[27] Yet, in view of Kipling's attitude to missionaries, this should come as no surprise. The missionary's wife in 'Lispeth' is another version of the persecuting evangelical woman of 'Baa Baa, Black Sheep' and Kipling's own remembered childhood. Like them, she is a hypocrite, cloaking self-interest and prejudice in a pose of toleration. The moral of

'Lispeth' is not that love ought to triumph over racial divisions. It is rather that evangelical cant should not deceive people into ignoring those divisions. The same point is given a hard edge in 'Baa Baa, Black Sheep', when Punch reflects on the indignities inflicted by 'the Woman's' choice of a school:

> He took stock of his associates. Some of them were unclean, some of them talked in dialect, many dropped their h's, and there were two Jews and a negro, or some one quite as dark, in the assembly. 'That's a *hubshi*,' said Black Sheep to himself. If I was with my father ... I shouldn't *speak* to those boys. He wouldn't let me. They live in shops. I saw them go into shops – where their fathers live and sell things.' ... He was thrashed at school before the Jews and the *hubshi*.[28]

Punch, Lispeth and young Kipling are all victims of the false doctrine of universal brotherhood.

Interpreters of Kipling's work also tend to ignore the precision of his political references. Often when he appears to be enunciating general principles he is commenting quite specifically on political figures and issues of the day. 'The Head of the District' personally targets Lord Ripon. His famous admonition to 'take up the white man's burden' addressed the United States on the occasion of the Spanish–American War. A Russian and a Frenchman figure as the villains of *Kim* because the leaders of those countries had recently formed a dual alliance that Kipling believed threatened British rule in India. (He did not foresee that within a very few years Britain would join them in the Triple Entente.) By locating the exact context of the poem 'Recessional', we can avoid the conventional reading of it as an elegiac comment on Empire and a reproach to jingoism. When Kipling wrote in *Something of Myself* that he felt during 'the Great Queen's Diamond Jubilee ... a certain optimism that scared me', he was far from registering a complaint about either militarism or imperial expansion.[29] He was scared by what 'men were telling me about affairs outside England'. There was 'trouble in South Africa after the Jameson Raid which promised ... further trouble. Altogether, one had a sense of "a sound going in the tops of the mulberry trees" – of things moving into position as troops move.' What England needed was a timely warning of the need for a military build-up. Otherwise, the Empire might fall to the barbarians.

This perception of an Empire threatened by upstart rivals and world war was the predominant strain of imperialism at the turn of the century.[30] It counted more for Kipling than any lust for colonial expansion. It provides a more convincing explanation for his antagonism to anti-imperial nationalist movements than racial theory. The 'Great Game', not just in India, but across the globe, was intended to prevent the British territory from falling into the hands of less worthy European imperial powers. The spy theme in *Kim* is not, as some would argue, a digression from the main story, but a central concern. Kipling really believed that misguided British do-gooders and Indian nationalism could deliver the subcontinent into the hands of much worse alien rulers.

Race

For a man so good at hating, it is remarkable how rarely Kipling injects the spirit of racial hatred in his work. To say that Kipling was a racist is like saying a mariner knows the sea. It reduces an extremely complex body of thought to a one-dimensional cartoon. Race for Kipling did not function primarily as a device for separating whites and blacks. Nor was it predicated on distinctions drawn between superior and inferior peoples. It permeated and explained the world. It was as useful for explaining the difference between a Yorkshireman and a Cornishman as for understanding Hindus and Pathans. 'Now, a Dalesman from beyond Skipton will forgive an injury', says the narrator of 'Pig', 'but a South Devon man is as soft as a Dartmoor bog. You can see from their names that Nafferton had the race-advantage of Pinecoffin.'[31] The villagers in the area round Kipling's home 'came of a smuggling, sheep-stealing stock, brought more or less into civilization within the past three generations'.[32] He himself was the product of a father with 'sage Yorkshire outlook and wisdom' and a mother 'all Celt and three-parts fire'.[33] Swedes made 'first-class immigrants' because their race had been hardened by ice and snow.[34] America had been racially weakened by the loss of a million strong men in the Civil War and by the turn of the century was being swamped by less fit immigrants.[35] Despite his frequent use of the term 'English' as a synonym for British, Kipling drew fine, if not always consistent, distinctions among the Celts and Saxons of the British Isles. Perhaps because he had seen at first hand the importance of the Irish as agents of Empire in India, he avoided the common tendency to view them as inferior to the Saxons. The hero of *Kim* is Irish on both sides of his family, 'Irish enough by birth to reckon silver the least part of any game'.[36] Young McTurk of *Stalky & Co.* is another kind of Irish. 'In his holidays he was viceroy of four thousand naked acres, only son of a three-hundred-year-old house, lord of a crazy fishing-boat, and the idol of his father's shiftless tenantry; yet given to crooning "Oh, Paddy dear, and did ye hear the news that's goin' round?" '[37]

The nastier forms of simple-minded racism tend, in Kipling's writing, to be ascribed to other people. It is the Boers who display the 'primitive lust for racial domination'. It is a hopeless regiment of city-bred cowards who ignorantly look forward to fighting '"niggers" – people who ran away if you shook a stick at them', and who, 'not knowing much of the nature of the Goorkhas', make the mistake of treating them as they would treat any other 'niggers'.[38] It is a Sikh in South Africa who objects to contact with 'all Kaffirs – filth unspeakable'.[39] It is a 'Khusru Kheyl tribesman' who regards educated Bengalis as 'hated and despised animals'. It is the Russian spy in *Kim* who dismisses Hurree Babu as a 'monstrous hybrid' of East and West.[40] Colonel Creighton warns Kim against picking up colonial prejudices at St Xavier's school:

> 'There is a good spirit in thee. Do not let it be blunted at St. Xavier's. There are many boys there who despise the black men.'
>
> 'Their women were bazar-women,' said Kim. He knew well there is no hatred like that of the half-caste for his brother-in-law.[41]

Kim's quick response is meant to drive home Kipling's point, which is that the white colonial racist is only one variety of a universal phenomenon. Anyone, says the narrator of 'Jews in Shushan', who 'believes in the Brotherhood of Man should hear' his Mohammedan servant grinding the word 'Jew' between 'his white teeth with all the scorn he dare show before his master'.[42]

The twentieth century teems with racial theorists who proceeded from that point to argue for segregation, ethnic cleansing or final solutions. Kipling never does. No one was meant to take at face value the famous dictum that 'East is East and West is West and never the twain should meet' (generally misquoted as never the twain *shall* meet). Nor was Kipling pointing a moral when he wrote, 'a man should, whatever happens, keep to his own caste, race and breed. Let the White go to the White and the Black to the Black. Then, whatever trouble falls is in the ordinary course of things – neither sudden, alien nor unexpected.'[43] Kipling interested himself most intensely in the alien and unexpected products of the collisions and intersections of difference. Empire provided unparalleled opportunities for exploring those themes.

He wrote more realistically and sympathetically about interracial romance than either Haggard or Conrad. Social convention, not the authorial voice, brings these pairings to sad conclusions.[44] Kipling took pains to paint the Indian partners as tender and caring. In 'Without Benefit of Clergy', Holden claims his Ameera is a happier mother than white women, who 'give their children over to the nurses'.[45] Kipling avoided hinting that love across the racial divide delivered special ecstasies. 'Much', he said, 'that is written about Oriental passion and impulsiveness is exaggerated and compiled at second-hand.'[46] Nor did

Kipling use colour as a key to understanding the behaviour of female characters. Bisra of 'Beyond the Pale', who was 'fairer than bar-gold in the Mint', is treated in much the same way as Ameera, whose colour is unspecified. The women of Kafiristan, 'fair as you or me', present Europeans with the same dangers of miscegenation as darker-skinned ones of other regions.[47] On the other hand, interracial sex in Kipling's fiction, like the colonial societies he knew, is a one-way traffic. White men consort with native women, never native men with white women.

While steering clear of E. M. Forster's theme of white women in company with educated Indian men, he took a keen interest in the indigenous elites. Rider Haggard kept his Africans in Africa, beyond the frontiers of colonial authority. Kipling writes of Indians working in offices, directing engineering projects, owning yachts and foiling foreign spies. He even brings some home to England. The university-educated Bengali male appears in three different guises. He first crops up in 'The Head of the District', as Mr Grish Chunder Dé, MA, a figure of fun designed to show the futility of using Indians to rule India. This man, 'who had been to England and charmed many drawing-rooms there', is hardly allowed to speak before being bundled off stage.[48] In *Kim*, the same fat man recurs as Hurree Chunder Mookerjee, an accomplished spy. He also holds an MA from Calcutta University, though his account of his education undermines the reader's confidence in that institution:

> he, an MA of Calcutta University would explain the advantages of education. There were marks to be gained by due attention to Latin and Wordsworth's *Excursion* ... Also a man might go far, as he himself had done, by strict attention to plays called *Lear* and *Julius Caesar*, both much in demand by examiners ... Still more important than Wordsworth, or the eminent authors, Burke and Hare, was the art and science of mensuration.[49]

Finally he reappears in 'The Finest Story in the World' as Grish Chunder, 'a young, fat, full-bodied Bengali, dressed with scrupulous care in frock-coat, tall hat, light trousers, and tan gloves'. Son of a retired official, his first degree paid for 'by the brutal Indian Government', he studies law in London while posing as the 'cadet of a royal house' and dining out on 'stories of the brutal Indian bureaucrats who ground the faces of the poor'.[50] This cynical radical is in every respect the intellectual and social equal of the story's narrator. Kipling never drew a more sympathetic portrait of a Liberal.

The Rao of Baraon in 'The Bridge Builders' represents another kind of elite, the pensioned-off Indian nobility of the formerly independent states. This young man dedicates his life to hunting and playing billiards with English gentlemen. 'He had been bear-led by an English tutor of sporting tastes for some five or six years, and was now royally wasting the revenues accumulated during his minority by the Indian government.'[51] Like Grish Chunder, he professes a thoroughly modern outlook; he finds religious ceremonies a 'dam-bore'. Kipling's critique parallels Marxist denunciations of a corrupt aristocracy bought by the colonial state. In the same story Kipling contrasts the uselessness of the rajah and his class with the practical skill of Peroo the Lascar, chief foreman on the bridge works. While some critics dismiss Peroo as a colonialist stereotype of the cooperative native, he is a far more complex creation than, for example, Gunga Din.

> It was Peroo who had saved the girder of Number Seven pier from destruction when the new wire-rope jammed in the eye of the crane, and the huge plate tilted in its slings, threatening to slide out sideways. Then the native workmen lost their heads with great shoutings, and Hitchcock's right arm was broken by a falling T-plate, and he buttoned it up in his coat and swooned, and came to and directed for four hours till Peroo, from the top of the crane, reported 'All's well,' and the plate swung home. There was no one like Peroo, serang, to lash, and guy, and hold, to control the donkey engines, to hoist a fallen locomotive craftily out of the borrow-pit into which it had tumbled; to strip, and dive, if need be, to see how the concrete blocks round the piers stood the scouring of Mother Gunga, or to adventure upstream on a monsoon night and report on the state of the embankment-facings. He would interrupt the field councils of Findlayson and Hitchcock without fear, till his wonderful English, or his still more wonderful *lingua-franca*, half Portuguese and half Malay, ran out and he was forced to take string and show the knots that he would recommend.[52]

No downtrodden water-carrier, this technical miracle-worker claimed to having once 'prayed to the low-pressure cylinder' in the engine room of a steamship – out of sheer wonderment at the technology. The story charts his progress from mere scepticism to downright rejection of the Hindu gods. Meantime, under the influence of opium the white engineer Finlayson dreams of supernatural beings. Peroo makes an instructive contrast with Joseph Conrad's portrayal of an African boiler-tender in *Heart of Darkness*. The narrator, Marlow, 'had to watch the steering, and circumvent those snags, and get the tin-pot [steamer] along by hook or by crook'.

> And between whiles I had to look after the savage who was fireman. He was an improved specimen; he could fire up a vertical boiler. He was there below me, and, upon my word, to look at him was as edifying as seeing a dog in a parody of breeches and a feather hat, walking on his

> hind-legs ... He squinted at the steam-gauge and at the water gauge with an evident effort of intrepidity ... He ought to have been clapping his hands and stamping his feet on the bank, instead of which he was hard at work, a thrall to strange witchcraft, full of improving knowledge.[53]

Employing similar material, the self-announced racist and imperialist Kipling delivers a powerful and imaginative portrayal of Indian intellectual capacity, while the supposed anti-imperialist Conrad serves up a racist cliché.

Gentlemanly chameleons

The conundrum posed by Kipling's work is to explain how a man who flew his hatreds, prejudices and his imperialism boldly from the masthead wrote as well as he did about India under colonial rule. A great many of his poems – for example, 'Song of the White Men' – would do very well as Brown Shirt marching songs. Yet, in an intellectual climate that generally pitted Europeans against an undifferentiated 'otherness' of subject peoples, Kipling slings a rainbow of diversity across the South Asian landscape. In seeking explanations, most serious critics have been driven, willy-nilly, towards the theories of another 'torpedo-bearded' psychiatrist, Sigmund Freud. Although he associated Freud with the 'intimacy of unclean deduction',[54] in many, many ways Kipling positively invites psychological investigation. Like the other artists in this study, he was not given to straightforward self-revelation. His autobiography promises only *Something of Myself*. His favourite device for story-telling is the inner narrator, someone who is not the author but is introduced by the author. Sometimes, as in 'Love of Women', he introduces a narrator who introduces another narrator who in turn tells someone else's tale. Frames within frames, boxes within boxes, make it hard to find subjects who speak on their own behalf, and virtually impossible to find the inner Kipling. Race is only one of several devices Kipling used to differentiate 'them' from 'us'.

The British Tommy – Private soldier Thomas Atkins – ostensibly celebrated in Kipling's army stories, is no more a subject than the Indian characters. He speaks a dialect, generally Irish or provincial, which can verge on the impenetrable. 'A little before I was inviladed from Burma, me an' four an'-twinty young wans undher a Lift'nint Brazenose, was ruinin' our dijeshins thryin' to catch dacoits. An' such double-inded divils I niver knew! 'Tis only a *dah* an' a Snider that makes a dacoit.'[55] Frequently the story hiding behind the dialect is not about Tommy at all, but about some fallen gentleman – a gentleman ranker – who once was 'one of us'. Thus Larry Tighe, the syphilitic Don Juan of 'Love of

Women', reveals 'by the turn av his spache whin he was not takin' care to talk rough that he was a gentleman ranker'.[56] And the mysterious marine, Vickery, who committed some monstrous, unnamed crime against the barmaid, Mrs Bathurst, was 'a superior man ... long, black-'aired, genteely speakin'.[57] Macklin in 'The Janeites', who lectures ''is superior officers up an' down' when drunk, gives his past away by ''is toff's voice'.[58] The use of Celtic, provincial or working-class characters as 'frame narrators' in stories of this type distances readers from them and from direct complicity in the inner action of the drama. Their function is the same as the Sikh narrator in 'A Sahibs' War', who simultaneously discloses and holds at arm's length the brutal revenge taken on a Boer family by British and Australian troops.

A vital difference between gentleman rankers – us – and Tommies – the others – is social mobility. Gentlemen have the power to rise and fall. Tommies stay put. In none of Kipling's stories do we meet a working-class person or common soldier who moves upwards on the social scale. They are as fixed in their identities and destinies as the racially and culturally anchored Indian characters. Gentlemen, on the other hand, move in fascinating and perilous ways. 'Strickland of the Police' is the master of a dozen dialects and disguises that enable him, when he wishes, to adopt any identity. He may curse like a Pathan horse-dealer without detection, whereas even a university-educated Bengali will give himself away in English by his funny accent. The adolescent gentlemen heroes of Kipling's public school stories possess the same ability at effortless adaptation. Thus Stalky replies in perfect provincial cadences to a gamekeeper's wife who treats his gang to berries and cream:

> 'Come yeou right in an' set down, my little dearrs,' said the woman. 'They'll niver touch my man. He'll poach 'em to rights. Iss fai! Fresh berries an' cream. Us Dartymoor folk niver forgit their friends '
>
> 'Us'll take un with us when we'm finished here. I reckon yeou'm busy. We'll bide here an' – 'tis washin' day with yeou, simly,' said Stalky. 'We'm no company to make all vitty for. Never yeou mind us. Yiss. There's plenty cream.'[59]

Less fortunate gentlemen fall rather than move. Tighe falls into dissipation. Trejago falls into a dangerous liaison. McIntosh Jellaludin and a host of others fall into drunkenness. Morrowbie Jukes falls into a crater full of demons. In Kipling's Indian newspaper office 'one met men going up and down the ladder in every shape of misery and success'.[60] The desire to rise and the fear of falling preoccupied Dickens and a great many other middle-class writers during the unsettling period of industrialisation and modernisation in Britain. The dramatisation of these hopes and fears reproduced in secular terms the evangelical

Protestantism that Kipling loved to hate. On the frontiers of Empire anxieties proliferated. You could lose not only your class position but your racial identity, your health, your mind, your very soul. An unimaginably vast distance separated the heaven of achievement from the hell of failure. Lose your hold on the bottom of 'the ladder' and you disappeared into a bottomless pit of perdition. Rise to the top and you ruled a territory bigger than France. ('You' being in all cases an educated, middle-class white man; other creatures who attempt to move are pitied, scorned or ridiculed.)

Persistent anxieties about identity and salvation give Kipling's early work a dangerous edge lacking in Haggard's imperial romances. Haggard's country gentlemen exult in their temporary roles as Kukuana or Zu-Vendis. We never fear that they may permanently lose caste. In Kipling's best work the heroes dizzily tread the edge of the abyss. 'The Man Who Would Be King' is particularly striking for the way it constantly threatens to dissolve the all-important lines separating 'them' from 'us'. Two ex-soldiers, Peachey Carnehan and Daniel Dravot, who have previously managed a hand-to-mouth existence as blackmailers and confidence men, decide to conquer a kingdom in Central Asia with twenty modern rifles and their knowledge of military drill. Playing on existing tribal divisions and similarities between the prevailing religion and Freemasonry, they achieve their goal, only to see their dreams dissolve when Dravot's marriage to a local woman destroys the illusion of their godlike powers.

At the head of the text stands a quotation ostensibly affirming the democracy preached by Freemasonry – 'Brother to a Prince and fellow to a beggar if he be found worthy' – which is immediately undercut by the narrator, who points out that the 'Law, as quoted, lays down a fair conduct of life, and one not easy to follow'.[61] This narrator, a journalist rather like Kipling in his Indian newspaper days, goes on to substantiate his observation with a series of contradictory assertions. First he soliloquises on class divisions in railway carriages.

> There had been a Deficit in the Budget, which necessitated travelling, not Second-class, which is only half as dear as First-class, but by Intermediate, which is very awful indeed. There are no cushions in the Intermediate class, and the population are either Intermediate, which is Eurasian, or native, which for a long night journey is nasty, or Loafer, which is amusing though intoxicated ... in hot weather Intermediates are taken out of the carriages dead, and in all weathers are most properly looked down on. (p. 217)

Having retailed the perils of 'Intermediate', he plunges into a description of how he nonetheless undertook a commission for someone of the Loafer class 'with an educated taste for whisky', solely on the basis of their common bond of Freemasonry. This particular Loafer, Peachey Carnehan, denounces the Indian government for putting bureaucratic obstacles in the way of economic development and the narrator is 'disposed to agree with him'. Carnehan's ideas about economic development include, as it turns out, skulduggery, fraud and blackmail in the Independent Native States, which, the narrator informs us, 'are the dark places of the earth, full of unimaginable cruelty, touching the Railway and the Telegraph on one side, and, on the other, the days of Harun-al-Raschid'. The rulers of 'the little rat-trap states of Central India or Southern Rajputna', he continues, are generally 'drugged, drunk, or diseased from one end of the year to the other' (pp. 220–1). Just as the reader is learning how to tell bogus kings from real ones, the narrator again pulls the rug out with ironic references to the European 'Empires and the Kings' who 'continue to divert themselves as selfishly as before'. He complains about having to hold up production of his little paper till all hours of the morning, waiting to get the latest telegram about 'a King or courtier or a courtesan'.

Distinctions of race are as fuzzy as distinctions of authority. Before setting off, the adventurers read that the inhabitants of Kafiristan 'think they're related to us English' (p. 227).[62] The speculation seems to be confirmed when they meet 'fair men – fairer than you or me – with yellow hair and remarkable well built'. The women, likewise, are 'fair as you or me'. When 'the Chiefs come round to shake hands … they were so hairy and white and fair it was just shaking hands with old friends'. Soon Dravot is convinced that they are 'white people – sons of Alexander [the Great] – and not like common, black Mohammedans' (pp. 227, 235, 237, 241–2). 'These men aren't niggers; they're English! Look at their eyes – look at their mouths. Look at the way they stand up. They sit on chairs in their own houses. They're the Lost Tribes, or something like it, and they've grown to be English' (pp. 243–4). Until the debacle of the marriage reveals the real distance between the rulers and the ruled, Dravot and Carnehan believe that the similarities between Masonic rites and the local religion are evidence of cultural as well as racial kinship.

Why does Kipling insist on blurring the lines that are so important to his conservative politics? Explanations vary according to the readers' interpretations of this exceptionally rich story. It is entirely plausible to argue that this is yet another of Kipling's cautionary tales about the dangers of crossing lines, especially lines that are almost invisible. 'The beginning of everything', the narrator tells us, was the promiscuous mixing of humanity in Intermediate class on the train from Mhow to Ajmir. Peachey and Daniel have been many things, 'soldier, sailor, compositor, photographer, proof-reader, street-preacher', not to mention 'boiler-fitters, engine-drivers, petty contractors' (p. 225). They have never, however, been gentlemen – even when engaged in impersonation. Dravot is 'a big man with a red beard, and a great swell he is. You'll find him sleeping like a gentleman with all his luggage round him in a Second-class apartment. But don't you be afraid' (p. 219). Their road to destruction through over-reaching ambition begins in India where they dress in white, pretending to a class status above themselves. It continues in Kafiristan where Dravot fatally ignores distinctions of race and culture: 'These men aren't niggers; they're English!' Viewed in this fashion, the story echoes the opening lines to 'Beyond the Pale': 'A man should, whatever happens, keep to his own caste, race and breed.'

An entirely different way of reading the story is to focus on the religious elements. Dravot goes to his death with a mock crown on his head. Peachey has nails driven through his hands, is 'crucified' between two trees and is last heard crazily singing a hymn.

> The Son of Man goes forth to war,
> A golden crown to gain;
> His blood-red banner streams afar –
> Who follows in his train?

Despised and rejected, men of the commonest sort attempt to inaugurate a kingdom where there shall be neither Jew nor Gentile. They gather followers as they go until they meet death at the hands of an outraged, Pharisaical priesthood. At one point Dravot gives the narrator Christ's promise, 'Half my kingdom shall you have, as the saying is' (p. 231). Interestingly, the reader is offered the choice of reading the religious elements in opposite senses. Taken seriously, the story is a trope of the Gospels with a lowly Christ crucified. Read the other way, it becomes one more comical tract against evangelical religion and its ridiculous premise of the equality of all believers. (Kipling was quite capable of holding both views simultaneously.)

From another highly plausible perspective the story reads as an allegory of empire. The conquest of Kafiristan, like the British conquest of India, is carried out by a few men whose strategy is to side with certain local rulers in their long-standing quarrels with other rulers. A locally recruited native army then maintains imperial overrule until a rebellion breaks out analogous to the Indian Mutiny of 1857 ('This business is our Fifty-Seven'). Again, however, there is doubt about what moral ought to be drawn from the tale. When all is lost, Dravot lashes out at failures in technology and personnel. 'It's your fault', he says to Carnehan, 'for not looking after your Army better. There was mutiny in the midst, and you didn't know – you damned engine-driving, plate-laying, missionary's-pass-hunting hound!' (p. 250). Carnehan, on the other hand, blames faulty ideology and policy. 'Dealings with a woman in foreign parts, though you was a crowned King twenty times over, could not but be risky' (p. 248). The policy of using Masonic ritual to control the priesthood, which Dravot had claimed would make 'running the country as easy as a four-wheeled bogie on a down grade' (p. 240), was not only contrary to strict Masonic law but also a very shaky cultural foundation for rulership. Carnehan seems to argue that kingship requires a reliable, invincible military. By simultaneously posing as a god and trying to assimilate his subjects to English values, Dravot had built a contradiction into the edifice of rule. That analysis squares with the posture Kipling adopts in 'The Head of the District' and other stories that condemn the policy of recruiting Indian personnel as equal partners in the project of imperial rule. A third lesson that will occur to thoughtful readers is that all projects of colonialism are fatally flawed.

Taken more literally, 'The Man Who Would Be King' reflects on the pitfalls of a particular variant of nineteenth-century colonialism. The prototype was the sultanate of Sarawak that Englishman James Brooke established in north Borneo – self-sufficient and independent of formal ties to Britain or any other European state. 'We have decided', Dravot and Carnehan state with intentional brutality, 'that there is only one place now in the world that two strong men can Sar-a-*whack*. They call it Kafiristan' (p. 226). Brooke's real-life adventure resonated with a venerable European power fantasy realised by Shakespeare in *The Tempest* and by Defoe in *Robinson Crusoe*. In *King Solomon's Mines* Rider Haggard's trio of adventurers had been treated as 'gods from the stars', but had ultimately rejected the prospect of opening up a country to be fought over by missionaries, gun-runners and gin peddlers. In the sequel, *Allan Quatermain*, the same fantasy had been carried to a greater extent by the same trio. At the end of the novel Sir Henry Curtis assumes the mantle of kingship with the express purpose of closing his happy realm to the dangerous forces of economic development.

Kipling completely alters the tone by changing the social class of his protagonists. Although Dravot burns half his beard to impress the natives (Captain Good had shaved half his beard in *King Solomon's Mines*) and the adventurers arrive in Kafiristan 'just as though we had tumbled from the skies', they parody the ideal English gentlemen of Haggard's tales. They are much closer to the grotesques of Conrad's 'Outpost of Progress' – a story that anticipated the horrors of *Heart of Darkness* but with a cast of characters incapable of engaging our empathy. Foredoomed by their class position, they lack the discipline and knowledge required to carry off their audacious project. Yet, like Haggard, Kipling returned again and again to the underlying quest for a magical place where an Englishman might experience the licentious joys of an alien culture without surrendering the mastery accorded to a ruler.

The lost delights of India

The necessity of control vs the attraction of licence is the premise on which Kipling's most compelling and enduring fiction is grounded. Sullivan puts it very well: 'At the core of Kipling's dualistic narratives is an alternation between mastery and its lack, control and its absence – an ambivalence acknowledged implicitly in Kipling's view of himself as artist split between controlled craftsmanship and daemonic possession.'[63] Kipling served up psychological explanation on a platter in autobiographical and fictional accounts of his own childhood. To recapitulate, a boy cossetted by love, warmth, colour and admiring servants is sent away by parents to a cold, dark England where strait-laced evangelical women call him Black Sheep and berate him for his sins. Although he learns through his later public school education the reasons why control of desire is necessary, he remains entranced by the attraction of the exotic. A psychoanalytic reading accepts this explanation – so far as it goes – but pushes on towards the things Kipling could not say except within the safe framework of his fiction. Kipling's recollected Indian paradise is a much-censored version of infancy. It acknowledges only innocent desires and ignores the child's delight in basic bodily functions, erotic desires for the mother, the resentment directed against the father whom he desires to displace. None of the blame for the pain associated with the repression of those forbidden desires and hatreds is ascribed to his parents.[64] It is all displaced onto the English place of exile: the 'house of desolation'. Significantly, he blames the boarding house and his first English school for failing to diagnose or treat his poor eyesight. That is to say, he associates the period of repression with going blind. The desire to see that which was repressed emerges first in his return to India as a journalist and subsequently in a series of stories in which psychologically dangerous subjects are visited through the eyes and words of an inner narrator who is not Kipling.

The most dangerous stories steer very close to the real lost world of infancy. 'Beyond the Pale' is ostensibly a simple tale about the perils of miscegenation. A white man's affair with a cloistered Indian woman is discovered; her relatives cut off her hands; the man is assaulted and nearly killed. However, it is embroidered with bizarre details. The

Englishman, Trejago, while engaged in 'aimless wandering', walks into Amir Nath's Gully, a nightmare site loaded with scatological imagery. It is hardly conceivable that anyone could enter it without conscious intent. The long narrow passage is lined with blank stone walls. At the entrance buffaloes wallow in 'blue slime'.[65] Beyond lies a 'big heap of cattle-food' over which Trejago 'stumbles' before finally arriving at a barred window. Behind it sits 'a widow, about fifteen years old', who had been praying to 'the Gods, day and night, to send her a lover'. After hearing her 'pretty little laugh' from behind the grate, Trejago whispers a verse from the *Arabian Nights*. She replies with another verse, entirely appropriate to the situation. Next morning an old woman, who is never seen again, throws a packet into Trejago's cart as he drives to work, 'not a clumsy compromising letter', but a bundle of objects whose meaning had to be decoded. 'No Englishman should be able to translate object letters', but Trejago is able to 'puzzle out' the meaning, which is that he should come at midnight to Amir Nath's Gully.

That night 'was the beginning of so many strange things, and of a double life so wild' that Trejago wonders later 'if it were not all a dream'. The heavy grate slides away from the wall, 'leaving only a square of raw masonry into which an active man might climb'. The couple make love in a room outside of which is heard 'the deep even breathing' of the mysterious old woman. Somewhere else sleeps the male relative Durga Charan. 'Who or what Durga Charan was, Trejago never inquired.' When the girl discovers that Trejago had gone driving one day with a white woman, she flies into a jealous rage and insists that all relations between them cease, even though she swears that 'on my soul and my Mother's soul, I love you'. Before he drops from the window ledge, 'she kissed his forehead twice'. When, a few weeks later, Trejago calls again at the grate, she holds out to him the stumps of her severed hands. 'Some one in the room grunted like a wild beast', and thrust 'something sharp' at him, cutting into 'one of the muscles of the groin'. In an addendum the narrator notes that

> One special feature of the case is that he does not know where lies the front of Durga Charan's house. It may open on to a courtyard common to two or more houses, or it may lie behind any one of the gates of Jitha Megji's *bustee*. Trejago cannot tell. He cannot get Bisesa – poor little Bisesa – back again. He has lost her in the City where each man's house is as guarded and unknowable as the grave; and the grating that opens into Amir Nath's Gully has been walled up.

If this were Kipling's only story of interracial love, or if all such stories ended in death and disaster, it might reasonably be supposed to express the combination of desire and desperate fear with which the white man in India approached forbidden liaisons. But Kipling wrote many stories of love and sexual coupling across the colour line that end very differently. He was plainly not afraid of sex. He did not hide the fact that India in his day was a place of almost inexhaustible sexual opportunity for white men.[66] He wrote knowingly, ironically and often sympathetically about the complications generated by the social exclusion of Indian sexual partners from polite society. So how to explain the weird and horrific aspects of 'Beyond the Pale'?

In psychoanalytic terms the story is an almost stereotypical Oedipal drama. It takes place in a sexualised landscape that juxtaposes a channel of food and excreta with a narrow passage to the feminine object of desire. It is a mysterious older woman who delivers a message of invitation that cannot be openly stated but must be decoded. The object of desire has been married yet is absurdly young and available. Trejago calls to her with a verse and she responds with another. (Kipling's mother wrote verses and he replied with volumes of them.)[67] Their lovemaking occurs at night in a small bedroom where the breathing of the older woman is clearly audible. Durga Charan is also nearby, though his identity is even more veiled. We are not allowed to know 'who or what' he was. The girl swears her love by her soul and her mother's soul. She says her final goodbye with two motherly kisses on the forehead. The penalty exacted for the violation of the beloved is a wound in the groin, a symbolic castration. Finally the house of lost desire is walled off forever – as unreachable as Ayesha and the cave of immortal fire in Rider Haggard's *She.*

Notice how many barriers Kipling sets up before he gives us his version of the Oedipal story. An inner narrator tells somebody else's tale. Trejago does not seek forbidden love; he stumbles accidentally into its presence. The castrating father figure is called an uncle but never glimpsed directly. The object of desire is further distanced by race. In other stories Kipling could write comically about impossible liaisons between older women and younger men in white Anglo-Indian society where convention set up bars to the sexual consummation of flirtations. His favourite memsahib, Mrs Hauksbee, is forever taking young men under her wing using, when she has to, her formidable powers of sexual attraction. In 'The Rescue of Pluffles' she talks to her young man 'after the manner of a mother, and as if there had been three hundred years, instead of fifteen, between them'.[68] 'Venus Annodomini' tells the story of 'Very Young Gayerson', who is prevented from making a complete fool of himself over an unnamed, apparently ageless beauty through the timely arrival of her grown-up daughter and his own father, who takes up the lovemaking he left off a generation earlier.

Sanitising the Raj

We are very close to the essence of Kipling's relation to India and imperialism. The circumstances of his upbringing led him consciously and vocally to associate India with the happiness of a lost paradise of infantile innocence. At the age of sixteen he was reunited with India and with his parents, but not the lost paradise. Instead he found personal insecurity, instability and fear.[69] The plainer of his *Plain Tales* expose the discontents of a colonial elite that constantly teeters on the brink of losing control. The stranger stories probe a chaotic world of subconscious fears as well as guilty fantasies of power and sensual gratification that Kipling strove to suppress but could not banish. He would not 'look bogey in the face' and reassess the tale he had told himself about his childhood. It seemed necessary to absolve his parents of blame for his exile and unhappiness. From all accounts he formed a close, supportive and loving association with them after his return. Kipling's private and personal problem therefore remained finding a way to approach the compelling world of lost infancy while holding the forces of guilt, fear and disintegration at bay. The solution was imperialism.

This accounts both for his ferocious hatreds and his lavish affection for multi-cultural India. A clear-eyed assessment of the threats to British rule on the subcontinent would have put the growth of Indian nationalism at the top of the list. Kipling puts it at the bottom, seldom mentioning it except to dismiss it. The fury of the Indian deserter who cries out to his comrades 'Come out of your tents, as I have done, and fight against the English', is later shown to be the result of a disappointment in love.[70] It moves none of his compatriots to anything more than anger against the dishonour brought to their regiment by a desertion from their ranks. Grish Chunder, the well-dressed Bengali law student in London, has dined out on 'stories of the brutal Indian bureaucrats who ground the faces of the poor'. He has also 'contributed cheap sedition' to a nationalist newspaper.[71] However, his nationalism is presented by the narrator as nothing more than a mask adopted to impress credulous English liberals. Likewise, the nationalists described to Kipling by an American ex-governor of the Philippines: 'His account of Filipino political "leaders", writing and shouting all day for "independence" and running round to him after dark to be assured that there was no chance of the dread boon being granted – "because then we shall most probably all be killed" – was cheeringly familiar.'[72] Over and over again, Kipling insists that the real threat to Empire comes from within the ranks of the rulers or from foreign powers. It comes from men who cannot hold their liquor or otherwise lose a grip on themselves. More dangerously, it comes from the missionaries and evangelicals who preach unrealisable ideals of brotherhood. From the liberals who would walk away from Empire because it is expensive and unnecessary, given the capacity of native peoples to develop their own institutions of self-government. From the pacifists who would leave the frontiers unpatrolled. From the arty crowd who would abandon their own aesthetic standards and ally themselves with the primitivism of the exotic. Therefore all these apostles of disintegration must be cordially hated.

With the passage of years Kipling moved away from the strange and painful subjects of his early Indian stories. This movement was probably psychologically necessary for the author, but to many readers it made his fiction less interesting. As Henry James wrote in 1897, 'in his earliest time I thought he perhaps contained the seeds of an English Balzac; but I have quite given that up in proportion as he has come steadily from the less simple in subject to the more simple – from the Anglo-Indians to the natives, from the natives to the Tommies, from the Tommies to the quadrupeds.'[73] In *Kim*, his last major work on India, Kipling packaged a cleaned-up reworking of his earlier stories. It is as important to notice what it deletes as what it reveals. Gone is all sense of the Indian government as a flawed and rickety apparatus of authority. Gone are the loafers, the drunks, the suicides, philanderers, adulterers and syphilitic soldiers. So are the vanishing houses, pits of demons, silver lepers and werewolves.

The circumstances of its writing also merit notice. At the age of twenty Kipling had conceived an idea for a picaresque novel of Indian lowlife built round the loafers at an imagined boarding house run by an Irish landlady who was to have given her name to the book: 'Mother Maturin'. The project was put aside forever, apparently at his father's urging. *Kim*, on the other hand, was completed with both his parents almost literally looking over his shoulder from their retirement cottage in England. He took his idea 'to be smoked over with my Father. Under our united tobaccos it grew like the Djinn released from the brass bottle.'[74] It would be a tale safe enough to be told directly without a frame narrator.

Kim, whose progress from street urchin to Secret Service agent for the Indian government is the subject of the novel, is conveniently shorn of parents. (His mother died of cholera soon after his birth and his Irish father perished not long afterwards from the combined effects of drink and opium.) He thus shares the infant paradise of Kipling/Punch but escapes the bitterness of exile. He subsequently acquires a number of ersatz fathers, none of whom appears with a wife in tow.

The most important is a Tibetan monk seeking enlightenment. In a significant scene Kim goes with the lama to see an expert in Buddhism who is, like Kipling's father, a curator with special expertise in that religion at the Lahore Museum. In a symbolic act of relinquishment, the curator presents his own spectacles to the short-sighted lama who will henceforth see with the eyes of a father. Next Kim is reunited with his birth-father's old regiment, thanks to a handful of papers he carries round his neck. This leads to his first meeting with the head of the Secret Service, Colonel Creighton, who oversees Kim's education as a gentleman at a Catholic private school (and is suspected by other officers of having a truly paternal interest in the child). A series of other adult males of various racial identities take paternal charge of the young man until he is finally reunited with 'his lama'.

In a sequence of episodes the plots and characters of Kipling's Indian short stories are recalled, sanitised and then dismissed. Colonel Creighton is a mild version of Strickland of the Police, an expert in disguises, local customs and dialects. Unlike Strickland, however – who 'knew too much' and went in for unsavoury practices that could have led to his dismissal from the service – Creighton is a loyal servant of the Crown who communicates directly with the Commander-in-Chief. The drummer boys who persecute Kim during his short stay with his father's old regiment are lifted from 'The Drums of the Fore and Aft'. They assume the bullying role of The Woman's son in 'Baa Baa, Black Sheep' without suggesting a direct parallel with Kipling's youthful traumas. Mahbub Ali, the horse-dealer and part-time spy, is recognisable as the vengeful husband of the story 'Dray Wara Yow Dee'.[75] But whereas the prototype issues a burning denunciation of the white man's patronising attitudes,[76] Mahbub Ali merely says to Kim, 'in the tone he used towards Europeans', 'What talk is this of *us*, Sahib? ... 'I am a Pathan; thou art a Sahib and the son of a Sahib.'[77] The educated Bengali is recycled in *Kim* as Hurree Chunder Mookerjee, alias Hurree Babu. Lacking the well-heeled suavity of Grish Chunder in 'The Finest Story in the World', he only pretends to talk seditiously of British misrule in order to mislead a Russian spy.

Women from earlier stories are also recalled and treated with an intriguing tenderness. The Woman of Shamlegh who, in the penultimate chapter, nurses Kim back to health after his affray with the foreign spies, turns out to be the same Lispeth who was led astray by missionaries in the first story of *Plain Tales from the Hills*. Though she has lost none of her bitterness against the hypocritical Christians and the Englishman who deserted her, she offers her love to Kim. He re-enacts the rejection – but without deception, thus redeeming to some extent the earlier betrayal.

'Good-bye', she says poignantly in English, knowing already the answer to her final question, 'you will come back again?' The old woman, 'high-born widow of a Hill Rajah on pilgrimage', who provides hospitality to Kim and the lama on the Grand Trunk Road, bears some similarities to the crone mother in 'Without Benefit of Clergy' and to the mysterious, silent old woman who throws the coded love message to Trejago in 'Beyond the Pale'. However, where the one was grasping and unfeeling, this old woman is a paragon of generosity. And she is anything but silent. From behind the safety of her widow's veil, she engages in rapier-sharp exchanges of wit with Kim and an English policeman – almost as if Mrs Hauksbee had been stained brown, aged twenty years and sent out on the road in Hindu disguise. Equally interesting is the treatment of the prostitute Huneefa, who administers to Kim the colour dye that will conceal his race during the course of his secret mission to the frontier. The episode provides the mechanism for fulfilling the 'wish fantasy' common to the subjects of this book that for the imperialist 'everything is possible, that one can go anywhere and be anything'.[78]

It begins just a few paragraphs after a schoolboy at St Xavier's has 'hinted very broadly that Colonel Creighton's interest in Kim was directly paternal' (p. 188). As the colonel is day-dreaming (like Kipling's father?) of being elected to the Royal Society for his ethnographic work, he is interrupted by Mahbub Ali who insists that at sixteen Kim is old enough to enter the Great Game. After all, he reminds the colonel, 'when I was fifteen, I had shot my man and begot my man' (p. 183). Mahbub next leads Kim to the prostitute Huneefa's house, taking care 'to point out how Huneefa and her likes destroyed kings' (pp. 188–9). This strong suggestion of a sexual initiation is followed by a most remarkable passage in which Kim is told to 'strip to the waist' so the skin dye can be applied and then fixed through magical incantations.

> Then the room filled with smoke – heavy, aromatic, and stupefying. Through growing drowse he heard the names of devils – of Zulbazan, Son of Eblis, who lives in bazars and *paraos,* making all the sudden lewd wickedness of wayside halts; of Dulhan, invisible about mosques, the dweller among the slippers of the faithful, who hinders folk from their prayers; and Musboot, Lord of lies and panic. Huneefa, now whispering in his ear, now talking as from an immense distance, touched him with horrible soft fingers, but Mahbub's grip never shifted from his neck till, relaxing with a sigh, the boy lost his senses.
>
> 'Allah! How he fought! We should never have done it but for the drugs. That was his white blood, I take it,' said Mahbub testily. 'Go on with the *dawut* (invocation). Give him full Protection.'

> *'O Hearer! Thou that hearest with ears, be present. Listen, O Hearer!'* Huneefa moaned, her dead eyes turned to the west. The dark room filled with moanings and snortings ... Huneefa, in some sort of drugged ecstasy, wrenched herself to and fro ...
>
> Huneefa's crisis passed, as these things must, in a paroxysm of howling, with a touch of froth at the lips. She lay spent and motionless beside Kim, and the crazy voices ceased. (pp. 190–2)

Among Kipling's earlier stories, it is 'In the House of Suddhoo' that presents the closest parallel to this scene. There a *jaddoo* (magic) ceremony also takes place in a harlot's room located just off a staircase above a small shop. While stupefying smoke from *huqas* fills the air, a magician with bangles on his ankles, 'stripped to the waist', turns himself into a blind, shapeless crawling thing, something like a snake that writhes horribly round the room before projecting the severed head of a baby into a basin of water.[79] In *Kim*, although the magician and the prostitute are collapsed into the same person, that person is likewise blind and shapeless: 'a huge and shapeless woman' with 'white and sightless eyes' and bangles round her ankles. The writhing thing on the floor and the beheading of a baby in 'The House of Suddhoo' call to mind a male sexual organ and a threat of castration. The shapeless figure of Huneefa is more inchoate (a female breast?) and thus far less threatening. Moreover, what she promises Kim is 'the full protection of the Road' just after Mahbub Ali has told him that 'Most true is it in the Great Game ... it is by means of women that all plans come to ruin and we lie out in the dawning with our throats cut' (p. 189).

It is surely not too fanciful to suggest that the threat which has been dispatched by Huneefa and the other female figures in *Kim* is that threat of an Oedipal reckoning which had haunted Kipling's earlier Indian stories. Through the excision of white older women of Mrs Hauksbee's set, longing for reunion with an Indian mother has been entirely projected upon women on the far side of the comforting racial divide. The widow of the Hill Rajah engages in flirtatious conversations that are rendered completely harmless by her age and wrinkles. The magical symbolic coupling with Huneefa enables Kim not only to withstand the wiles of the women against whom Mahbub Ali has warned him, but also the more serious attractions of Lispeth who, despite her age and her two husbands, is still sexually available. Not just in *Kim*, but in many of the earlier stories, being suckled by an Indian woman provides protection for the 'native-born', the men, he insists, who should form the elite of imperial rule. The Sikh trooper of 'A Sahibs' War' points out that his commander, Lieutenant Corbyn, had such an upbringing, recalling affectionately: '*he* was a little baba, sitting upon a wall by the parade-ground with his ayah – all in white, Sahib – laughing at the end of our drill. And his father and mine talked together.'[80]

The unnamed narrator of the same story had a wet nurse who 'was a Surtee woman from the Bombay side'.[81] The old widow in *Kim* asks the knowledgeable English policeman, 'Who suckled thee?' When he gives an appropriate reply, 'A *pahareen* – a hillwoman of Dalhousie, my mother', she reflects that 'these be the sort to oversee justice. They know the land and the customs of the land. The others, all new from Europe, suckled by white women and learning our tongues from books, are worse than the pestilence. They do harm to Kings' (p. 82). We know, on the other hand, from the story 'Without Benefit of Clergy' that the white memsahibs never suckle their own children.[82] The boys Kim admires at St Xavier's are white children of the land whose 'every tale was told in the even, passionless voice of the native-born, mixed with quaint reflections, borrowed unconsciously from native foster-mothers, and turns of speech that showed they had been that instant translated from the vernacular' (p. 133).

By putting Kim under the paternal care of a celibate Buddhist mystic, and projecting all the maternal care of his infancy onto Indian foster mothers, Kipling liberated his creation from the inner conflicts that so profoundly troubled him on his first return to India and which endlessly haunt the stories from that time. Kim can 'dive into the happy Asiatic disorder' (p. 69) without peril. And although we are told that Kim 'had known all evil since he could speak', in reality he has been given 'the full protection of the Road' against certain kinds of unthinkable thoughts. In the earlier Indian stories Kipling strung high-tension wires between the necessity to maintain imperial self-control and the temptation to succumb to the forces of irrationality, mystery and darkness. In *Kim* the tension is gone. India's mysteries are harmless and the only real threats to imperial hegemony come from outsiders: nasty foreign villains and bumbling greenhorns from Britain who have no knowledge of Indian life and customs. We know that neither Kim nor his 'native-born' fellow sahibs will fall into drunkenness, cowardice, self-hatred or any of the other thousand and one perils that beset the white subjects of his *Plain Tales from the Hills*.

Edward Said marvelled that Kipling wrote so well about India in Kim while maintaining the historically untenable position that 'Indian reality required, indeed beseeched British tutelage more or less indefinitely'.[83] It is equally important to notice that Kipling's position on governance made the real business of ruling India virtually impossible. The only men with the right stuff 'to oversee justice' are the handful of native-born, Indian-suckled white men who possess a perfect command of a dozen vernacular tongues and an encyclopaedic knowledge of local ethnography. No one born or trained in Britain can possibly know enough to belong to this holy, incorruptible knighthood. The mission of these native-born Templers is not to transform India but to hold it against forces of change massed at its borders. Their associates in the business of rule are the people of India themselves who staff all the lower positions. The question Kipling does not put in *Kim* is, what then is the point of the imperial connection? We do not know the answer because he never wrote again on India.

Notes

1 Rudyard Kipling, *Collected Stories* (London: Everyman, 1994), p. 621.
2 Ibid., p. 628.
3 On 4 December 1919, Rider Haggard wrote concerning the Bolshevik revolution: 'Kipling, who has been lunching here today, is of opinion that we owe all our Russian troubles, and many others, to the machinations of the Jews'; Morton Cohen (ed.), *Rudyard Kipling to Rider Haggard: The Record of a Friendship* (London: Hutchinson, 1965), p. 110.
4 'Introduction', in Rudyard Kipling, *Kim*, ed. by John Bayley (London: Everyman, 1995), p. xix.
5 Rudyard Kipling, *Something of Myself* (London: Penguin, 1992 [1936]), p. 36.
6 Charles Carrington, in *Rudyard Kipling: His Life and Work* (London: Macmillan, 1978), p. 50, points out that the incident related in the autobiography, where Kipling is required to wear a placard reading 'Liar', is actually borrowed from *David Copperfield*.
7 Kipling, *Collected Stories*, p. 429.
8 Ibid., p. 373.
9 Ibid., p. 32.
10 Ibid., p. 699.
11 Ibid., p. 277.
12 Kipling, *Something of Myself*, p. 62.
13 Ibid.
14 Kipling, *Collected Stories*, pp. 173–4.
15 Kipling, 'The drums of the fore and aft', in ibid., pp. 98–9. The description prefigures widespread criticism of Britain's 'racial deterioration', as exemplified in soldiers recruited for the Boer War.
16 Kipling, 'The strange ride of Morrowbie Jukes', in ibid., pp. 311–34. For a perceptive reading of this story as an allegory of colonialism, see Zohreh T. Sullivan, *Narratives of Empire: The Fictions of Rudyard Kipling* (Cambridge: Cambridge University Press, 1993), pp. 70–7.
17 Kipling, *Something of Myself*, pp. 39, 45. See also Sullivan, *Narratives of Empire*, p. 116.
18 Kipling, *Something of Myself*, pp. 87–8.
19 Ibid., p. 88.
20 Ibid., p. 82.
21 Kipling, 'On Greenhow Hill', in *Collected Stories*, p. 59.
22 Kipling, 'The head of the district', in ibid., p. 206. See also *Kim*, pp. 234–5: 'But the war was not pushed. That is the Government custom.'
23 Kipling, *Something of Myself*, p. 165.
24 Ibid., p. 129.
25 A point made at length in the story 'A sahibs' war'.

26 Kipling, *Something of Myself*, p. 131.
27 Sullivan, *Narratives of Empire*, p. 24.
28 Kipling, *Collected Stories*, pp. 425, 432.
29 Kipling, *Something of Myself*, p. 120.
30 Bernard Porter, *The Lion's Share* (London: Pearson, 2012), pp. 108–11; Norman Etherington, *Theories of Imperialism: War, Conquest and Capital* (London: Croom Helm, 1984).
31 Kipling, *Collected Stories*, p. 37.
32 Kipling, *Something of Myself*, pp. 139–40.
33 Ibid., p. 86.
34 Ibid., p. 152.
35 Ibid., p. 109.
36 Kipling, *Kim*, p. 40.
37 Kipling, 'In ambush', in *Collected Stories*, pp. 508–9.
38 Kipling, 'The drums of the fore and aft', pp. 106, 116–17.
39 Kipling, 'A sahibs' war', in *Collected Stories*, pp. 531, 534, 536.
40 Kipling, *Kim*, p. 253.
41 Ibid., p. 127.
42 In Kipling, *Collected Stories*, p. 211.
43 Kipling, 'Beyond the pale', in *Collected Stories*, p. 17.
44 Nor does Kipling use 'inner' or 'frame' narrators to point a moral. Although in the story 'To be filed for reference', the ruined, alcoholic Oxford man, McIntosh, lives with an Indian woman, his downfall is not in any way ascribed to her agency.
45 In Kipling, *Collected Stories*, p. 165.
46 Kipling, 'Beyond the pale', p. 17.
47 Kipling, 'The man who would be king', in *Collected Stories*, p. 237.
48 Kipling, 'The head of the district', p. 190.
49 Kipling, *Kim*, p. 173. The name may have been suggested by Harish Chandra Mukherjee (1824–61), a Bengali journalist and patriot. Burke and Hare were not authors at all, but men convicted of murdering tramps and selling their bodies to medical dissectors. Kipling, who did not go to university, is also deprecating the utility of liberal studies for Indians.
50 In Kipling, *Collected Stories*, p. 278.
51 'The bridge builders', in ibid., p. 472.
52 Ibid., p. 443.
53 Joseph Conrad, *Heart of Darkness*, in *Heart of Darkness and Other Tales* (Oxford: Oxford University Press, 1990 [1899]), p. 187.
54 In 'Dayspring mishandled', in *Collected Stories*, p. 846.
55 Private Mulvaney in 'The taking of Lungtungpen'; R. Kipling, *Plain Tales from the Hills* (London: Macmillan, 1891), p. 105.
56 In Kipling, *Collected Stories*, p. 75.
57 'Mrs Bathurst', in ibid., p. 584.
58 In Kipling, *Collected Stories*, p. 739.
59 'In ambush', p. 516.
60 Kipling, *Something of Myself*, p. 72.
61 'The man who would be king', in *Collected Stories*, p. 217; subsequent quotations from this edition.
62 Kipling was, of course, familiar with the linguistic work of Max Müller, who argued for the kinship of Aryan peoples stretching from Europe to the Indian subcontinent.
63 Sullivan, *Narratives of Empire*, p. 28.
64 He seems to have entirely accepted the idea that his exile was necessary for reasons of health as well as education. See his stories that deal with happy infants who are monarchs of all they survey until they are carried off by some Indian disease: 'Without benefit of clergy' and 'The story of Muhammad Din'.
65 This and the following quotations come from 'Beyond the pale', in *Collected Stories*, pp. 17–23.

66 Ronald Hyam, *Empire and Sexuality: The British Experience* (Manchester: Manchester University Press, 1990).

67 In the same paragraph of *Something of Myself* (p. 44), Kipling writes of his childhood: 'I understood that my Mother had written verses, that my Father "wrote things" also ... and I learned all sorts of verses for the pleasure of repeating them to myself in bed.'

68 Kipling, *Plain Tales from the Hills*, p. 54.

69 Angus Wilson, *The Strange Ride of Rudyard Kipling* (New York: Viking, 1977), pp. 102–7; Sullivan, *Narratives of Empire*, pp. 66ff.

70 'On Greenhow Hill', p. 47.

71 'The finest story in the world', in *Collected Stories*, pp. 278–9.

72 Kipling, *Something of Myself*, p. 149.

73 Quoted in R. Gottlieb, 'Introduction' to *Collected Stories*, p. xvi. Others argue vociferously that Kipling's writing got better and more interesting.

74 Kipling, *Something of Myself*, pp. 115–16.

75 However, in that story the name Mahbub Ali is given to another man.

76 He replies thus to an offer of money in *Collected Stories*, p. 137:

> Fire burn your money! What do I want with it? I am rich and I thought you were my friend; but you are like the others – a Sahib. Is a man sad? Give him money, say the Sahibs. Is he dishonoured? Give him money, say the Sahibs. Hath he a wrong upon his head? Give him money, say the Sahibs. Such are the Sahibs, and such art thou – even thou ... And now I pray you, give me permission to depart. Great favour and honour has the Sahib done me, and graciously has he shown his belief that the horses are stolen.

77 Rudyard Kipling, *Kim*, ed. and intro. by John Bayley (London: Everyman, 1995); subsequent quotations from this edition.

78 Edward Said, *Culture and Imperialism* (New York: Vintage, 1994), p. 158. Said goes on to note how T. E. Lawrence in *The Seven Pillars of Wisdom* expresses this fantasy over and over, 'as he reminds us how he – a blond, blue-eyed Englishman – moved among the desert Arabs as if he were one of them.'

79 His 'eyes were rolled back till you could only see the whites of them'; *Collected Stories*, p. 8.

80 'A sahibs' war', p. 533.

81 Ibid., p. 532.

82 Kipling, *Collected Stories*, p. 165.

83 Said, *Culture and Imperialism*, p. xxi.

CHAPTER THREE

How Herbert Baker created an architecture of imperial power

Herbert Baker resembles other Edwardian artist imperialists in his politics, affiliations and personality. Though he wrote a great deal about his life's achievements, he revealed little about his inner self. His closest friends remarked on his extraordinary reserve. Even when controversy swirled about his work, he kept his feelings under wraps. The commissions he won secured his reputation as the pre-eminent exponent of imperialism in British architecture, but he wrote precious little about his intentions or the means by which he realised them. Understanding how he expressed imperialism in his work requires close attention to his designs and finished buildings in relation to the sites on which they stand. The process by which he arrived at the highest expression of imperial power was gradual. As he progressed from an exponent of the English Arts and Crafts Movement to neo-classicism informed by study of Greek and Roman architecture, he became intensely interested in the way his architecture could interact with landscape in elevated situations. Another imperialist architect might have chosen to express colonial overrule through buildings that subjected indigenous motifs to an overarching European schema. Baker took a different tack. Using locally quarried stone he made his imperial compositions appear to grow from the ground on which they stood – as though British dominion had existed from time immemorial. Using a variety of architectural techniques acquired during his early years in Cape Town, he conveyed the idea of domination through buildings set in elevated positions that suggest command posts for watchers who see everything but are not themselves seen. Many of his buildings contain unsuspected inner sanctums, not expressed in the exterior form, that hint at some kind of psychological drama being played out. It is as though the authority so confidently expressed on the outside harbours at its core some vulnerable essence that must be protected or contained at all costs.

Figure 1 Herbert Baker from *The State* (1909)

Baker and Rhodes

Baker was Cecil Rhodes' Albert Speer – architect, confidant and utterly devoted acolyte. Within weeks of his arrival at Cape Town from England in 1892, thirty-year-old Baker had met Rhodes and been commissioned to 'build my house'. What fame and fortune Baker might have won without Rhodes cannot be known. He came to South Africa after befriending a future great, Edwin Lutyens, but with no significant work behind him. Rhodes carried Baker bodily up to the celestial reaches of his profession. Commissions came thick and fast, first from Rhodes himself, then from the De Beers group of companies.

The impress of his work still weighs heavy on streets of Cape Town. Standing by the National Library at the corner of Queen Victoria Street and Wale Street you can see his City Club, the Mutual Life Assurance Building, St George's Cathedral and, of course, the Rhodes Building – today the Mandela Rhodes Building (Figure 2).

Proceed eastwards round the base of Table Mountain, you will pass Groote Schuur, the house that launched his work with Rhodes (now the official residence of the state president), and the 'Woolsack', which he prepared as a summer residence for Rudyard Kipling (now occupied by

Figure 2 Mandela Rhodes Building, Cape Town

Figure 3 'Woolsack', University of Cape Town, the cottage Rhodes commissioned Baker to build for Rudyard Kipling

University of Cape Town bureaucrats) (Figure 3).[1] A little farther on lie the great mansions he built for the lesser political and financial magnates of South Africa, including James Rose Innes (Figure 4) and Abe Bailey.

Lift up your eyes unto the hills and you will see Rhodes Memorial which Baker regarded as so important that he gave it a prominent place in the official portrait commemorating his work on the Bank of England in the 1920s.

Baker's rise did not end with Rhodes' death. Accompanying South Africa's High Commissioner, Lord Milner, to the conquered Transvaal in the wake of the Anglo-Boer War, he became part of the celebrated 'Kindergarten' of youthful administrators, which he treated quite seriously as an order of modern-day chivalry. His draftsman's pen transformed the cityscape of Johannesburg as it had Cape Town in the previous decade. At the downtown meeting place of labour and capital he built the monumental rail station. On high ridges to the north of the town he designed, as he said, 'for men of wealth on the Rand' who

Figure 4 J. Rose Innes house, Cape Town

'realized their responsibility and built large houses'. His South African career climaxed with the Union Buildings at Pretoria, a commission that launched him on a further trajectory as the foremost architect of Empire. With Lutyens he designed the complex of government buildings at New Delhi. Back in London, he not only rebuilt – some would say ruined – the Bank of England in the City but also made a significant impact on the Trafalgar Square precinct. South Africa House stands on the square itself, the former Royal Empire Society building in adjacent Northumberland Square and India House not far away at Aldwych. Sharing Rhodes' dream of bringing young men from the Dominions to study in the mother country, he built student facilities at London House, at Downing College, Cambridge and at Rhodes House in Oxford.

By and large, posthumous critical opinion has been no kinder to Baker than to Rhodes. While in South Africa the term 'Herbert-Baker style' is still used by real estate salesmen to tout almost any house built between 1895 and 1925, his work elsewhere has been slighted or ignored. Baker's Secretariat Buildings in New Delhi are generally regarded as inferior to Lutyens' viceregal palace. The late works in Britain are admired, if at all, for the fine craftsmanship displayed in exterior masonry and interior fittings. Nikolaus Pevsner's *Pioneers of Modern Design* (first edition, 1936) did not mention Baker, even though he was still alive and actively engaged on large projects. In part Baker's loss of public esteem stemmed from his association with Rhodes and the idea of Empire. His continued adherence to classicism and publicly stated scorn for modernism alienated the rising generation of architects. However, more is required to explain the disjuncture between his triumphs in South Africa and the lukewarm reception accorded to his projects in England. A vital point of difference was his inability to use English sites as he had done in South Africa and India. Through Rhodes' patronage Baker learned how to project ideas of imperial power by making his neo-classical buildings interact theatrically with the dramatic South African landscape. No such effects could be achieved on the flat urban plots where he built in England. This chapter examines the steps by which he advanced from experiments in picturesque historical idioms to a commanding, even crushing deployment of European classicism in rugged, elevated situations.

Just thirty years of age, Baker had travelled to the Cape to visit a brother who had got into financial difficulties with an orange plantation. Thanks to family connections he was introduced to Cape society by a member of parliament, Louis Vintcent. At dinner Baker found himself seated opposite Rhodes, at that time near the pinnacle of his career.[2] Not only had he secured control of the Kimberley diamond fields for his De Beers Consolidated Mines, he was prime minister of the Cape Colony and director of the British South Africa Company that had leveraged a mineral concession from Ndebele king Lobengula into a Royal Charter for the government of the territory he modestly named Rhodesia. To top it all off he too had invested in the nascent Cape citrus industry. With so much to talk about Baker was abashed to find himself virtually tongue-tied in the presence of The Colossus. No matter. Rhodes, famously susceptible to attractive young men, enquired after him. 'I like the look of that young man', Rhodes reportedly said, 'he doesn't talk too much.'[3] A few days later he offered him the commission to convert an old Cape Dutch estate high on the slopes of Table Mountain into the stately home known as Groote Schuur.

A most literary architect, Baker went on to write on Rhodes (*Cecil Rhodes, by His Architect*) and an account of his own life in *Architecture and Personalities*. Only his own personality went unexplored. Eloquent on paper, he floundered in conversation and in social situations. The silence Rhodes noticed was often in evidence. Edwin Lutyens found that 'beneath his reserved and serious manner', he was 'prone to be moody and introspective'.[4] An admirer complained in the 1930s that aside from his year of birth, 'he gives much less information about himself in the ordinary books of reference than most architects'.[5] Aside from his idolisation of Rhodes, the only relationships about which he wrote passionately were with the members of Milner's Kindergarten in South Africa and, following the Great War, with Lawrence of Arabia. Eight to twelve years older than the rest of the young men recruited by Milner to work in the reconstruction of the Transvaal following the Anglo-Boer War, Baker was colloquially termed grandpa. He also lacked their university education. But his prowess at the manly sports

A "KINDERGARTEN" GROUP, IN FRONT OF THE HALL CHIMNEY OF GOVERNMENT HOUSE.

Back row : Lionel Curtis, Nel Hichens, Peter Perry, Hugh Wyndham, Herbert Baker, Geoffrey Dawson.

Sitting : Lord Selborne (Governor-General), Robert Brand, Patrick Duncan, Lady Selborne, Lord Long (Secretary of State for the Colonies), Richard Feetham.

On Floor : Philip Kerr, John Dove, Dougal Malcolm.

Figure 5 A Kindergarten group

Figure 6 Baker's chest

of cricket, athletics and horsemanship commanded admiration. He likewise shared their almost religious devotion to the idea of Empire. During their years of close association the Kindergarten resembled a celibate order of imperial chivalry. Two never married and most of those who did arrived late at the altar: Baker and several others well into their forties. Baker celebrated the Kindergarten in a neo-medieval chest he devised as their gift to Lord Selbourne, Milner's successor as South African High Commissioner (Figure 6).

It is tempting to interpret the gift as an act of personal concealment. The very idea of a heavy chest suggests a place where valuables are locked away. In this case the chest functions as a hiding place for the names of the brotherhood. Putting his name last in a non-alphabetical list, Baker hides best of all.

Much of his architecture deals in calculated concealments and revelations. Early domestic commissions reflected South African conditions that, for the privileged, have always required defence against theft and control of servants. Baker's design for attached houses in the Cape Town suburb of Mowbray displays his practical attention to considerations of security and racial distance (Figure 7). Unlike contemporary

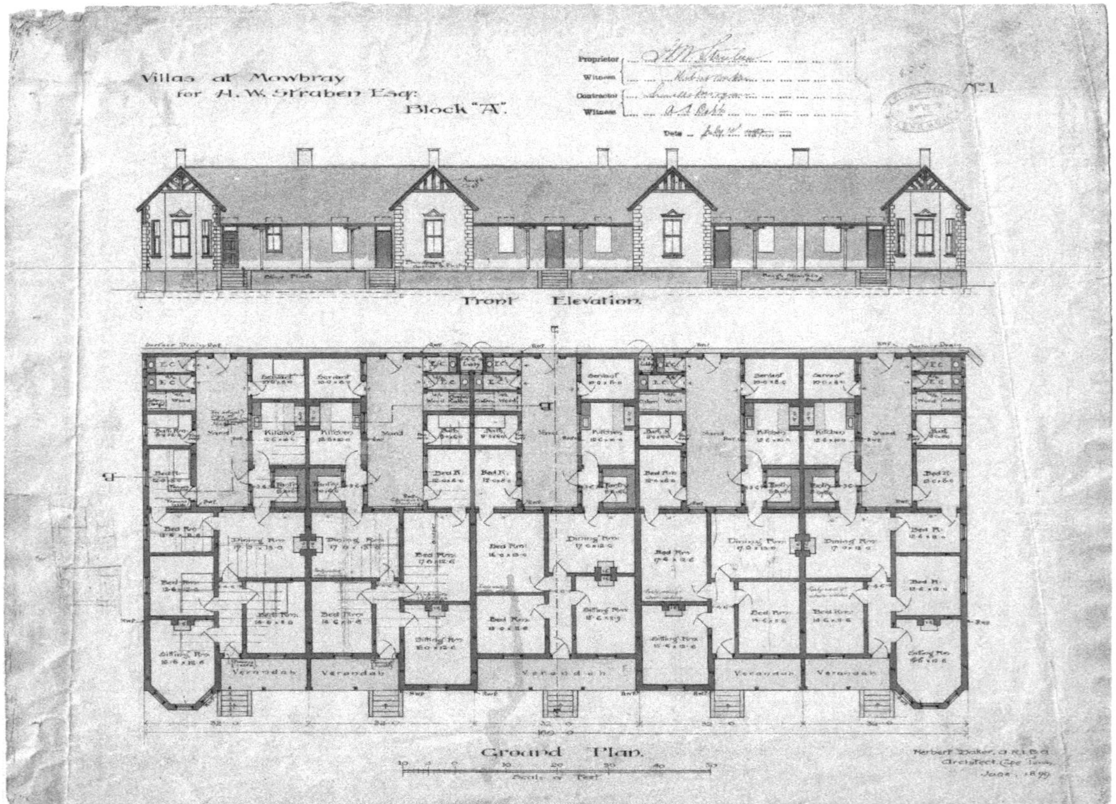

Figure 7 Mowbray Villas for H. W. Struben

equivalents in England, Australia, the United States or Canada, each four-bedroom 'villa' presents a forbidding wall to its outer perimeter boundary. The live-in, undoubtedly black servant is pushed to the extreme rear corner, as far as possible from the nearest white bedroom, and close to the rear entrance, which she would be expected to use, and the open court from which she must gain access to the kitchen, cistern and pantry. There can be no question of family and servant using the same toilet, so there are two. The practical business of servicing the unplumbed earth closets decrees they should be side by side – despite the racial proximity this entails.

Even when large sites accorded more room to sprawl in the mansions Baker built for wealthy clients, the same considerations led to their tight enclosure of space. In the Hutchins residence (Figure 8) and James Rose Innes' house (Figure 4) the rear servants' areas are walled round; entrances are kept to a minimum. Baker's cavernous porches add to the impression of a guarded place. The arched and deeply recessed entrance was a favourite device of late-nineteenth-century architects such as Frank Furness in the United States and Norman Shaw in England, whose work Baker admired. In a South African context it worked to suggest a vantage from which to look out on a potentially threatening

Figure 8 E. Hutchins house

Figure 9 House at Wynberg

exterior. The Hutchins house and another at Wynberg (Figure 9) deploy versions of the deeply recessed porch at both ground and upper levels.

In tall commercial buildings the recessed porch could be reworked as an elevated portico with enhanced dramatic effect. Recessed spaces figure on four of the five storeys of Baker's Mutual Life Insurance building in Cape Town (Figure 10). At ground level an arcade shields the lobby from prying eyes. At the next level a narrower set of arches appears to promise access to a generous viewing platform. And on the fourth level we see offices offering privileged access to a space where executives could see out, but where, because of the narrow line of sight afforded from the street, they could not be seen. Again, the concept was unoriginal but skilfully employed by Baker to epitomise corporate power – as does the Rhodes Building (Figure 11). Even more than the Kindergarten's gift chest, it functions as a box of treasures and secrets. The exterior of this square edifice, while offering some upper-storey lookouts, gives no hint of its hollow centre, which is a sunlit atrium extending vertically from top to bottom (Figure 12). Apart from a grand boardroom and a huge safe (presumably for De Beers diamonds), the

Figure 10 Mutual Life Insurance Building, Cape Town

main feature of the ground floor was, in Rhodes' time, a carved soapstone bird mounted atop a pedestal (Figures 13 and 14).

To Baker and Rhodes, the bird represented their view of their mining and colonisation enterprises. Like many of their generation, they regarded the ruins at Great Zimbabwe as the work of an ancient white civilisation that had exported gold from the Central African interior to the Mediterranean via the Indian Ocean and the Red Sea. The soapstone carved birds found at the ruins linked these supposed predecessors to their current schemes of imperial expansion. Today, when archaeology

Figure 11 Rhodes Building: De Beers offices

has decisively confirmed that Africans built Great Zimbabwe and related complexes, we view the bird in the Rhodes Building in quite a different light. It stands for the diamonds seized by the De Beers monopoly through the exploitation of African migrant workers; for the treasures looted from Zimbabwe; for the racial theories that denied African capacity to build in stone and insisted that some unknown ancient white civilisation must have been responsible. The secret at the centre of the Rhodes Building is the expropriation of Africa's Iron Age heritage.

Baker's domestic architecture often features an inner sanctum at the heart. At Groote Schuur the hidden retreat is Rhodes' marbled private bathroom with its enormous bath: eight feet long and carved from a single block of granite. According to his biographer it simultaneously catered to Rhodes' obsession with cleanliness and his emulation of the Roman emperors with whom he identified.[6] Unlike his Spartan bedroom and roughly furnished main rooms, the bathroom hints at

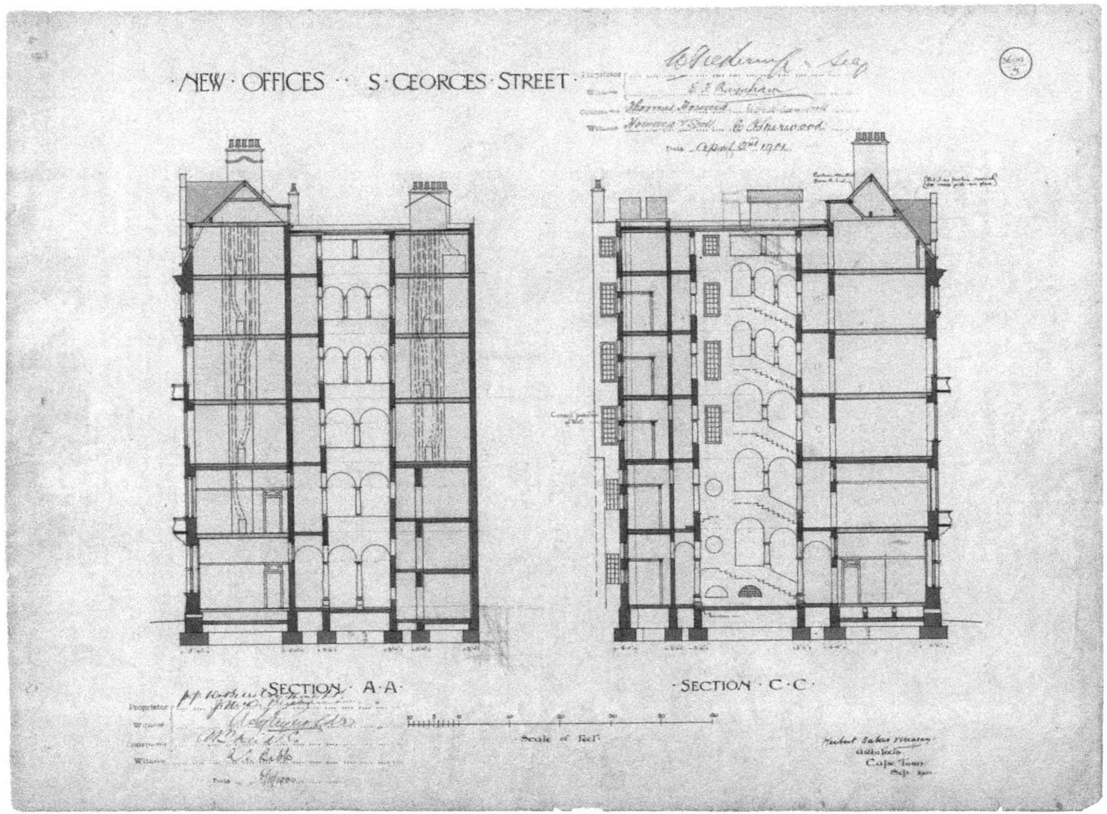

Figure 12 Rhodes Building, vertical cross section

Figure 13 Rhodes Building atrium

an opulent fantasy of naked indulgence. This can probably be attributed entirely to the imperious client, but Baker most likely bears sole responsibility for the secluded shrine concealed within 'Rust-en-Vrede', the stately home he designed for Cecil Rhodes' friend Abe Bailey. Bailey counted among the wealthiest of the 'Randlords' who made their fortunes through development of the Witwatersrand gold fields. He selected a site at Muizenberg adjacent to the site of Rhodes' seaside retreat. He was forty years of age when he commissioned Baker to create a mansion suitable for entertaining on a grand scale, but was hardly present during the planning. When not attending to business

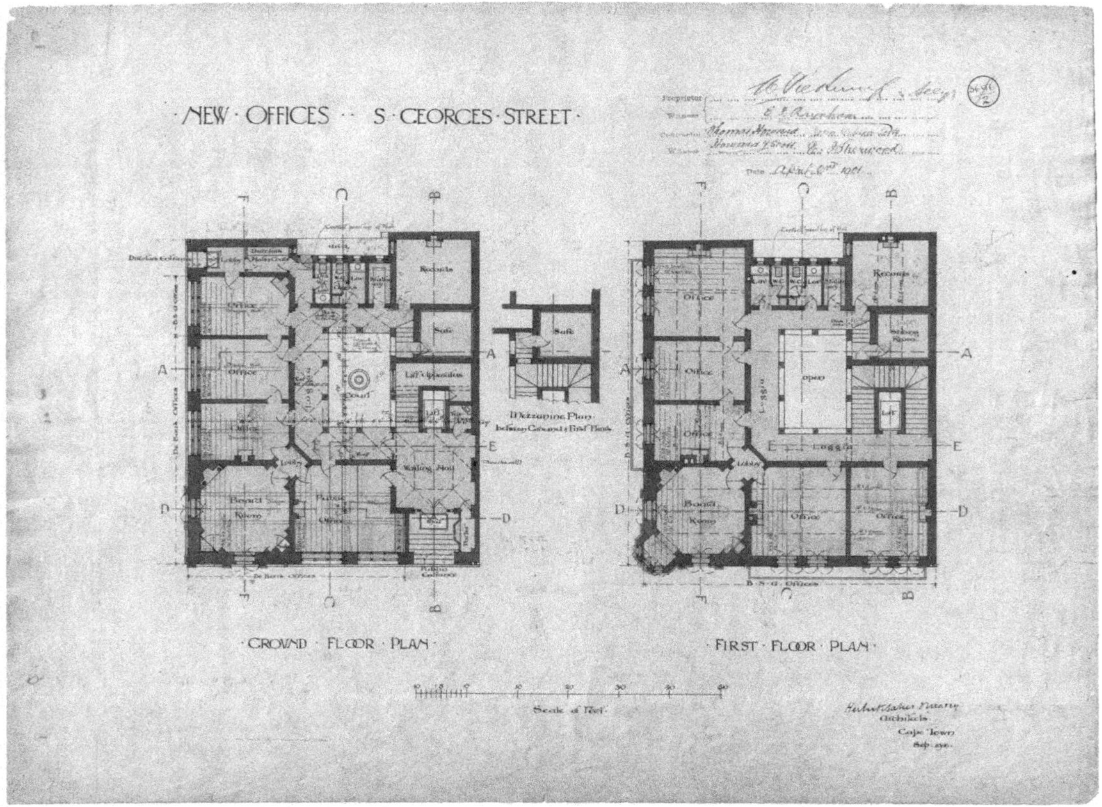

Figure 14 Rhodes Building ground-floor plan

in Johannesburg, Bailey was off to Britain or touring Europe. The furnishing of the library epitomises his distance from the project. When Baker's firm called attention to the need to fill empty bookshelves, the task was assigned to the clerk of works on the project, who first tried to borrow books by the yard from Cape Town booksellers. Finding this impossible, he drew up a list of books by suitable authors, including Haggard, Stevenson, Kipling and Conan Doyle, which he instructed a bookseller to buy at a set price of three shillings and sixpence per item.[7] A similar process governed the supply of artworks, with an emphasis on old views of the Cape.[8] There is no evidence that Bailey himself took any part in their selection, nor even in the layout of the house. Baker can thus be assumed to be the sole author of its innermost sanctuary, a room walled with marble with a fireplace set deep within a church-like apsidal alcove (Figure 15).

Apart from the gift chest, Baker gave the fullest expression of the Kindergarten as a secular order of chivalry in 'The Stonehouse', set high on a ridge in Johannesburg. Planned with Lionel Curtis, it was to be a place where 'he and I and other friends could live together'.[9]

Figure 15 Inner sanctum of Abe Bailey house, Rust-en-Vrede

Figure 16 'The Stonehouse', Parktown, Johannesburg, 1902

Because the growth of trees during the last century has greatly softened the appearance of the house, the most appropriate view is this early photograph (Figure 16). It presents as a fortress, walled on all sides, including, as in Baker's Cape Town houses, the servants' quarter. Stairs provide access to viewing platforms at the upper level, from which the eye might wander imaginatively over the gold mines that drove the imperial engine of South Africa, or north towards the vast beckoning spaces of unconquered Africa.[10] Characteristically accessed by stairways invisible from outside, the viewing platforms offer vantages from which the inhabitants may see without being seen (Figure 17).

What went on in the enclosed social spaces of the ground floor could be neither glimpsed nor guessed from outside. Although the plan shows a rectangular dining table, the ideals of Baker, Curtis and friends would have been better expressed in a round table, the name Curtis would give to the journal on imperial affairs he founded in 1910 and which recalled the legends of Camelot.

By choosing to build in stone quarried from the ridge, the architect employed another characteristic device to make new money and new power appear grounded in the ancient landscape they dominated. For millennia Parktown ridge had been the abode of African chiefs. From the 1840s its sovereigns had been Afrikaner republicans opposed to British rule. Milner's frantic building following the

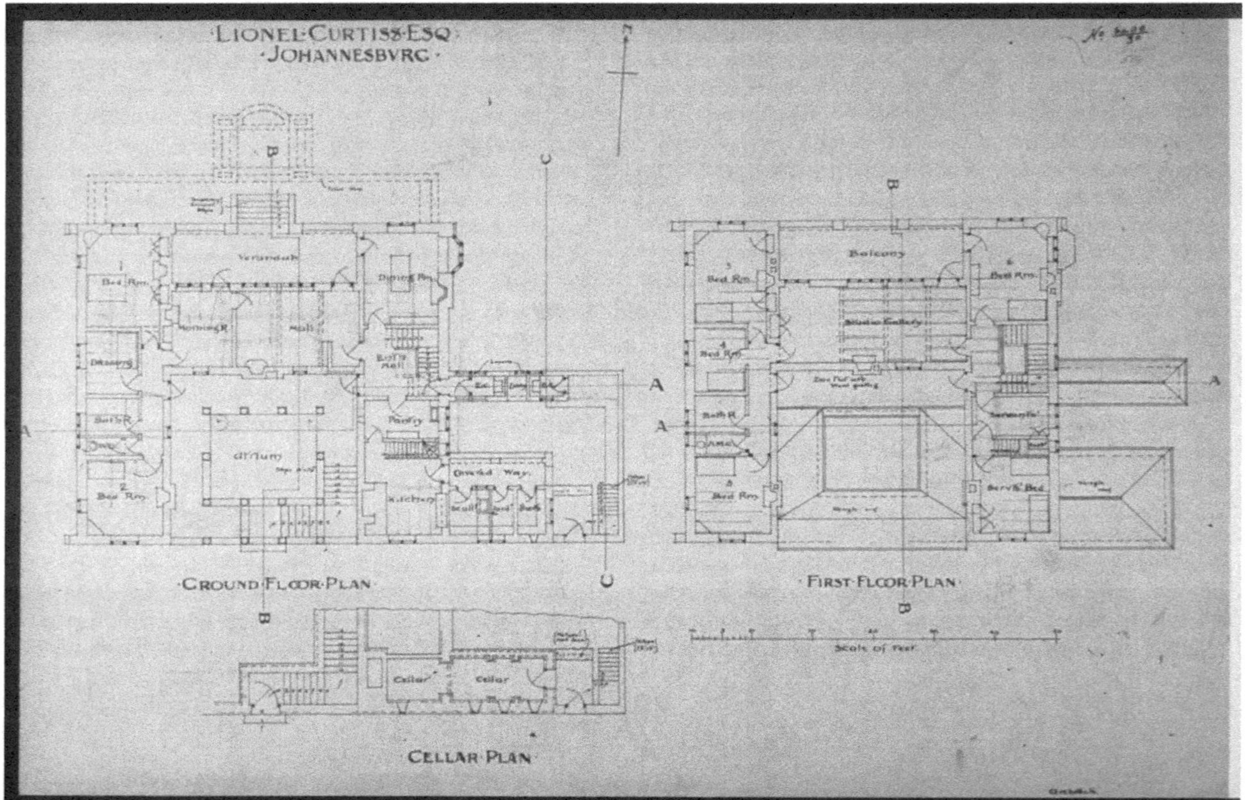

Figure 17 Plan of 'The Stonehouse'

second Anglo-Boer War and the mansions Baker strewed along the ridge proclaim a foreordained Empire as rooted in the bedrock as any vanished hegemony. Pointedly ignoring the black presence, they enact the consequences of the conquest on which the whole politico-economic edifice rested.

Baker's marriage in 1904 put an end to the Stonehouse conception of a shared residence for the Kindergarten; it became the family home. It continued to stand, however, for the symbolic relationship between his buildings and the interior psychological essence he so deliberately strove to brick in. The soft centres he built into so many of his houses speak of the 'gentleness' many of his friends discerned at the core of his being, and of the timidity that could overwhelm him in the presence of forceful characters such as Rhodes and Lutyens.

After the move to Johannesburg his domestic work shrank, displaced by great public commissions realised in a classical idiom. Their style and the principles employed in their siting also owed much to Rhodes. The defining moment in Baker's later architectural education followed a typically imperial commission that Rhodes penned on one of his architectural sketchbooks during the early stage of the South African War:[11]

> March/1900
>
> I desire you to see Rome, Paestum, Agrigentum, Thebes and Athens. I am thinking of erecting a mausoleum to those who fell at Kibrly [Kimberley], a bath and a copy of Paestum. Your expenses as to trip will be paid and in case ɏ I undertake any of these thoughts you will receive the usual architects fee for supervision of 5 per cent
>
> C J Rhodes

The revelation of classical landscapes

The immediate results of Baker's grand tour were somewhat comical schemes for the Kimberley war memorial. Rhodes had been among those besieged by Boer forces in 1899. De Beers company engineers and foundry workers tried to counter the Boers' long-range artillery with their own big gun, which quickly became known as Long Cecil.

The phallic implications were obvious to the soldiers and workers of Kimberley. Even more so when Baker put the gun into his memorial designs. One, based on the ruined Temple of Aruns (Figure 18), places the canon between enormous upright cylindrical pillars. Kipling was quick to approve 'the Phallic suggestion of the pillars'.[12] Viewed from above in cross section the diagram provokes mirth.

Although it kept the gun, the final realisation of the Kimberley Memorial (1904) gave Baker practice in neo-classical style, but offered

Figure 18 One of Baker's designs for the Kimberley war memorial

no opportunity to work with the landscape (Figure 19). The profounder effects of Baker's Mediterranean trip showed up in his thinking about scale, style and landscape, causing him to abandon forever the 'teaching of Ruskin and his disciples' to which he formerly adhered.

> 'Sketch, sketch, sketch!' was the motto given to students by Scott and Street, the great architects of the Gothic revival, and architects and the public forgot that the greater and eternal qualities of the art are scale, balance and symmetry, orderly arrangement, and a simplicity which subordinates details of design to a big conception and to the demands of surrounding nature.[13]

There can be no doubt that it was Rhodes who pushed Baker towards building for imperial purposes in classical forms, but what impressed Baker so profoundly was not the classical idiom itself, but the way the buildings he saw interacted with their natural settings. Though he was at pains to praise the Romans for their perfection of an imperial order in architecture, it was the interplay of built form and landscape in Greek sacred architecture that fired his imagination.

> The effect of the Parthenon, crowning the skyline of the Acropolis, the symbol of all the Greek held sacred, designed to be seen over the sea and the plains of Attica, is a supreme instance of the value of restraint

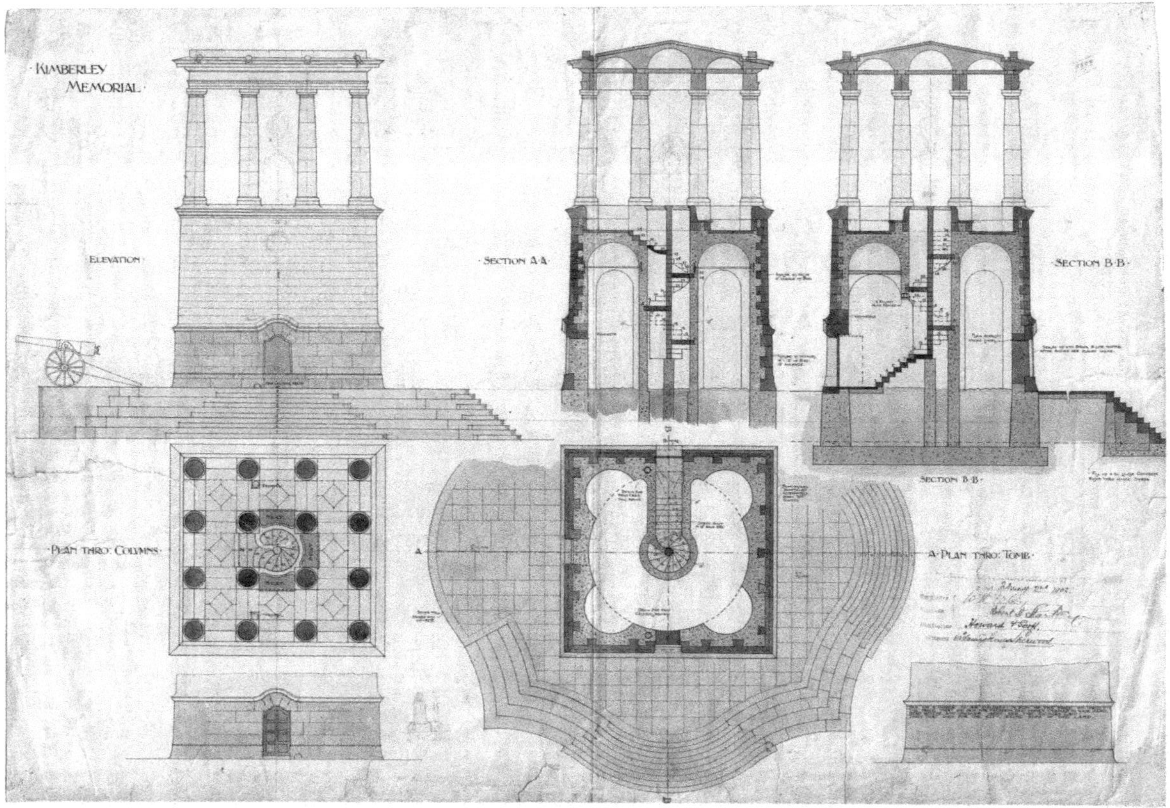

Figure 19 Detail of final design for Kimberley Memorial with 'Long Cecil' separately mounted

> and subordination to an idea in architecture ... Its nobility, apart from the sculpture, depends primarily on the simple row of seventeen similar lintel-spanned columns ranged along the top, and in scale with the steep cliff which formed the Acropolis.[14]

It is very important to stress that not everyone will perceive these relationships in the same way. With few texts to guide him, Baker drew his own lessons from the mute ancient sites. The precise nature of his perception can be better understood by contrasting his perceptions with those of a more recent architectural scholar. Fifty years after Baker's four-month jaunt round the Mediterranean, a young American, Vincent Scully, proceeded on a longer study trip backed by an equally impressive patron – the Fulbright fellowship programme. He seems to have been unaware of Baker, for as late as 1979 he lamented that publications on Greek sites continued to ignore the relationship between temples and surrounding nature: 'I am ... somewhat exasperated by recent publications of Greek sites. The landscape still does not exist so far as their authors are concerned ... Such obdurate blindness now seems hardly less than humanistically irresponsible.'[15] What most impressed Scully about the Greek temples was the way they seemed to him to celebrate the forms of the gods and goddesses inhabiting the sacred sites. Quoting Herman Melville and clearly under the influence of Freud and D. H. Lawrence, Scully saw the landscape in sexual terms.

> Thebes is a hidden city, closely set into the *deep folds* of the land ... On the northern side it is more open, but even when approaching from this direction one is finally surprised at the size of the city and the actual height of its acropolis hill, since intervening folds of the land had allowed only a small portion of it to be visible before. From the north, however, it can be seen that Thebes is set on a *mounded hill* near the southern end of its enclosing valley and that directly on axis to the south rise the *notched cleft*, the broad horns, and the *rounded masses* of Mount Cithairon.[16]

On Mount Mathia, 'The symbols of the goddess were explicit: the cone or mound and the horns seen across intervening swells of land.'[17] And at Therapne, 'The hill of the Menelaion is not the highest or the furthest projecting of these mounds, but it is the central one and the most perfect in shape. The remains of the later temple upon its high, deeply stepped platform still give the impression, when seen from the valley or from the other hills, of *a nipple on a breast*.'[18] If Baker noticed anything similar, he kept it to himself. What he emphasised was the way the Greek sites were designed as places from which to see and to be seen (Figure 20).

> The Greeks at the height of their artistic development ... had a wonderful eye for *impressive effect from a distance*, especially from the sea. Athens, Agrigentum, Selinus, had groups or rows of temples ranked along

Figure 20 Selinus from the sea as imaginatively reconstructed

> the skylines of cliffs which overlooked the town, the harbour and the sea. The carefully studied scale of these temples was large enough to *impress the beholder* from a distance with the beauty and glory of the city. It is easy to imagine how the Greek sailor, 'the merry Grecian coaster', returning from a long sea voyage must have venerated his home.[19]

Scully and Baker agreed in seeing the Greek sites as processional spaces, but conceived the ancient processions in quite different terms. Scully imagined a worshipper moving among the temples with unexpected and spiritually significant views unfolding on all sides:

> the altars may be so placed or the approaches so arranged that the temple carries the eye east, west, north, or south toward a significant shape [in the landscape] and can be seen with it ... Indeed, multiple combinations, specific and unformularized, occur almost everywhere ... and can be grasped only through the direct experience of each site as a 360° whole.[20]

Baker imagined the ancient processions in far more linear terms, again with an emphasis on 'imposing effects' (Figure 21):

> The greatest skill was displayed at Athens ... A steep flight of steps up the cliff led to the great colonnade of the Propylaea. On one side of this stood the little Temple of Victory, and on the other a sculptured monument: these two balanced each other, standing out clear against the sky on spurs of the cliff. Above on the flat top of the rock were the Doric Parthenon and the Ionic Erechtheum, again balancing each other on either side, each being carefully placed so as to have the most imposing effect as seen, the Parthenon from the harbour and sea, and the Erechtheum from the city.[21]

Figure 21 Procession to the Acropolis as envisaged by Baker

On the other hand, Scully and Baker appreciated with equal vivacity the effect that can be achieved by a processional ascent in which the most important built form is alternatively hidden and disclosed. Using the same example of the Acropolis at Athens, Scully imagines how at one point in the procession:

> The Parthenon has dropped entirely out of sight behind the hill, but as the procession curved around toward the south side its pediment would have slid out above the slanting walls below it. Then it would have disappeared again as the procession left its horses and its chariots and came on foot to Mnecicle's Propylaia.[22]

The final lesson Baker took from his travels was the way in which a variety of built forms could be deployed across an elevated site to 'impress visitors from a distance'. The sites that astonished Baker were precisely those that Scully recognised to have been designed for theatrical effect: Selinus in Sicily and Pergamon in western Turkey. Each was strung along an elevated platform. Scully insightfully related these sites to the problem of planting colonial cities in regions that lacked the scale and sacred associations of the Greek homeland (Figure 20). Selinus in his opinion represented the Greek architects' solution to the difficult problem of 'tying the city to an identifiable horizon ... the temples which crowned the two hills were clearly intended to form solid reference points for each other. In the otherwise rolling and fluid landscape, opening on one side to the empty reaches of the sea, the temples gave stability and scale to the town between and behind them.'[23] It was, he observed,

> perhaps a dilemma faced by rich colonial peoples everywhere: how to bring a new and vaster landscape into civilized order without perverting the values upon which that order was based; how to conquer barbarism without becoming barbarized oneself; how, perhaps most of all, to make use of vaster sums of money than had ever been available at home without expressing the power of the money rather than the power of the god.[24]

This was for Herbert Baker a non-problem. His pseudo-temples would unashamedly express the power of the money, and – if they contained any gods – they were the spirits of Rhodes and the political masters he served. To reiterate, when he looked upon Selinus he saw 'rows of temples ranked along the skylines of cliffs' whose 'carefully studied scale' aimed 'to impress the beholder from a distance with the beauty and glory of the city'.[25] He longed to achieve similar effects in South Africa, but recognised the problems of scale and belonging that Scully noticed in colonial landscapes:

> If Table Mountain were on a much smaller scale the temples might be imagined crowning the flat ridge of the mountain and the horns of its crescent, the Devil's Peak and the Lion's Head. But Table Mountain would dwarf any work of human hands which attempted to vie in scale with it. It would be easier to imagine a Pergamos or Halicarnassus growing out of any semi-circle of the cliffs that stretch from Muizenberg to Simon's Town, or rising from any of the encircling hills of Pretoria or Bloemfontein.[26]

Rhodes Memorial

The classical site that impressed him most of all, and from which he drew the basic form of Rhodes Memorial, was the late Hellenistic complex of Pergamos (modern Pergamon) in Asia Minor (Figure 22).

Although he had not visited it, he knew the place through Reginald Blomfield's book, *The Mistress Art*, and reconstructions published by French scholars.[27] The key line for him in Blomfield's text observed that 'the general result, as seen from the plain, was this: the Royal Palace and garden, the temple of Athene, and the immense Altar of

Figure 22 Pergamon: reconstructed model

Zeus formed one immense composition on the segment of a curve, lining the ridge and encircling the theatre in the hollow on the breast of the hill below.' Baker would arrange his Union Buildings in Pretoria in just this way on an almost identical site. But prior to that he was given his first opportunity to show what he could do with classical forms and landscape in 1905 when the Rhodes Memorial Committee, approving his initial sketches, allocated £20,000 for a building that 'would last forever'.[28]

To sum up so far, Rhodes sent Baker to study classical models as inspirations for Boer War memorials. Baker did that and more. He believed the ancient sites had taught him three ways in which the interplay of building and landscape could give visual expression to imperial power:

1 The architect should seek out elevated sites where the buildings could impress observers from a great distance.
2 Buildings should be arranged on the landscape as processional spaces in which important elements would be alternately hidden and disclosed during the visitor's ascent.
3 When opportunities arose to build large complexes, these should be arranged in a platform conforming to the folds of an undulating ridge that commanded large views from above and respectful admiration from below.

Baker believed he was carrying out the spirit of instructions communicated to him by Rhodes himself prior to his death. The burial site in the Matopos should be in the centre of a 'Druidical circle' of boulders, adjacent to the memorial Baker had designed to commemorate the dead of the Matabele War. ('I advised him to put the monument just outside the boulders, leaving the "Druidical circle" as the open portico to the monument. The inside I hinted should be left as a sacred place for another purpose. He silently agreed. I knew his 'thoughts' with regard to this Heröon for the great dead of Rhodesia, and felt that he himself should be in the central spot; and it is there he ... lies.') Baker was outraged that while he was absent in England, the war memorial was moved to a more distant and lower spot; 'it was never designed to be looked down on'.[29] He made sure that mistake was not repeated with Rhodes Memorial. There was no doubt that the building would occupy an elevated position on Table Mountain.

> In many talks I had with Rudyard Kipling, when he spent the southern summers at the Wool-sack, we discussed the sites and sculpture for the memorial. Lord Grey had suggested a colossal statue on the Lion's Head promontory to be seen from Capetown and the sea. But on that beacon-hill it would have been invisible from his own beloved mountain side.[30]

Baker's writings emphasise Rhodes' pantheistic regard for the mountain. He had once dragged an organist outdoors in the midst of a luncheon party, pointed to the peak above and demanded, 'Put that into your music; it's so big, no artist can paint it.'[31] Baker placed the building well above Groote Schuur so that trees on an adjacent property could not obscure it.[32] Visitors were meant to approach the building from below where the building would be seen outlined against Devil's Peak.

All of Baker's decisions about materials reflected his desire to make the memorial appear to grow from its site, as he had done with the Stonehouse. A nearby quarry supplied the stone. The lowest rank of masonry is formed of rough, undressed blocks slanting upwards from the base. Baker asked that Watts' statue, *Physical Energy*, and the bronze lions that line the ascending stairs be treated before delivery to display a green patina of corrosion. He was alarmed by a reddish colour that emerged for unknown reasons in later years and recommended chemicals be used to restore the green hue.[33] When inscriptions were carved in the 1920s, Baker instructed that they should be hand-rubbed with earth to make them seem ancient.[34] These decisions seem political and ideological rather than aesthetic. The building falsely asserts that the white man was no intruder but belonged to the landscape. Rhodes had liked that idea. According to Baker,

> the archaeology of Rhodesia cast a great spell over his romantic mind. He clung to the belief in its historical connexion with the early northern civilizations of Egypt or Phoenicia, linked directly or indirectly by some

> seafaring nation of the Arabian Sea. Evidence of such a link existed, he thought, in the Birds carved in soapstone, reminiscent of the Egyptian Hawk, on the tall stone posts which stood like sentinels round the ramparts of the ruins at Zimbabwe.[35]

Rhodes placed a soapstone carved bird like that installed in the Rhodes Building (Figure 13) in his prime ministerial cabinet room to remind his fellow ministers 'that many centuries looked down upon their deliberations'. Another stands atop Rhodes House in Oxford. Baker's design for the Kimberley Memorial based on the Tomb of Aruns (Figure 18) reminded Rhodes of the conical tower in the 'Great Enclosure' of the Zimbabwe ruins (Figure 23).[36] Embedding Rhodes Memorial in the primordial rock of Table Mountain was a defiant and deliberate act of cultural appropriation.

But it is above all in the siting and arrangement of the building that Baker most clearly demonstrated what he had learned about the projection of imperial power through the interplay of structure and landscape. The germ of an idea for the memorial went back to a project of the 1890s to place a lion house on the grounds of Groote Schuur, as part of Rhodes' scheme for zoological and botanical gardens that would celebrate his achievements as similar menageries had graced the palace of Versailles and other royal residences of Europe. An early

Figure 23 Conical tower at Great Zimbabwe

plan suggests that the cages might be arranged in a descending series of enclosures on the mountainside (Figure 24). By the time Rhodes dispatched Baker on his travels, the idea had been developed into a project for recreating the ruined temple of Paestum, through which the lions would be allowed to roam at will (Figure 25).

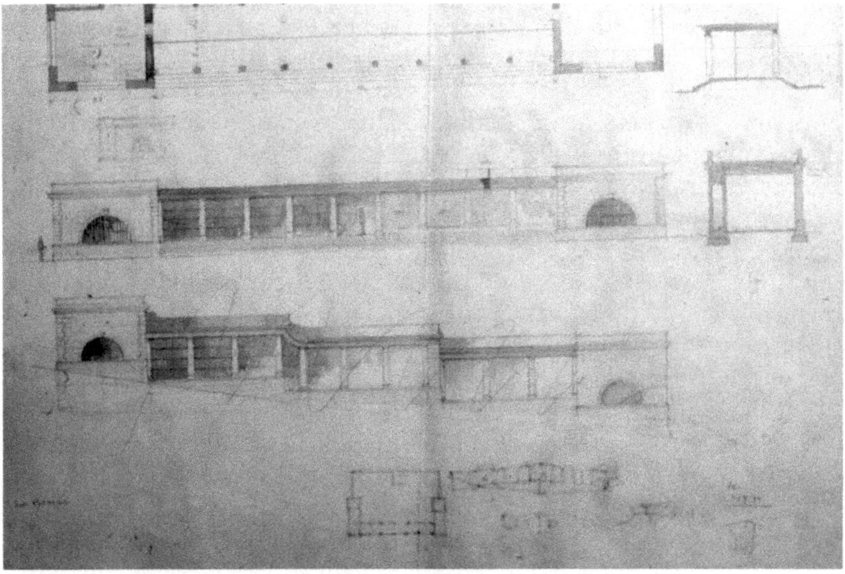

Figure 24 Initial lion house plan for Groote Schuur

Figure 25 Ruins at Paestum, Temple of Poseidon, sketched by Baker as possible basis for lion house at Groote Schuur

> The lion house was planned to be a spacious and beautiful building: a Paestum temple was in his mind where the king of beasts would be admired in his natural strength and dignity. The old Roman in him pictured the beauty of lions moving through great columns, and he was quite unperturbed, when warned of the sanguinary fights which would ensue.[37]

After Rhodes' death the unrealised project was reshaped into the memorial. Because Rhodes had once called his attention to the avenue of sphinxes at the Egyptian ruins of Karnac, Baker decided that guardian lions of Egyptian form should sit atop huge stone blocks descending the hillside in the same fashion he had originally suggested for the big cats' cages (Figure 26). Although Baker would have no French sculptor for the project ('their work, tho technically brilliant, is licentious'), he recognised their skill with animal forms, and therefore chose the Englishman, J. W. Swan, who 'trained at Paris under big men & has I believe some of their skill'.[38] Swan also received the commission for the bust of Rhodes that was to sit in a central niche in the inner sanctum of the colonnade.

The building was based on the Altar of Zeus at Pergamon (Figures 22 and 27). Very likely the choice of the godhead's altar was deliberate. Kipling had written to Baker of Rhodes, 'I don't think that anyone who did not actually come across Him with some intimacy of detail can ever realize what He was. It was his Presence that had the power.' Baker noted that 'the capitals are significant'.[39] When conferring with Swan about the bust to be installed in the memorial, he pointed out the similarity between Rhodes' head and that of the Roman Emperor Titus, a similarity Baker believed Rhodes had also noticed.[40]

Baker's reshaping of the Pergamon altar for a temple to his own god/emperor reveals everything he had so far learned about projecting imperial power from an elevated site. The steep-pitched steps of the theatre offer access to the upper complex at Pergamon. The Altar of Zeus sits apart on a horizontal platform set at an oblique angle. Wishing to reproduce what he had seen at Agrigentum in Sicily, Baker put his Altar of Zeus/Rhodes in a very different position. He combined stairs and temple in a single structure and placed them theatrically against the background of Devil's Peak (Figure 28). The pitch of the stairs is markedly steeper than at the original as reconstructed at the Pergamon Museum in Berlin (Figure 29).

As a result the colonnades of the original become exceptionally deep porticos. Until the approach begins the visitor can have no clear view of anything that might be happening there. The device used in the upper storeys of some of his commercial buildings is generated on

Figure 26 Egyptian lion and J. Swan's version of it on the steps of Rhodes Memorial

a vastly exaggerated scale. Once again we may imagine the elevated porticos inhabited by watchers who see all but cannot themselves be seen. What these unseen watchers contemplate is nothing less than the whole of Africa spreading out to an infinite horizon. Kipling applauded Baker's preliminary sketches and pushed him to go even farther: 'being florid in my tastes I should like, against the dark green

Figure 27 Temple of Zeus at Pergamon (detail of reconstructed model)

Figure 28 Rhodes Memorial with steep stairs as pictured by Baker

Figure 29 Reconstructed Temple of Zeus, Pergamon Museum, Berlin

Figure 30 One way up. Visitors struggle up the stairs of Rhodes Memorial on opening day

[of the mountainside] a vermillion entablature and columns sheathed in bronze after the insolent Egyptian fashion. Something that to the vulgar suggested Cape to Cairo and to others – other things.'[41]

Baker's design provides but one choice to the visitor who makes the processional ascent of those stairs (Figure 30). One may pass to the right or to the left of G. F. Watts' statue, *Physical Energy*, but thereafter the line of ascent is rigidly determined. In a passage of great perceptiveness, Vincent Scully identifies this effect as a product of Roman imperialism that is far removed from Greek sensitivity to the gods inhabiting the forms of the land. He describes the Temple of Fortune at Praeneste (Figure 31), south of Rome, in phrases that could be applied word-for-word to Baker's memorial.

> The elements at Praeneste are rigidly symmetrical, as those at the Greek sites are not. The central axis of movement at Praeneste is fixed, and the parts are therefore distributed as the definers of symmetrical spaces to left and right according to an internal spatial principle. That principle, while decisive, is based upon the desire for a kind of security which the Greek had normally been willing to deny himself. The parts on the left echo, that is, the parts on the right, so that it is not the intensity of specific actions in the landscape but the careful orientation of the participant in an interior hierarchical order which determines the placement of the elements of the whole ... the Roman truth is more than that: insofar as Praeneste and its Imperial progeny create both security and dominion at vast scale, mass scale, in fact, appropriate to the objectives of a military empire and indicating that there are no true alternatives at all for human action but only a single way from which all else, however elaborate, must develop.[42]

Nicholas Thomas has written in rather similar terms about British imperialism, manifested at home by bureaucratic surveillance and abroad by the construction of visions of order: 'Some of those who visited Cairo in the early and mid-nineteenth century complained that

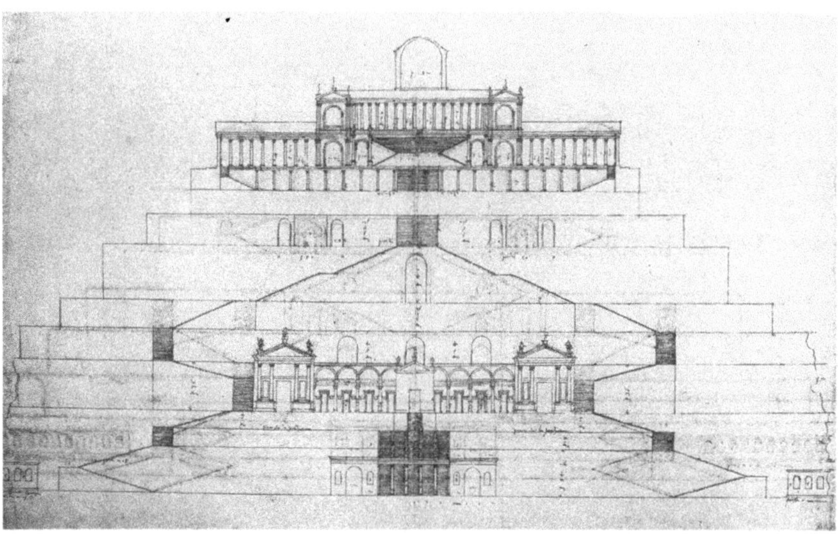

Figure 31 Praeneste drawing by Palladio, sixteenth century

the narrow and disorderly alleys precluded any overview, any sense of the totality; while later colonial architecture created interiors and exteriors, positioned an observing subject, and thus created "an appearance of order, an order that work[ed] by appearance".'[43]

The uncanny climax to the visitor's ascent of Rhodes Memorial is the realisation that there is no one there. A small bust of Rhodes stands in an apsidal niche reminiscent of the soft centres we have noted in other buildings. Nothing else. This citadel defies assault because, like the structure of Empire itself, the power it expresses lies beyond the reach of ordinary assailants: distributed in a network of money, military force and information stretching beyond South Africa to the ends of the earth.

A surprising testimony to Baker's success in projecting an idea of imperial power in the abstract, as opposed to *British* imperial power, is the support he gained from defeated Boer generals Smuts, Botha and Hertzog, who dominated the politics of the white supremacist state after the creation of the Union of South Africa.[44] Smuts championed Baker's plans for the Union Buildings; even in old age he liked to pass by Rhodes Memorial on his daily climb up the mountain. When Baker arrived on a trip from England in the 1920s, Prime Minister Hertzog had cars waiting at the dock to whisk him and his family up to Rhodes Memorial. Saul Dubow has called attention to the way agreement on a shared 'beautiful land' helped unify Afrikaner and English statesmen in the aftermath of war.[45] Baker played a major part in this imaginative enterprise. It may be that the choice of a classical idiom appealed to Smuts, Botha and Hertzog, because it recalled a shared European heritage rather than recognisable British models. And, though they did not say it, they may have grasped the way Baker's buildings, through their calculated placement on hillsides, expressed the power they shared over the African people. If Baker's deep porticos call to mind omniscient watchers who are not seen, by the same token subjugated peoples are the absolutely necessary element required to complete the vast tableau.

Union Buildings, Pretoria

Baker achieved this effect on a much larger scale in the Union Buildings at Pretoria, a project that took shape even as Rhodes Memorial was rising on the side of Table Mountain. He was commissioned without a competition and

> given a free hand in suggesting sites in and around the city. I was shown the block of land which the Government had bought in the centre of the city, where the Museum and Town Hall now stand. But with the high

> ideals we all had at the time I thought this site unworthy of the capital buildings of a united South Africa. So I explored the surrounding kopjes [hills] and selected two ideal sites overlooking the valley where Pretoria lies.[46]

One was a flat sunlit hilltop with scope for later extensions and extensive gardens. The other ran along a narrow ridge, had no room for extensions, was shrouded in shade for much of each day and would require gardens to be laid out below – if there were to be gardens at all. Baker's fixation on the Greek buildings he had studied led him to choose the more difficult site. It would dominate the city 'as did the Acropolis the city of Athens'. It contained 'a natural concave depression in the rock platform such as the Greeks might have chosen for an open-air theatre'. The 'vision of what a building here might be brought to my mind Segesta with its temple and theatre, and of Agrigentum with its rows of temples on the hillside' (Figure 32).

It would have 'the dignity and nobility of city set upon a hill'. That is to say, it would 'impose' and 'impress'. It would be a place from which to see and be seen. The narrowness of the building site provided no scope for a 360° interaction with the hill on which it stood. Nor was

AGRIGENTUM : SHOWING SITE OF TEMPLES ON EDGE OF CLIFF.

Figure 32 Agrigentum

Figure 33 Sketch for the Union Buildings, as published in *The State*

there much scope for interaction between the various elements within the complex. Necessity decreed that the Union Buildings would form a stage set with an amphitheatre at the centre-point. Baker obviously gloried in the theatricality. While he keenly appreciated the changing vistas that would open and close before the physically fit visitors ascending the central stairs, he allowed only a single processional line of approach (Figures 33–35).

The similarity to what Scully identified as the imperial 'Roman truth' of Praeneste – 'there are no true alternatives at all for human action but only a single way' – is striking. This can readily be seen by juxtaposing Baker's plans with a drawing of the Praeneste ruins surmounted by the Renaissance Barbarini Palace (Figure 36). Perhaps Baker knew the site, but there is no question of plagiarism here. Baker enthusiastically sought precisely the imperial effect that Scully so deftly differentiates from the Greek way of seeing.

Baker also incorporated the deep colonnaded porticos he had employed in Rhodes Memorial. Once again the visitor confronts the impression of elevated watchers who see everything but are not themselves seen. Only this time there is no possibility of joining the watchers on their shaded platforms. These adjoin offices assigned to the mighty office-bearers who may only be approached via well-guarded doors and corridors. Even more than in Rhodes Memorial, there is a suggestion that the visitor who ascends the processional stairs in search of the seat of power will find the object of the quest constantly receding into an unattainable distance.

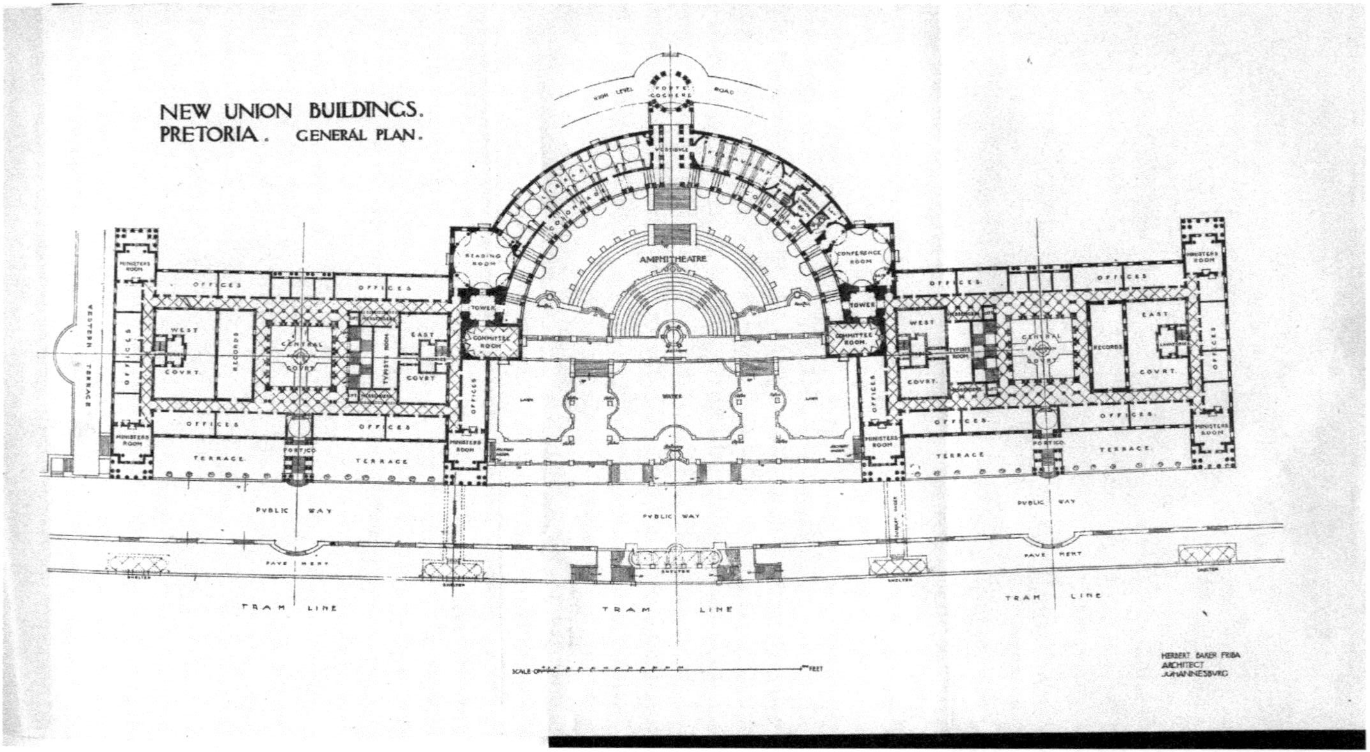

Figure 34 Layout of main buildings, Union complex

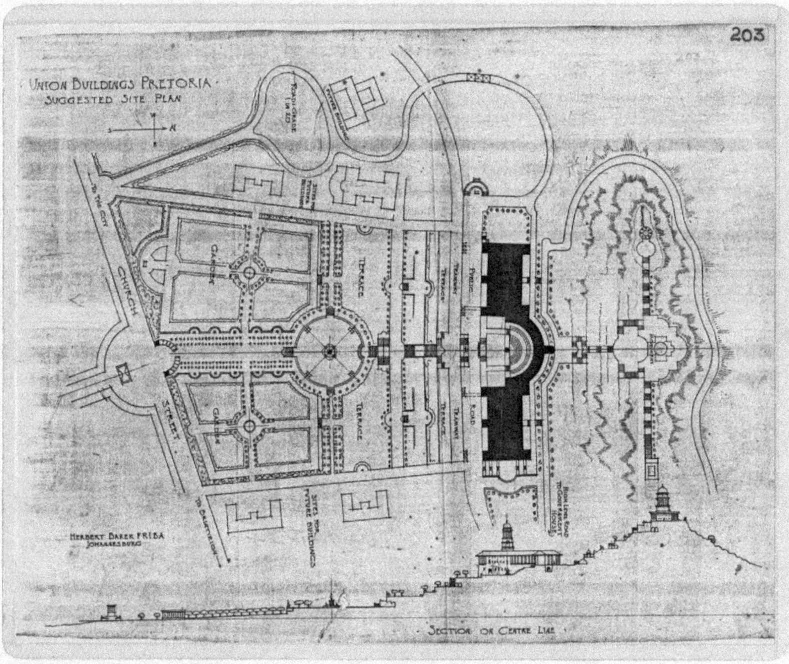

Figure 35 Union Buildings site plan with gardens and elevation

It is also noteworthy that Baker strove here as in Rhodes Memorial to anchor new buildings to a spurious ancient European past. He envisaged two sham Greek temples (never built) to sit on the peaks above the main complex (Figure 38).

The view from the central terrace towards Pretoria and the South African Highveld is commanding in the military sense. In precolonial times Africans chose such sites for their homes and cattle byres because raiders might be seen from afar and missiles rained down on them.[47] Baker perceived the symbolic power of the site, as evidenced by the photograph he presented to the Royal Institute of British Architects titled 'The Sentinel' (Figure 39).[48] As with Rhodes Memorial, the greatest tribute to his success was the way in which Britain's defeated enemies enthusiastically seconded his ideas. Far from regarding the commanding position as an expression of Britain's triumph in the late war, General Smuts walked the hillside with the architect and joined in the widespread praise for the ensemble as symbolising the reconciliation of 'the two races' of South Africa – by which, of course, was meant the English and the Dutch. The negotiated terms of peace

Figure 36 The Roman way of seeing: Praeneste and Baker's Union Buildings

Figure 37 Portico-loggia at the Union Buildings

ensured that Africans would continue to be denied participation in the governance of the country. Thomas Metcalf has drawn attention to their exclusion from the built and symbolic programme of the Union Buildings.[49] Considered from another point of view the bellicose posture of the complex makes sense as a statement of white supremacy in an ongoing struggle.

In the early stages of Baker's design work, it had not yet been decided that the branches of the Union government would be scattered – as they eventually were – with parliament sitting in Cape Town, the high court in Bloemfontein and the executive in Pretoria. He contemplated a home for the parliament in a domed capitol located behind the central colonnade that links the eastern and western buildings. In this situation it would be a dominant element viewed from the city, but would be invisible to visitors as they ascended the terraces. He explained his intentions in a letter to Lutyens: 'The dome would be seen from the town and valley but not from the terraces – but must there be no surprises in architecture? no hiding and then revealing? It all grew from that colonnade!'[50]

Hiding and then revealing can in retrospect be discerned as the dominant strategy of Baker's work since his arrival in South Africa. It shows up in the early domestic and commercial buildings and gets carried further after the epiphany of his Mediterranean tour when he grasped that the power of classical architecture derived in large part

Figure 38 Sham temples for the Union Buildings

from its deployment within a stepped and rugged landscape. The awesome sight of ruined buildings from the sea gives way, on disembarking, to a complex experience of hiding and revealing as the visitor ascends, like the throngs of ancient sacral processions through continually altering points of vantage until at last the acropolis is disclosed in all its majesty. The chasm separating Baker's architectural vision of Empire from that of his old friend Lutyens remained unknown to them until their collaboration in New Delhi threw it into sharp relief and

Figure 39 'The Sentinel': A view over Pretoria from the terrace of the Union Buildings, *c.*1911

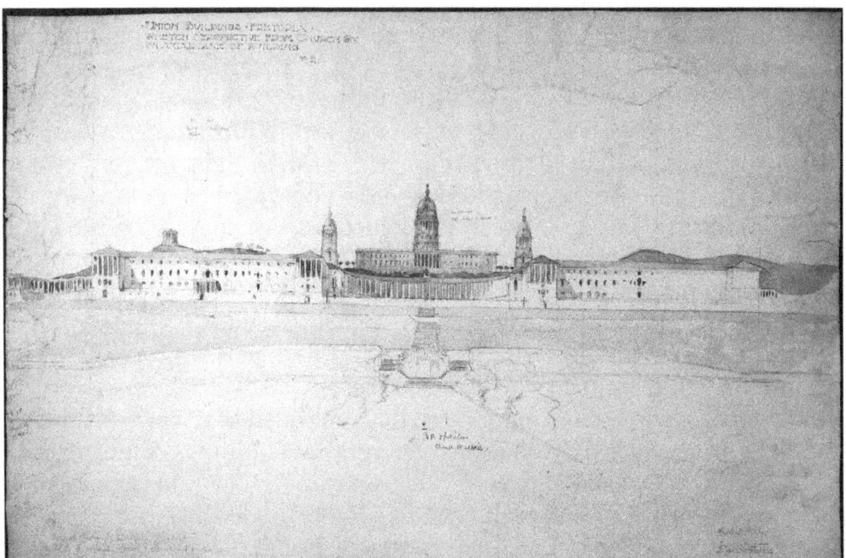

Figure 40 Baker's 1909 perspective drawing of Union Buildings incorporating a domed capitol and high court chambers

became the cause of one of the most notorious quarrels in the history of architecture.

Showdown at New Delhi

The dispute, which has been superbly recounted in Robert Grant Irving's *Indian Summer*, concerned the angle of approach to the Viceroy's palace, whose design had been confided to Lutyens.[51] Baker's main task was the design of the Secretariat Buildings housing the principal government departments. The chosen site, Raisina Hill, lacked the craggy grandeur of Table Mountain or the kopjes of Pretoria, but offered some possibilities as a processional space. Lutyens' palace would sit on a plaza atop the hill, while the offices of Baker's Secretariat would be split into two lower buildings sitting either side of the avenue of approach.

By the time of their collaboration both architects had abandoned Ruskin, Morris and the Arts and Crafts Movement in favour of a return to classicism. As Lutyens put it in a letter to Baker back in 1903, 'in architecture, Palladio is the game!! It is so big – few appreciate it now, and it requires training to value and realize it. The way Wren handled it was marvellous.'[52] On hearing the news of the New Delhi commission, Baker wrote, 'It is really a great event in the history of the world and of architecture, – that rulers should have the strength and sense to do the right thing. It would only be possible now under a despotism – some day perhaps democracies will follow ... Hurrah for despotism!'[53] With his London experience, a domed viceregal palace would have brought to Lutyens' mind the gentle ascent to Wren's St Paul's via Ludgate Hill. Baker strove for something like his invocations of imperial domination in South Africa. Without at first realising what he had done, Lutyens signed off on an angle of ascent that ensured that in the final approach his building would momentarily disappear almost completely from sight.

When he saw the finished model, he concluded that Baker's motive had been to focus attention on *his* Secretariat Buildings. Fuming that he had been 'Bakerized', Lutyens declared war.[54] He would not be satisfied until the avenue was bulldozed to a lesser angle that would enable his building to be kept continually in view. Rendered practically mute by the ferocity of Lutyens' assault, Baker fell back on practical arguments based on the expense of re-engineering the site. In the end he prevailed with the Viceroy's backing, but without ever clearly articulating the vision of the imperial architecture he had forged in South Africa and sought to recreate for the Indian capitol. Far from wishing

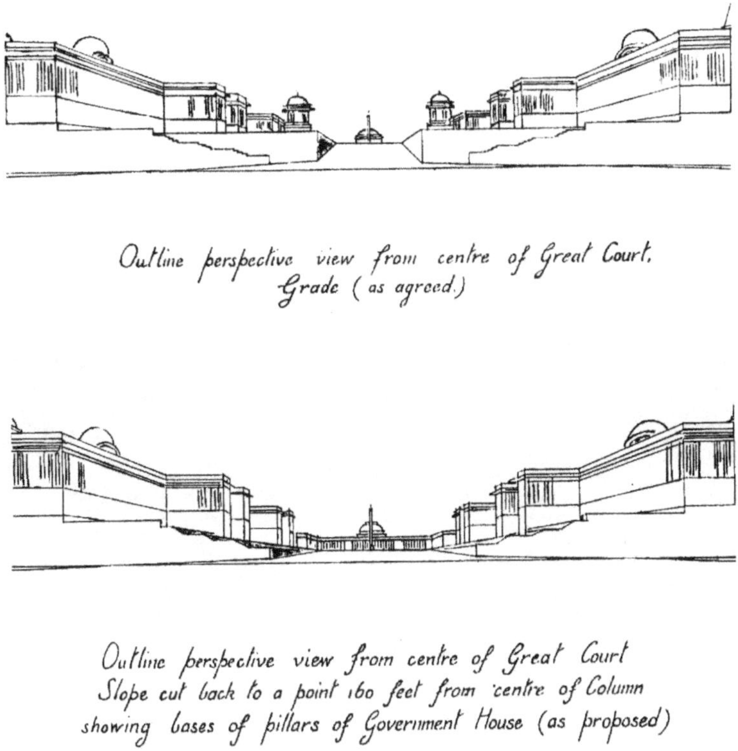

Figure 41 1916 drawings by W. H. Nicholls showing agreed approach to Government House, New Delhi

to upstage Lutyens, he envisaged the revelation of the central palace as the culmination of a procession towards the sacral majesty of imperial power (Figures 41–44).

The dispute centred on the way Baker had determined a line of ascent that causes Lutyens' viceregal palace to be alternatively concealed and revealed. Lutyens believed this reflected Baker's vain desire to spotlight his Secretariat Buildings that lined the ceremonial way to the top. Coming from horizontal England and lacking Baker's South African vision, Lutyens completely misunderstood Baker's intention, which was to use landscape to enhance the ultimate revelation of Government House.

Almost all accounts of the six-year battle neglect Baker's practice of representing imperial power through interaction with landscape and the role his Secretariat Buildings actually play in a processional

Figure 42 Lutyens' viceregal palace, New Delhi, seen from afar

Figure 43 Viceregal palace obscured on the approach between Baker's Secretariat Buildings

Figure 44 Viceregal palace fully revealed

ascent towards Lutyens' building. Is it fair to say that Baker's arrangement makes the twin blocks of the Secretariat the focus of attention? David Cannadine dismisses them as 'over-blown, windy, ponderous Edwardian Baroque, salted and spiced with Indian motifs which were decorative but not integrated'.[55] And so they may be if considered in isolation. However, Baker positioned them to face north and south at right angles to the 'Processional Way'. A full frontal view differs profoundly from that seen on the controversial gradient of Raisina Hill.

From this angle most of Baker's buildings lie hidden, as does the machinery of the Indian Raj spinning busily behind those mighty walls (Figure 46). These ramparts, which rise from the plain, resemble 'an embattled stronghold, as though Indian nationalism and the debilitating breadth of the landscape rendered all building defensive by necessity'.[56] His trademark elevated porticos seem, if anything, more unattainable and intimidating than at Rhodes Memorial or South Africa's Union Buildings. The real cause of the misunderstanding between the two old

Figure 45 Baker's Northern Secretariat with pool and gardens

Figure 46 Southern facade of North Secretariat Building as seen from ground level on the approach to viceregal palace

friends may have been Baker's deeper commitment to Empire and the expression of political power in architecture. As Irving remarks:

> Unlike Lutyens, whom he thought concentrated his intellectual talents on abstract and geometrical qualities to the neglect of human and national sentiment, Baker felt that content in art was of the first importance. In building New Delhi, therefore, English classical architecture in the manner of Inigo Jones and Wren should be adopted in order fearlessly to 'put the stamp of British sovereignty' on the subcontinent of India.[57]

As Baker expressed it himself in a draft of an article on 'Architecture and Empire':

> Our rule confers order, progress and freedom within the law to develop national civilizations on the lines of their own tradition and sentiment: so in architecture there is infinite scope within the limits of order, true science, and progress for the widest self-expression in every field of art; but without the orderly control of the great principles, there might result a chaos in the arts such as in governments which History records our rule was ordained to supersede.[58]

Baker uses pseudo-Mughal cupolas and arches much as he used the carved Zimbabwe bird in South Africa, to express that vision of a classical British order controlling the potential chaos of alternative visions. They cannot be integral to the structure, as Cannadine seems to wish, because Baker would never allow them to be. The Secretariat looms like a fortress not just defensively, but offensively. As with the Union Buildings, the expression of power is meaningless without reference to the colonial subjects who inhabit the larger landscape.

On his return to England, Baker won commissions for a range of large projects, none of which won him much praise from his peers. Though Baker never admitted it, the failure of these huge commissions owed less to failures in design than to his inability to work with the kind of landscapes he had found in Africa and India. To take an example, the street facade of Rhodes' House, Oxford, seems a most unhappy marriage of classicism and the picturesque tradition in late-nineteenth-century country-house building (Figure 47). Lacking an elevated podium, the colonnaded entrance cannot evoke visions of potent unseen watchers.

South Africa House in London fails to inspire for similar reasons (Figure 48).[59] Constrained by its adjacent streets, there was no opportunity for deep elevated porticos. Here they are narrowed to mere balconies. The roughcast lower storey afforded some protection during anti-apartheid demonstrations of the late twentieth century, but is not visually intimidating. There is no landscape to facilitate theatrical

Figure 47 Rhodes House, Oxford

Figure 48 South Africa House, Trafalgar Square, London

effects. Above all, the building does not work in conjunction with an implied chaotic subject population who require the heavy hand of law and order. At the democratic headquarters of Empire, Imperial Power needs no visual representation. Big effects are reserved for Buckingham Palace and the Houses of Parliament.

Herbert Baker: architecture and personality

Baker, despite being an author and connoisseur of literature, left little that might provide a basis for a psychological exploration of his inner life. Even when writing about his own buildings he confined his observations to questions of technique and symbolism. There is nothing like the grandiloquent theorising about architecture, self-expression and society that poured from his great contemporary, Frank Lloyd Wright. Yet Baker constantly challenges us with suggestions that he has put his deepest self into his buildings. From his first tentative ventures in South Africa, he experimented with deep recesses and hidden secrets. Some of the secrets concerned the mundane business of tucking the work and living places of black servants into walled yards. Others expressed the ruling class's preoccupation with surveillance and privacy. However, the soft centres he built within commercial buildings and mansions for mining magnates served no necessary functions. Like the gift chest from the Kindergarten, they suggest a wish to closet the innermost Herbert Baker from prying eyes. The urge to conceal and hide may have something to do with his hero-worship of Rhodes and T. E. Lawrence and the fanatical devotion he displayed to the companionship of the Kindergarten, particularly in the original concept for 'The Stonehouse'. Whatever it was, when realised in architecture, it spoke a central truth about British imperialism. The emphasis on control, order, grandeur, elevated vantage points and hidden places where unseen governors devised their plans proclaimed an ideal of colonial domination that could never be and never was implemented. Too few pretended to decree the destinies of too many. The uncanny way that power constantly recedes from view in Baker's buildings, the way it alternatively hides and shows itself, the emptiness at the heart of Rhodes Memorial – all betray the weakness that haunted the most vociferous proponents of Empire. There were never enough soldiers, battleships, resources, markets. If the work of shoring up the defences ceased even for a moment, rivals would attack, assassins would infiltrate, subjects would rebel. The world has seen many versions of architecture devised by fearful rulers to bully people into accepting their subordinate status. Herbert Baker did it as well as anyone.

Notes

1 Correspondence, photos and drawings from Baker's firm were donated by the successor to his Cape Town practice, Kendall and Earle, to the University of Cape Town (UCT). Formerly known as the Kendall and Earle Collection, they are now held in Special Collections as the Herbert Baker Collection.
2 Robert Rotberg, *The Founder: Cecil Rhodes and the Pursuit of Power* (Oxford: Oxford University Press, 1988), p. 381.
3 Daniel M. Abramson, 'Baker, Sir Herbert (1862–1946)', *Oxford Dictionary of National Biography* (Oxford: Oxford University Press, 2004), online edn, May 2009 (www.oxforddnb.com/view/article/30547, accessed 11 April 2013).
4 Christopher Hussey, *The Life of Sir Edwin Lutyens* (Woodbridge: Antique Collectors' Club, 1989), p. 181.
5 Charles H. Reilly, *Representative British Architects: Leading Figures from 1930s Design* (London: B. T. Batsford, 1931), p. 47.
6 Rotberg, *The Founder*, p. 383.
7 D. F. Ellis to Baker and Massey, 10 September 1904, box 33, Kendall and Earle Collection, UCT.
8 Darter, Brothers and Company, Fine Art Dealers, Cape Town to Baker and Massey, 20 December 1904, box 33, Kendall and Earle Collection, UCT.
9 Herbert Baker, *Architecture and Personalities* (London: Country Life, 1944), pp. 48–9.
10 For Baker's intentions in this house and others along the Parktown ridge, see Jeremy Foster, *Washed with Sun: Landscape and the Making of White South Africa* (Pittsburgh: University of Pittsburgh Press, 2008), pp. 152, 172–6.
11 A facsimile of the letter is reproduced following p. 15 of Herbert Baker, *Cecil Rhodes by His Architect* (London: Oxford University Press, 1934). The writing of the commission in Baker's sketchbook suggests that it followed a conversation on the subject. It may well be that Rhodes' instructions owed something to Baker's suggestions, as well as Rhodes' ideas garnered from his travels. In a letter about the Cape Town cathedral project written in 1899, Baker wrote that 'wherever a Greek colony was founded on the shores of the Mediterranean, we find there to this day beautiful stone built temples, eloquent witnesses to the greatness of their builders'; Baker to Rev. Phillip Legg, 11 March 1899, box 78, Kendall and Earle Collection, UCT.
12 Kipling to Baker, 22 September 1900, in Thomas Pinner (ed.), *The Letters of Rudyard Kipling, Vol. III: 1900–10* (London: Macmillan, 1996).
13 Herbert Baker, 'The architectural needs of South Africa', *The State* 1 (1909), 512.
14 Ibid., 514.
15 Vincent Scully, *The Earth, the Temple, and the Gods*, rev. edn (New Haven, CT: Yale University Press, 1979 [1962]), pp. ix, xvi.
16 Ibid., pp. 29, 32–3; my emphasis.
17 Ibid., p. lxii.
18 Ibid., p. lx.
19 Baker, 'Architectural needs', 514; my emphasis. Baker, unlike Scully, travelled from place to place by sea. It was therefore perfectly understandable that he should emphasise the sailor's point of view.
20 Scully, *Earth, the Temple, and the Gods*, p. 45.
21 Baker, 'Architectural needs', 514; significantly, to illustrate his view of the Acropolis in that article, Baker chose a drawing depicting an ascending procession.
22 Scully, *Earth, the Temple, and the Gods*, p. 178.
23 Ibid., p. 192.
24 Ibid., p. 144.
25 Baker, 'Architectural needs', 514.
26 Ibid., 517.
27 Ibid., 515–16. Baker mistakenly places it on the coast; it is actually located at an inland site. Baker would later work with Blomfield on First World War memorials.
28 Michael Keath, *Herbert Baker: Architecture and Idealism 1892–1913, The South African Years* (Gibraltar: Ashanti, 1993), p. 125.

29 Baker, *Cecil Rhodes*, pp. 125–6.
30 Ibid., p. 130.
31 Paul Maylam, *The Cult of Rhodes: Remembering an Imperialist in Africa* (Claremont, South Africa: David Phillip, 2005), p. 51.
32 Ibid., p. 31. When he returned to South Africa in 1927, one of Baker's first suggestions for refurbishment of the site was that more trees be removed: 'I consider it to be of urgent importance a good deal of tree cutting should be done round the Rhodes Memorial'; Report on Visit to the Cape, 5 August 1927, box 73, Kendall and Earle Collection, UCT.
33 Ibid.
34 Kendall to McKillop & Co., 15 September 1927, box 73, Kendall and Earle Collection, UCT.
35 Baker, *Cecil Rhodes*, pp. 103–5.
36 Ibid., p. 53.
37 Ibid., pp. 46–7.
38 Baker to F. Massey, 24 June 1907, box 73, Kendall and Earle collection, UCT.
39 Baker, *Architecture and Personalities*, pp. 28–9.
40 Baker, *Cecil Rhodes*, p. 133.
41 Quoted in Keath, *Herbert Baker*, pp. 131–2.
42 Scully, *Earth, the Temple, and the Gods*, pp. 210–12.
43 Nicholas Thomas, *Colonialism's Culture: Anthropology, Travel and Government* (Oxford: Polity Press, 1994), p. 111. The interior quotation is from Timothy Mitchell, *Colonising Egypt* (Cambridge: Cambridge University Press, 1988), p. 32.
44 Baker, *Cecil Rhodes*, p. 70; *Architecture and Personalities*, pp. 21, 59.
45 Saul Dubow, 'Imagining the new South Africa', in D. Omissi and A. S. Thompson (eds), *The Impact of the South African War* (London: Macmillan, 2002), pp. 86–9.
46 Baker, *Architecture and Personalities*, p. 58.
47 N. Etherington, *The Great Treks: The Transformation of Southern Africa, 1815–1854* (London: Longman, 2001), pp. 18–19.
48 Christopher Vernon, 'Projecting power on conquered landscapes', in N. Etherington (ed.), *Mapping Colonial Conquest: Australia and Southern Africa* (Perth: UWA Press, 2007), pp. 150–6.
49 Thomas R. Metcalf, *An Imperial Vision: Indian Architecture and Britain's Raj* (Berkeley: University of California Press, 1989), p. 194.
50 Quoted in Keath, *Herbert Baker*, pp. 177–8.
51 Robert Grant Irving, *Indian Summer: Lutyens, Baker and Imperial Delhi* (London: Yale University Press, 1981).
52 Keath, *Herbert Baker*, p. 91.
53 Quoted in ibid., p. 195.
54 For a full account of the dispute, see ibid., chapter 7.
55 David Cannadine, 'Sir Edwin Lutyens', in *The Pleasures of the Past* (London: Collins, 1989), p. 115.
56 Irving, *Indian Summer*, p. 282.
57 Ibid., p. 278.
58 Ibid. From an article drafted for the *Round Table*, but for some reason not published; Baker collections, Owletts, Cobham, Kent.
59 This was not entirely Baker's fault. His original, arguably much better design was rejected by the Fine Arts Commission for failing to harmonise with adjacent buildings; Roy Macnab, *The Story of South Africa House* (Johannesburg: Jonathan Ball, 1983), pp. 25, 27.

CHAPTER FOUR

Joseph Conrad: Kipling's secret sharer

Some might argue that Joseph Conrad does not belong in this collection of conservative artists of empire. Born a subject of the Russian czar, educated as a Polish patriot, steeped in French literature, a wanderer on the seven seas during his chosen career as a ship's officer, Conrad is a long stretch from every stereotype of Englishness. Fellow seamen, mocking his stylish dress, fastidious manners and heavy accent, called him 'the Russian Count'.[1] Viewed from another perspective, however, Conrad is simply the extreme case among this book's company of outsiders who aspired to be imperial insiders. Once established as a writer, Conrad clothed himself in tweeds, found a rural cottage, sent his sons into the army and generally did what he could to perfect the outward image of countrified gentility. When in his novels he assumed the narrative voice of Captain 'Charley' Marlow, no one could hear his accent.

Conrad resembles other subjects of this book in his explorations of the limits of discipline and civilisation as instruments for keeping raw nature and animal savagery under control in the individual psyche and the wider world. However, by pushing his characters to the edge of sanity in far away places, he himself was pushed towards the more extreme and challenging conclusion that imperialism cannot work any better in real-life government than the individual superego can succeed in its vain attempts to silence the wanton demands of the id.

Conrad, Kipling and politics

It is not his lifestyle but his supposed political opinions that have led so many scholars to set him apart from the rest of the imperial artists. Conventional opinion opposes Rudyard Kipling the imperialist to Joseph Conrad the anti-imperialist. Just as *Kim* occupies the first rank among 'novels of empire', *Heart of Darkness* heads almost every list of literary critiques of colonialism. Some of Conrad's closest friends shared the common view. His publisher, Edward Garnett, pointed to Kipling as '*the* enemy ... *the genius of all we detest*'.[2] Understanding Conrad's complex attitude to colonialism entails understanding why he rejected that view. In a letter to one of his radical friends he wrapped an appreciation of Kipling in his customary irony:

> Mr Kipling has the wisdom of the passing generations – and holds it in perfect sincerity. Some of his work is of impeccable form and because of that little thing he shall sojourn in Hell only a very short while. He squints with the rest of his excellent sort. It is a beautiful squint; it is a useful squint. And – after all – perhaps he sees round the corner? And suppose Truth is just round the corner like the elusive and useless loafer it is?[3]

It is significant that at the precise moment that Conrad was most deeply engaged in exploring problems posed by European political and commercial adventuring in the tropics, he was also studying Kipling. In or about 1898, when *Lord Jim* and *Heart of Darkness* were taking shape, he wrote an essay on Kipling.[4] Had the manuscript survived it would be much easier to trace Kipling's influence on his own thinking. However, there is enough evidence to indicate that Conrad's regard for his rambunctious contemporary was deep and continuing. He knew Kipling's prose well enough to suspect that John Buchan's story 'The Far Islands' had borrowed freely from Kipling's tale, 'The Finest Story in the World'.[5] In praising the 'impeccable form' of some Kipling stories, he was most likely acknowledging the debt that both writers owed to Maupassant.[6] One of Kipling's lifelong complaints against the English literary establishment was its slender knowledge of French work;[7] his enthusiasm for Conrad's *Mirror of the Sea* testifies to his admiration for a fellow craftsman.[8] Conrad declined nomination for the Order of Merit in 1919, arguing 'strongly that Kipling is the right person'. Evidence abounds in Conrad's letters and fiction to show that he shared a great many of Kipling's characteristic conservative political beliefs – and his pet hates.

Both Conrad and Kipling loathed evangelical Christianity. Kipling's autobiography traces his hatred back to the matron of the English home where he was sent to board as a child.[9] Male and female versions of that loveless killjoy crop up throughout Kipling's work. Conrad is equally tough on preachers. Many of the troubled souls who crop up in his fiction are identified as 'sons of arch-priests' or parsons: the half-mad 'Harlequin' in *Heart of Darkness*; Captain Leggatt in 'The Secret Sharer'; Razamov in *Under Western Eyes* (whose mother is daughter of an arch-priest); Jim in *Lord Jim*. Lay preachers are represented by the fanatical cook in *The Nigger of the*

'Narcissus' who makes ridiculous and revolting efforts to 'save' the dying Jimmy. In his first novel, *Almayer's Folly*, Conrad took up Kipling's theme of dark-skinned girls betrayed by mission education and hypocrisy. Almayer's wife, who was pulled from a Malay pirate ship by Captain Lingard and sent to a Samarang convent school, reverts to her 'savage nature' after experiencing racial prejudice. Her daughter, Nina, repeats the experience when, after Protestant schooling, she is sent home because she aroused the sexual interest of young white men. Like Kipling's Lispeth she reviles her betrayers and all white men, telling a Dutch lieutenant, 'I hate the sound of your gentle voices.' Her mother's advice is precisely that of Kipling's Lispeth: 'forget their friendship and their contempt; forget their many gods.'[10] Conrad's most subtle jibe at missionaries is the contrast drawn in *Lord Jim* between Jim's gleaming white figure on the dark shore of Patusan and 'the dark dot of the mission-house on a white beach'.[11]

Conrad and Kipling shared a hatred for Liberals, liberalism, socialists and do-gooders of all complexions. Kipling reviled Gladstone, the Liberal prime minister, for 'calling down brimstone upon the British Dominions' and for appointing another Liberal, Lord Ripon, to be Viceroy of India. Liberal principle, Kipling observed, 'ends not seldom in bloodshed'.[12] For Conrad, Gladstone's victory in the general election of 1885 meant that 'the great British Empire went over the edge'; he expected that the 'newly enfranchised idiots' who had voted Gladstone in would soon bring about the triumph of socialism and despotism.[13] Kipling caricatured Liberal idealism in the figure of 'The Member for Lower Tooting', who wanders 'about India in pot-hat and frock-coat' proclaiming the need for 'a duly qualified electoral system and a general bestowal of the franchise'.[14] In a similar fashion Conrad attacked Samuel Plimsoll's parliamentary crusade against the overloading of merchant ships. One of the seamen in *The Nigger of the 'Narcissus'* recalls a ship's crew who were sentenced to six weeks' hard labour for refusing duty, all because they listened to 'a fatherly old gentleman with a white beard and an umbreller'.

> Said as how it was crool hard to be drownded in winter just for the sake of a few pounds more for the owner – he said. Nearly cried over them – he did; and he had a square mainsail coat, and a gaff-topsail had too – all proper. So they chaps they said they wouldn't go to be drownded in winter – depending on that 'ere Plimsoll man to see 'em through the court. They thought to have a bloomin' lark and two or three days' spree. And the beak giv' 'em six weeks – coss the ship warn't overloaded. Anyways they made it out in court that she wasn't. There wasn't one overladed ship in Penarth Dock at all. Pears that old coot he was only on pay and

> allowance from some kind people, under orders to look for overladed ships, and he couldn't see no further than the length of his umbreller.[15]

Needless to say, a man who could suspect the social-democratic ambitions of a Gladstone or the mild philanthropy of a Plimsoll was unremittingly harsh in his judgement of more radical reformers. The anarchists of Conrad's *The Secret Agent* are portrayed as the dupes of self-seeking, twisted schemers and oppressive foreign governments. And in all literature there could be no crueller portrait of the labour union organiser than the shabby figure of Donkin in *The Nigger of the 'Narcissus'*.

> They all knew him! He was the man that cannot steer, that cannot splice, that dodges the work on dark nights; that, aloft, holds on frantically with both arms and legs, and swears at the wind, the sleet, the darkness; the man who curses the sea while others work. The man who is the last out and the first in when all hands are called. The man who can't do most things and won't do the rest. The pet of philanthropists and self-seeking landlubbers. (pp. 12–13)

The man who comes within a whisker of destroying the ship yet thrives on shore 'by discoursing with filthy eloquence upon the right of labour to live' (p. 172).

Kipling and Conrad both scorned literary society, though Kipling was more direct in his denunciation of those who 'dealt in pernicious varieties of safe sedition' while acting as 'purveyors of luxuries to the "Aristocracy"'.[16] Conrad in *The Arrow of Gold* served up a devastating account of Parisian artistic circles. The London society both writers craved was not Bohemia but Clubland: Kipling at the Saville Club, and Conrad at the Athenaeum (his membership fees paid by the press baron, Lord Northcliffe). Conrad shared Kipling's antipathy to pacifism: 'I am not a peace man, nor a democrat', he proclaimed to his socialist friend, R. B. Cunninghame Graham, and went on gratuitously to remark that whenever opportunity offered he warned young people against the dangers of social-democracy.[17] Quite probably the shared antipathy to democracy explains the general hostility Kipling and Conrad displayed towards America and Americans. Though Kipling married an American and lived for a time in New England, he reviled the country for its violence, its immigrants and 'the overwhelming vacuity of the national life'.[18] And even though American readers would eventually give Conrad the financial security he craved, it is hard to find a sympathetic American character in all the pages of his fiction. Ex-Confederate Captain Blunt of *The Arrow of Gold*, who 'lives by his sword', the Yankee cut-throat with 'homicidal and conceited smile' in *Lord Jim* and Holroyd, the hypocritical financier of *Nostromo*, rank among the nastiest of his villains. 'America is ungovernable', Decoud asserts in *Nostromo*. 'Those who worked for independence have ploughed the sea.'[19] In letters to friends Conrad denounced Theodore Roosevelt and imagined a conflict between Germany and the United States as the best of all possible wars.[20] Lifelong hostility to Wilhelmine Germany partly explains Conrad's support for British arms in the Boer War, even though he found laughable Kipling's public comment that the conflict was being fought for democracy.[21] In a letter to a Polish relative he made his stance uncharacteristically plain:

> That they [the Boers] are struggling in good faith for their independence cannot be doubted; but it is also a fact that they have no idea of liberty, which can only be found under the English flag all over the world. *C'est un peuple essentiellement despotique,* like by the way all the Dutch. This war is not so much a war against the Transvaal as a struggle against the doings of German influence. It is the Germans who have forced the issue … You are mistaken in saying that it is the Government who sends soldiers. The English Government has no right to make a single Englishman move, if he does not consent to it.[22]

On a whole range of other political issues Conrad staked out conservative positions that even Kipling might have hesitated to embrace. During his time in France in the 1870s Conrad despised the politicians of the Third Republic; his political sympathies were all with 'the imperialists', that is, the Bonapartist pretenders to the throne lost by Napoleon III in the debacle of 1870.[23] While Kipling cautiously endorsed America's attack on the moribund Spanish Empire in 1898 as taking up 'the White Man's Burden', Conrad cheered 'Viva L'Espagna', without reflecting on the consequences for ordinary people living under Spanish rule in Cuba or the Philippines.[24] He shared with his collaborator Ford Madox Ford a ferocious antipathy to contemporary feminist politics.[25] After the First World War he expressed admiration for what Mussolini was doing in Italy.

In short, there is little in Conrad's letters, his rare public pronouncements or his fiction that can shift his politics even fractionally to the left of Kipling's. Although it would be rash to situate him, as someone once did, on 'the lunatic fringe of conservatism',[26] Conrad's general political stance was, as Albert Guerard succinctly observed half-a-century ago, more or less what might be expected from 'a deeply conservative mind'.[27] The long tradition of stubbornly reading Conrad's political pronouncements against the grain partly reflects a reluctance in some quarters to admit that conservative minds can be interesting and is partly a judgement that anti-imperialism and conservatism don't mix. Evaluations of Conrad's politics have been further complicated by an acrimonious, late-twentieth-century American squabble about his place in the so-called 'literary canon'. Critics of the canon charged that the group of authors most studied in universities reflected the dominance of Western cultural values and consequently underrepresented women, minorities and most non-European authors. Defenders of the canon replied that long-dead writers should not be judged according to political fashions of the present era, and that, in any case, the passage of time will eventually democratise the list of greats. Conrad's work has been at the core of this muddled debate ever since the highly regarded African novelist Chinua Achebe remarked in a 1974 public lecture that *Heart of Darkness* is shot through with racist judgements on Africans.[28] While conservatism and nationalism can be countenanced in canonical writers, it is now almost as difficult to admit racists to the pantheon as to praise Stalinists and Nazis. Emphasising Conrad's anti-imperialist credentials provides an important counterweight to Achebe's accusation of racism.

The toolbox of literary theory contains many ingenious devices that can be used to distance Conrad's fiction from the political principles he consistently espoused in the other arenas of his existence. Any argument that Conrad intended to express a particular opinion in his novels can be dismissed as 'the intentional fallacy'. When Marlow expresses conservative opinions, it can easily be demonstrated that he is not Conrad, but an imagined narrator. And even when all the inner narrators are shown to echo, as if with one voice, the Blimpish opinions Conrad so often propounded in political conversations with friends, it is possible to argue that the text lives a life independent from its creator and may, in subtly coded ways, subvert its own ostensible message.[29] The same tools can, of course, be used to show that 'The White Man's Burden' is an anti-imperialist tract or even that *Mein Kampf* had nothing to do with Adolf Hitler's political beliefs. In fact, similar devices have been employed to argue that when, in *King Solomon's Mines*, the white men leave Kukuanaland and King Ignosi vows that no others shall be admitted in future, Rider Haggard was really laying the intellectual groundwork for the conquest of Africa. The reason why Conrad – unlike Kipling or Haggard – is so often read against the current of the author's personal conservatism is that a legion of admiring readers want to preserve his place in the rankings of the great and the place of *Heart of Darkness* as the pre-eminent literary critique of empire.

Situating *Heart of Darkness* and *Lord Jim* in historical context requires more than just careful reading of the texts. The stories and the characters that people them must be understood in relation to Conrad's other fiction, to his professed political beliefs and to the many varieties of Western adventure in the tropics that flourished at the end of the nineteenth century. It is helpful to pursue the comparison with Kipling because it illuminates the very particular way in which Conrad engaged with European imperialism. Kipling took all the British Empire as his subject. He wrote stories and poems about international rivalries in Central Asia, British officials in India, the Imperial Federation Movement in the colonies of white settlement, the social milieu of Himalayan hill stations and the conduct of the Anglo-Boer War. Above all, he wrote about the defence of Empire against the threats posed by internal and external enemies. Conrad wrote nothing at all about British colonies. Not a single story. Though the time he spent as a ship's officer in Australian ports far outweighed his brief stays in the Indonesian archipelago and his unhappy months in the Congo, he evidently did not regard the imperial enterprise in established colonies as a fit subject for his pen. Sydney, Singapore, Western Australia and Queensland each get a mention in *Lord Jim*, but the nature of British rule in those places is not explored.

Conrad, like Haggard, chose to write mainly about the world not yet annexed by European powers. Unlike Haggard, he did not seek it out as a terrain for fantastic or supernatural encounters. He used it to test the mettle of isolated, lonely Europeans brought face to face with other races and cultures. Thus the subject of his first novel was Almayer, 'the only white man on the east coast' of Borneo. Kipling rarely ventured into such locales, but in one famous story gave them a memorable name drawn from the Bible. In his tragi-comedy, 'The Man Who Would Be King', two white 'loafers' engage in crooked dealings in the 'Native States', i.e. those Indian states not brought under direct British rule. They 'are the dark places of the earth, full of unimaginable cruelty, touching the Railway and the Telegraph on one side, and, on the other, the days of Harun-al-Raschid'.[30]

The dark places of the earth. There was a phrase to reverberate in the imagination. Especially when coupled with references to unbridled greed, corrupt dealings in railways and cruel, licentious tales from the *Arabian Nights*. While it was common enough in the late-Victorian era to speak of 'darkest Africa' and other heathen lands 'awaiting the light of Christian truth', it is striking that Joseph Conrad should employ exactly Kipling's words in the opening pages of his two most important works about the futility of private adventuring beyond the frontiers of settled government. In *Heart of Darkness* Marlow looks round at the gathering London gloom and reflects that 'this also has been one of the dark places of the earth'. *Lord Jim* begins in Singapore, where seamen can be found living 'in a crazy maze of plans, hopes, dangers, enterprises, ahead of civilisation, in the dark places of the sea'. Indeed, much of what Conrad wrote in the first decade of his life as a professional author can be read as an extended, though deadly serious, commentary on the themes of 'The Man Who Would Be King'.

Tom Lingard in *Almayer's Folly* is cast in the mould of Rajah Brooke of Sarawak. He is 'Rajah-Laut' – the King of the Sea' and, for a time, arbiter of the 'Sambir' on the east Borneo river 'he had discovered'.[31] Petty trading in 'Manchester goods, brass gongs, rifles and gunpowder' gives him the wealth necessary to fund his philanthropic hobby of interfering in other people's lives. Though possessed of undoubted courage and humane intentions, Lingard's judgement is invariably wrong. He mistakes a fierce young Malay pirate for a sweet maiden, sends her off to Singapore for a convent education and then marries her to the feckless Dutchman, Almayer, who looks after 'his river'. Unfortunately, the girl has taken on 'only the superstitious elements of the religion'. Back among people of her own race, she reverts to the habits of 'half-savage womankind'. Not only does she become, before her youthful beauty wilts, the lover of the local rajah, but, in an act of symbolic cultural renunciation, she burns the European furniture and fittings of her house. Almayer henceforward pins all his hopes on his daughter Nina, whom he hopes to marry one day to some respectable burgher of Amsterdam. Repeating her mother's story, Nina is sent for a Christian education to Singapore, where she suffers racial slights that turn her against all white men save her father. She finds a better, truer love in the arms of a dashing Balinese prince. His daring attempt to smuggle gunpowder back to his homeland is ruined by enemies who tip off a Dutch naval patrol. Almayer fails in his attempt to dissuade his daughter from fleeing with her prince. His lifelong dream destroyed, he takes up opium-smoking with the local 'Chinaman' (another of Lingard's failed experiments) and soon finds the death he seeks.

Even the most sympathetic reader must notice that the clichés of late-Victorian racism saturate the book from beginning to end. White men go to pot in the tropics. Education is wasted on savages. Christian teaching confers only a veneer of civilisation. Oriental women lose their looks. The Chinese spread opium addiction. The Malay rajah is lazy, incompetent and corrupt. Babalatchi, his adviser, is cunning and treacherous. Taminah the slave girl has a 'half-formed, savage mind, the slave of her body' (p. 116). Conrad sums up Nina and her mother with an identical phrase: 'half-savage womankind' (pp. 22, 37), notwithstanding that the daughter is half-European by birth. That in turn echoes the message of 'The Man Who Would Be King': whatever the racial mixture, miscegenation is the ultimate disaster.[32]

The enduring interest of the book lies elsewhere – in the figure of Tom Lingard and Conrad's nuanced analysis of a 'dark place' on the edge of Europe's imperial horizon. Although Conrad had spent only a few days in the vicinity of the Berau River, which supplied the model of Lingard's river,[33] Almayer's story was embedded in a real imperial context. The Dutch claims to most of Borneo were dubious, based on coastal exploration rather than real occupation. Rajah James Brooke himself had twice offered to put Sarawak under the protection of Belgium. King Leopold II, who came to the throne in 1865, regretted that his timid subjects had turned their backs on that opportunity. From the moment he became king he schemed to create, as a private individual, the empire his bourgeois countrymen had scorned. In the early 1880s both Leopold and a British North Borneo Company were testing the limits of Dutch claims. Arbitration settled the boundary between Dutch and British claims, while Leopold had to be satisfied with the Congo as a testing ground for his experiments in private enterprise imperialism. An important legacy of the British North Borneo Company was the influence it had on the chartered company schemes of George Goldie and William Mackinnon in Africa.[34]

Almayer's Folly makes astute political comments on this short-lived scramble for Borneo. What happens on the ground is determined by the private initiatives of local rulers and traders, not by cartographic inscriptions penned in Europe. It is striking that 'natives' in the strict sense of the term hardly figure in Conrad's story. The local rajah and his adviser Babalatchi are recent arrivals on the scene. So are Tom Lingard and his Arab rival for supremacy on the river. (Conrad's model for Abdulla was the Singapore merchant who owned the ship on which he himself had first sailed to Borneo.) This is not the Manichaean world of settler colonialism where everyone is either a settler or a native. Capitalism in 'Sambir' is a game that all can play, regardless of colour or religion. The alternative to European colonial rule is not indigenous self-determination but subjection to some invading private freebooter, Malay, Arab or English.

Conrad is interestingly ambivalent in his appraisal of Dutch colonial rule. The idea that innocent people might be oppressed is subjected to ironic derision:

> The Nakhodas of the rare trading praus ascending the river paid visits to Lakamba, discussing with that potentate the unsettled state of affairs, and wagged their heads gravely over the recital of Orang Blanda [Dutch] exaction, severity, and general tyranny, as exemplified in the total stoppage of gunpowder trade and the rigorous visiting of all suspicious craft trading in the straits of Macassar. Even the loyal soul of Lakamba was stirred into a state of inward discontent by the withdrawal of his license for powder and by the abrupt confiscation of one hundred and fifty barrels

> of that commodity by the gunboat *Princess Amelia*, when, after a hazardous voyage, it had almost reached the mouth of the river … Reshid's wrath was principally directed against Almayer, whom he suspected of having notified the Dutch authorities of the desultory warfare carried on by the Arabs and the Rajah with the up-river Dyak tribes. (p. 48)

The defect of the regime is not its strength, but its weakness. Almayer hopes for the advent of the British North Borneo Company because the Dutch have 'no grip on this country' (p. 138). The Dutch officers accompanying the boundary commission readily admit their deficiencies. 'If we had a dozen boats we could patrol the creeks; and that wouldn't be much good … we haven't enough hold on this coast' (p. 145). Lacking resources to govern well, they fall back on the use of intermediaries, allowing the shifty, corrupt Rajah Lakamba to fly their flag. 'Almayer's Folly' is the name the Dutch seamen confer on the big house he builds in the expectation that it will be wanted by 'the future engineers, agents, or settlers of the new Company'. In a larger political sense Almayer's folly is his belief that things would be better under the governance of a chartered commercial company.

In the absence of anything but the pretence of European overrule, the destiny of places like Sambir depends on the quality of the strong men who venture there. Tom Lingard is the best of that diverse lot, but his grandiose schemes of improvement are invariably defeated by his own defective judgement, inadequate resources, his foolish agents, the plots of his rivals and the pervading tropical environment of decay. That leaves weak men like Almayer alone to face the darkness and their own inner demons.

Conrad's second novel, *An Outcast of the Islands*, explores similar problems in the same setting. However, it raises the stakes by pitting a god-like Lingard against a demonic opponent. Peter Willems is another philanthropic project gone wrong, a cabin boy from Rotterdam whom Lingard has set up in a Macassar business and married to the half-caste, illegitimate daughter of a European trader. Petty embezzlement ruins that career, but Willems is given another chance as assistant to Almayer on the river. Lingard glories in his accomplishments as an aspiring Rajah Brooke. 'You see, Willems, I brought prosperity to that place. I composed their quarrels, and saw them grow under my eyes. There's peace and happiness there. I am more master there than his Dutch Excellency down in Batavia ever will be when some day a lazy man-of-war blunders at last against the river.'[35] Willems is no more impressed with Lingard's benevolence than Almayer. Left to themselves among their perpetually scheming neighbours, these hopelessly inefficient commercial agents while away their time in mutual recrimination.

Forgetting the wife and child he has left behind in Macassar, Willems falls under the spell of Aïssa, daughter of the blind pirate Omar. Like Haggard's Ayesha, this pale-skinned woman traces her ancestry back to the Middle East and possesses fatal powers of attraction.

In other respects she resembles one of Kipling's lessons in the perils of miscegenation. In a letter to his literary confidante Marguerite Poradowska, Conrad described Willems as a man whose vanity causes his 'fall, his sudden degradation into physical enslavement by a completely savage woman'. 'I've seen that!' he added, as if to underscore his repulsion. In other hands Aïssa might have been made a tempting example of sexual opportunities waiting beyond the frontiers of civilisation. Conrad emphasises instead the unwholesomeness of her allure. She is the personification of tropical nature itself, 'which wants the sunshine but works in gloom; which seems to be all grace of colour and form, all brilliance, all smiles, but is only the blossoming of the dead; whose mystery holds the promise of joy and beauty, yet contains nothing but poison and decay' (p. 70). At their first encounter, Willems is 'charmed with a charm that carries with it a sense of irreparable loss, tingling with that feeling which begins like a caress and ends in a blow' (pp. 68–9).[36] It is he who surrenders to her, not she to him. And after the surrender, the transformation of his being is underscored by his urge to drink the muddy water of the river. 'His face felt burning. He drank again, and shuddered with a depraved sense of pleasure at the after-taste of slime in the water' (pp. 72–3). This slime is more than just mud. It is the very slime of primeval nature from which life first evolved. Willems' depraved thirst for Aïssa and the slime is the thirst for the primitive in himself that lurks unsuspected beneath the surface of civilised life.

However, it is not to primeval Darwinian struggles that the narrative now turns but to a poisoned Eden convulsed by conflicts between good and evil. When Willems' attempt to set himself up as an independent trader is thwarted by Almayer, he allies himself to Tom Lingard's enemy, the Arab trader, Abdulla. Lingard's monopoly on trade is broken when Willems reveals the secret of the channel that enables shipping to enter the river. The final confrontation between Willems and Lingard is elevated to Miltonic heights. Alone with Aïssa in his gloomy cottage, Willems comes to hate both the woman and her people: 'carried away by the flood of hate, disgust, and contempt of a white man for that blood which is not his blood, for that race which is not his race; for the brown skins; for the hearts false like the sea, blacker than night' (p. 152). The serpent that has poisoned his paradise is literally the 'old Adam' within, comically manifested in Willems' Adam's apple, a 'bone, sharp and triangular like the head of a snake', which darts 'up and down under the skin of his throat'. Lingard stalks the scene, larger than life, terrible in his wrath. Willems 'had no idea that the man would turn out to be so tall, so big and so unapproachable. It seemed to him that he had never, never in his life, seen Lingard' (p. 257). Yet the punishment Lingard exacts is not death but abandonment: 'You are my mistake. I shall hide you here.' Willems is only finally delivered from his hell on earth when Almayer provokes Aïssa to a murderous rage by confronting her with Willems' wife and child.

Its twisted plotting and metaphysical pretensions make *An Outcast of the Islands* one of Conrad's least admired novels. But it is essential reading for anyone curious to know more about what overwhelms Kurtz in *Heart of Darkness*: 'the powerless disgust, the surrender, the hate.' It is also noteworthy for its further analysis of the complex interplay of trade and politics in this (literally) godforsaken corner of Southeast Asia. The boast of the free-enterprise colonialist, Lingard, that he has brought peace and prosperity to the river, is a hollow sham; his judgement of his authority is as defective as his judgement of people. Lakamba is, like Lingard, a merchant adventurer from far away. He becomes rajah by overthrowing the authority of Patalolo, himself a usurper who had 'shaken off his allegiance to the Sultan of Koti'. Babalatchi, ironically described as a 'statesman' and 'prime minister', is another alien: ex-pirate and sometime merchant seaman on ships plying the Indian Ocean trade. His hatred for white men reflects not the sullen resistance of a colonial subject but resentment at their interference 'with the manly pursuits of throat-cutting, kidnapping, slave-dealing, and fire-raising, that were the only possible occupation for a true man of the sea' (p. 52). He plots to introduce Abdulla to the river partly in revenge for a defeat once suffered at the hand of Lingard, but mainly to promote Lakamba's defeat of Patalolo. Once that is accomplished, success will be sealed by applying 'to the Orang Blanda [the Dutch] for a flag; for a recognition of their meritorious services; for that protection which would make them safe for ever!' That is to say, the avowed object of this hater of white men is to bring formal Dutch overrule to the district.

Patalolo's response to his deposition is not to regret the advent of European colonial masters, but to abuse Lingard for not calling in the British. Lingard had prevented him 'from asking for a flag that would have been respected' (p. 172). This episode calls to mind a famous might-have-been in the history of the British Empire. Stamford Raffles, founder of Singapore, had effectively annexed Dutch Indonesia during the Napoleonic wars.[37] The general peace settlement after Waterloo restored Dutch authority. Conrad's emphasis on the weakness and inefficiency of the Dutch appears to align him with the expansionists who regretted the retrocession of Raffles' magnificent conquest. On the other hand, the climax of the struggle for power in Sambir is a farcical battle of flags that mocks the empty pretensions of European colonial powers. Willems, acting on no authority but his own, raises the Dutch flag while announcing that the people would henceforward be under the protection of 'the Great White Ruler in Batavia' (p. 179). In retaliation, Lingard's 'Chinaman', Jim-Eng, raises the Union Jack and offers to fight any man who dares to attack it. 'They are only black fellows', he tells Almayer. 'We white men ... can fight everybody in Sambir.' Lingard expresses surprise that Abdulla should have let Willems raise the Dutch flag: 'Hang it all! ... Abdulla is British!'

The colonisers behind the flags are invisible and the indigenes hardly figure. The struggle for Sambir is fought out among a motley crowd of interlopers: Lingard and his agents; the footloose pirates Babalatchi and Omar (Aïssa's father); Abdulla the Singapore merchant; Patalolo the usurper; Lakamba, the Malay intruder. Divided by colour, geographical origin and religion, they are united only in their thirst for money and power. They represent not the imposition of alien order but the chaos brought by the inexorable advance of the world capitalist economy and new technologies. These uncontrolled freebooters may from time to time raise European flags of convenience, but they are the antithesis of civilisation. In this and all the other 'dark places of the earth', white skin and Western education provide only the flimsiest bulwark against the forces of disintegration. Lingard survives, despite his misconceived liberalism, because of the discipline of seamanship and his simple-minded faith in the verities learned in childhood:

> Lingard had never hesitated in his life. Why should he? He had been a most successful trader, and a man lucky in his fights, skilful in navigation, undeniably first in seamanship in those seas ... To Lingard, simple himself – all things were simple. He seldom read. Books were not much in his way, and he had to work hard navigating, trading, and also, in obedience to his benevolent instincts, shaping stray lives he found here and there under his busy hand. He remembered the Sunday-school teachings of his native village. (pp. 197–8)

Conrad saw clearly enough that Lingard, like the stalwart heroes of G. A. Henty's books for boys, was the exception. Willems was the rule: the weak man who cannot resist the siren call of savagery.

Although the mix of character types varies in Conrad's early fiction, his perspective on political issues beyond the frontiers of civilisation remains constant. 'An Outpost of Progress' once again sends two European adventurers into one of the dark places of the earth. Kayerts and Carlier conspicuously lack the reckless courage of Kipling's

Carnehan and Dravot. Compared to these morons, even Almayer and Willems seem models of efficiency. Set down by the managing director of a trading company at a hopeless post far up an African river, they swiftly fall to pieces. After one of their black employees tricks them into selling some of their own labourers into slavery, they fall to quarrelling about trifles. One shoots the other, and then hangs himself. Readers can readily identify 'the Great Civilizing Company' with King Leopold's commercial venture in central Africa, whose deficiencies Conrad had witnessed at first hand during the period he spent employed as a steamboat captain on the Congo River. The story afforded Conrad splendid opportunities to shoot at the old enemies: liberalism, philanthropy and evangelical Christianity. Kayerts and Carlier are at first buoyed up by the article they find in an 'old home paper' on 'Our Colonial Expansion'.[38] It 'spoke much of the rights and duties of civilisation, of the sacredness of the civilising work, and extolled the merits of those who went about bringing light, and faith and commerce to the dark places of the earth'. However, 'the contact with pure unmitigated savagery, with primitive nature and primitive man, brings sudden and profound trouble into the heart' (p. 6). Soon Carlier is raving 'about the necessity of exterminating all the niggers' (p. 25). The message is one beloved of Kipling and John Buchan: scratch a liberal and you will expose a hypocrite.

A secondary theme of 'Outpost' is another conservative dogma: the idealistic efforts of humanitarians to improve the lot of savage peoples are a waste of time because savages are unimprovable. There are no sympathetic portraits of Africans in this story. Physically they may be 'fine animals' (but 'Pah! Don't they stink'). The local chief's reaction to the white men's madness is to offer 'extra human sacrifices to all the Evil Spirits'. The labourers contracted to work for the company come from 'a very distant part of the land of darkness and sorrow'; they are 'not happy, regretting the festive incantations, the sorceries, the human sacrifices of their own land' (p. 17). The slave traders are Imbangala, cannibals of legendary ferocity. Worst of all is the educated African, Henry Price, who arranges the sale of the company's workers. Significantly he comes from Sierra Leone, a colony founded as a utopian experiment by late-eighteenth-century humanitarians who believed that the spread of education and Christianity would help to suppress the African slave trade.[39] Price seems to represent Conrad's judgement on that experiment. He 'spoke English and French with a warbling accent, wrote a beautiful hand, understood bookkeeping, and cherished in his innermost heart the worship of evil spirits' (p. 3). The point that his civilisation is only a veneer is underscored by the fact that he is known to other Africans not by his baptismal name, but as

Makola. 'Makola', we are told, is 'a civilized nigger ... very neat in his person' (p. 19). The morning after his sale of slaves, he is seen conspicuously washing his hands.

Much hangs on the way we appraise Conrad's use of the word 'nigger'. Discussions of his work generally maintain a judicious silence on the subject. Yet 'nigger' was not a word serious writers would employ without reflection, even in the late-Victorian era. For instance, Rider Haggard's character Allan Quatermain states in the opening chapter of *King Solomon's Mines* that he will 'scratch out the word'. Conrad, like Buchan, used the word without apparent embarrassment. This is not simply the practice of inner narrators such as Marlow. It was Conrad who titled his third novel, *The Nigger of the 'Narcissus'*. Any discussion of racism in 'Outpost of Progress' or *Heart of Darkness* must take that into consideration, along with such private observations as Conrad's Congo diary entry for 4 July 1890: 'features very Negroid and ugly.'[40] In *Heart of Darkness* we meet 'strings of dusty niggers with splay feet', 'the old nigger' whom gentle, quiet Captain Fresleven whacks to death, the other 'beaten nigger' who groans in the bush, the 'quarrelsome band of footsore sulky niggers' following the Eldorado Exploration Expedition.[41] There are, in addition, several young men whose chief offence seems to be that they, like Henry Price in 'Outpost', have risen above their ordained racial station. With a hint of homophobia, Marlow resents the white manager of the central station – a man who 'inspired neither love, nor fear, nor even respect', but rather 'uneasiness' – for allowing his '"boy" – an overfed young negro from the coast – to treat the white men, under his very eyes, with provoking insolence' (pp. 163–4). There is also 'the fool-nigger' of a helmsman who 'dropped everything, to throw the shutter open and let off that Martini-Henry' (p. 201). And of course the fireman who caught Achebe's sensitive eye:

> He was an improved specimen; he could fire up a vertical boiler. He was there below me, and, upon my word, to look at him was as edifying as seeing a dog in a parody of breeches and a feather hat, walking on his hind-legs ... He squinted at the steam-gauge and at the water gauge with an evident effort of intrepidity ... He ought to have been clapping his hands and stamping his feet on the bank, instead of which he was hard at work, a thrall to strange witchcraft, full of improving knowledge. (p. 187)

This passage manages the economical feat of simultaneously damning the fireman along with every misguided philanthropist who ever tried to 'improve' Africans through education. It echoes an element in European thinking about race at least as old as Prospero's perceived reward for educating Caliban: that the misshapen savage now knows how to curse his benefactor and aspires to mate with his daughter. More proximately, it resonates with a celebrated mid-century essay by Thomas Carlyle on 'the Nigger Question'.[42]

Conrad and Carlyle

In the guise of an imaginary address to an anti-slavery meeting, Carlyle had attacked West Indians for refusing to work on sugar plantations. If, he argued, the main result of the abolition of slavery was that ex-slaves could luxuriate in idleness, then forced labour should be reinstituted. African Negroes had created perplexing problems by their stubborn refusal to die out as aboriginal peoples had done in the Americas and the Antipodes:

> This certainly is a notable fact: the black African, alone of wild-men, can live among men civilized. While all manner of Caribs and others pine into annihilation in presence of the pale faces, he contrives to continue, does not die of sullen irreconcilable rage, of rum, of brutish laziness and darkness, and fated incompatibility with his new place; but lives and multiplies, and evidently means to abide among us, if we can find the right regulation for him. (p. 471)

Unless they made their labour available at affordable rates, liberated blacks did not deserve to occupy the lands that hard-working white men had made fruitful.

> Till the European white man first saw them some three short centuries ago, those Islands had produced mere jungle, savagery, poison-reptiles and swamp-malaria; till the white European first saw them, they were as if not yet created, – their noble elements of cinnamon, sugar, coffee, pepper black and grey, lying all asleep, waiting the white enchanter who should say to them, Awake! (p. 484)

Carlyle's imagined orator claims not to be racially prejudiced:

> Do I then, hate the Negro? No; except when the soul is killed out of him, I decidedly like poor Quashee; and find him a pretty kind of man. With a pennyworth of oil, you can make a handsome glossy thing of Quashee, when the soul is not killed in him! A swift, supple fellow; a merry-hearted, grinning, dancing, singing, affectionate kind of creature, with a great deal of melody and amenability in his composition.

What 'kills the soul' is the misguided benevolence of philanthropists and the insistence of economists that the price of labour must be fixed by supply and demand. If planters must be ruined by the outrageous wage demands of idle black workers, then economics is truly a 'Dismal Science'. (The famous phrase was coined in this essay.)

Equally preposterous are the wage claims made by white working girls in England:

> Who has not heard of the Distressed Needlewomen in these days? We have thirty-thousand Distressed Needlewomen, – the most of whom cannot sew a reasonable stitch; for they are, in fact, Mutinous Serving-maids, who, instead of learning to work and to obey, learned to give warning: 'Then suit yourself, Ma'am!'

The male equivalent of these insolent young women is the 'overfed White Flunky' who refuses to enter long-term contracts, preferring instead to jump from employer to employer depending on the pay:

> Disloyal, unheroic, this one; *in* human in his character, and his work, and his position; more so no creature ever was. Pity is not for him, or not a soft kind of it; nor is any remedy visible, except abolition at no distant date! He is the flower of *nomadic* servitude, proceeding by month's warning, and free supply-and-demand; if obedience is not in his heart, if chiefly gluttony and mutiny are in his heart, and he has to be bribed by high feeding to do the shows of obedience, – what can await him, or be prayed for him, among men.

Carlyle's remedy for the evils of the needlewomen, the white flunkeys and the West Indian idlers is simply to state that 'he or she that will not work, and in the anger of the gods cannot be compelled to work, shall die!' In the event that the British government can find no way to force labour in the West Indies, Carlyle forecasts that private enterprise will take matters in hand:

> I see men, the rose-pink cant all peeled away from them, land one day on those black coasts; men *sent* by the Laws of this Universe, and inexorable Course of Things; men hungry for gold, remorseless, fierce as the old Buccaneers were; – and a doom for Quashee which I had rather not contemplate! The gods are long-suffering; but the law from the beginning was, He that will not work shall perish from the earth. (p. 486)

In Conrad's novel *The Nigger of the 'Narcissus'* Carlyle's essay goes to sea. Although Conrad steers his novel well away from exotic coasts he freights it to the gunwales with imperial meaning.[43] James Wait, the 'Nigger' on the ship *Narcissus*, is a West Indian and thus a descendant of slaves. Like the plantation workers whose strike action inspired Carlyle's 'Occasional Discourse', his refusal to work is a central issue. The ship's cook who tries to 'save' Wait through Christian preaching calls to mind the evangelicals who stopped the seaborne slave trade and whose programme to end the trade at the source itself inspired a host of interventions in Africa, beginning with the Sierra Leone colony and culminating in David Livingstone's efforts to 'open a way for commerce and civilisation'. 'Repent, repent!' he cries. 'I can't bear to think of you. I hear the call to save you' (p. 172). Donkin, the odious leader of the shipboard strike, knows how to play skilfully on the slogans popularised by evangelical philanthropy. His fellow seamen share out to him their own meagre belongings because he is, after all, 'a man and sailor' (p. 13), just as the African was, in anti-slavery pamphlets, 'a man and a brother'. Donkin is likewise described as 'the pet of philanthropists'. His opposite is the grizzled old sailor, Singleton. Laconic, obedient, fearless, it is he who steers the ship to safety in a storm. He is literally a survivor from the days of the slave trade. He can look back to days as terrifying as anything in Carlyle's nightmare vision of the future:

> He [Singleton] waited, made a contemptuous gesture. – 'I have seen rows aboard ship before some of you were born,' he said, slowly, 'for something or nothing; but never for such a thing … a black fellow … I have seen them die like flies.' He stopped, thoughtful, as if trying to recollect gruesome things, details of horrors, hecatombs of niggers. They looked at him fascinated. He was old enough to remember slavers, bloody mutinies, pirates perhaps …! (pp. 191–2)

Conrad heaps a characteristic burden of multiple symbolic meanings on the figure of James Wait. There is nonetheless much to be said for taking him at face value as a black man and a product of the Atlantic slave trade. Were it not for his racking, tubercular cough he might be reckoned a splendid specimen of a man: 'calm, cool, towering, superb'. Admiration for the muscular physique is balanced, however, by contempt for the visage. 'He held his head up … a head powerful and misshapen with a tormented and flattened face – a face pathetic and brutal: the tragic, the mysterious, the repulsive mask of a nigger's soul.' In a later passage, Wait is described as 'animal-like … A thing of instinct' with 'the unthinking stillness of a scared brute'. The challenge he poses for the rest of the crew is concisely stated when he answers the first roll-call. 'Wait … I belong to the ship' (pp. 23–4).

The *Narcissus* stands in a broad sense for the British Empire (if not the whole human race). England is likened to 'a mighty ship … a ship carrying the burden of millions of lives … mother of fleets and nations! The great flagship of the race' (pp. 242–3). Though the ship's cargo consists of pigs – suggesting the 'swinish multitude', 'the vast Gadarene swinery' that Carlyle's essay derides – Conrad's narrator claims that 'the august loneliness of her path' lends 'dignity to the sordid inspiration of her pilgrimage'. Deciding whether Wait 'belongs to the ship' depends, as in Carlyle's essay, on his fitness for work. As the crew's initial suspicion that he is malingering gives way to a belief he may be genuinely ill, their benevolence breaks over him in waves. Shipmates take him meals, lend him clothing and risk their lives to save him when the *Narcissus* turns on its side. A rough seadog becomes as 'sentimentally careful of his nigger as a model slave-owner' (p. 207). The cook's evangelical, philanthropic heart swells 'with tenderness, with comprehension, with the desire to meddle, with anxiety for the soul of that black man, with the pride of possessed eternity' (p. 170). Perversely, Wait answers all this attention with complaints and curses. Only the squalid Donkin, who openly accuses him of fraud, inspires some fellow feeling:

> Donkin abused him to his face, jeered at him while he gasped; and the same day Wait would lend him a warm jersey. Once Donkin reviled him for half an hour; reproached him with the extra work his malingering gave to the watch; and ended by calling him 'a black-faced swine.' Under the spell of our accursed perversity we were horror-struck. But Jimmy positively seemed to revel in that abuse. (p. 45)

It takes a little time for their partnership to develop. 'Don't be familiar', Wait warns at their first meeting. 'We haven't kept pigs together' (p. 31). But soon they are keeping 'the pigs' in line with complementary claims. Wait weakens the ship through his absence from duty and his power of arousing time-consuming benevolence. Donkin engages in a continuous campaign against obedience and discipline.

He is the very model of Carlyle's White Flunky. Joining the *Narcissus* after running away from an American merchantman, 'Nomadic servitude' is his way of life. This is the man Carlyle warned should not be pitied – 'the pet of philanthropists' – who has only to appear in his ragged clothes to create 'a wave of sentimental pity' among the ship's crew (p. 12). 'Dismal, unheroic', with 'gluttony and mutiny in his heart', Donkin's speciality is the 'right of labour to live'. In that sacred cause, he demands the masts be cut in the storm to save the crew, an action that would have almost certainly sent the ship to the bottom. And when the danger has passed, he has no thanks for the captain whose seamanship had saved them all: 'He [Donkin] told us we were good men – a "bloomin' condemned lot of good men." Who thanked us? Who took any notice of our wrongs? Didn't we lead a "dorg's loife for two poun' ten a month?" Did we think that miserable pay enough to compensate us for the risk to our lives and for the loss of our clothes' (p. 148). Carlyle complained democracy gave Judas Iscariot as much chance at the ballot-box as Jesus Christ ('Judas looks him in the face; asks proudly, "Am not I as good as thou? better, perhaps!"'). Donkin complains about an officer's language in just such words. ''Ear 'im; that's the way they tawlk to hus ... Comin' the mate hover hus. We are as good men as 'ee!' (p. 112). At heart he is a racist, revolted by Wait's boast that white girls prefer 'coloured gentlemen'. Nonetheless he raises a mutiny in the name of Wait's right to work, painting utopian pictures of a world where all would be equal and 'every lonely ship would travel over a serene sea, manned by a wealthy and well-fed crew of satisfied skippers' (p. 152).[44] The cynicism of Donkin's sloganeering about solidarity between black and white workers is exposed by his theft of Wait's money when Jimmy's weak chest at last expires.

Alone among the ordinary seaman, Singleton remains unmoved by Donkin's doctrines of class hatred. He is immune as well to the invitation Wait presents to wallow in benevolent sentiment. This old man who had once seen blacks 'die like flies' tells Wait to 'get on with your dying'. 'Don't raise a blamed fuss with us over that job. We can't help you' (p. 61).

Wait's passing is as portentous as his first appearance. He dies just in sight of land, as Singleton had predicted. The island shimmering in the distance is Flores, westernmost of the Azores. There, long ago, Columbus had been told that strange beings washed ashore from the west – unlike any men known in Europe. There too, at the very dawn of the Atlantic slave trade, slaves had grown sugar for Portuguese planters. At Wait's death, the slack sails of the long becalmed *Narcissus* begin to stir. Clearly, it had been he who had caused the ship to *wait*. But, unlike the albatross whose *weight* dropped from the neck of the Ancient Mariner when that accursed sailor looked with a benevolent eye upon shimmering slimy sea serpents, it is the *removal* of a temptation to benevolent sentiment that enables the *Narcissus* to move again. Wait's corpse, covered in the Union Jack, stubbornly refuses to slide down the plank until stirred by the Banshee-like wail of an Irish sailor.[45] Once it has slid beneath the waves, a fair wind speeds the ship home.

Here Conrad and Carlyle part company. The 'Occasional Discourse' argued that, as the Negro appears fated to live and multiply, his white masters must find 'the right regulation' that will put him to work. The officers of the *Narcissus* can find no formula for restoring Wait to servile health. He must die if the ship is to attain its European destiny. The political implications of the ending are ambiguous. Conrad may be drawing a Darwinian moral: 'the flagship of the race' cannot afford to be burdened by representatives of 'a dying race'. Yet by draping Wait's corpse in the Union Jack, he also suggests that Britain had performed some service by extending the protection of its flag to weaker peoples. There is, as well, just a hint of Kipling's trope upon the story of Caliban, 'half devil and half child'.

> Take up the White Man's Burden
> And reap his old reward
> The hate of those ye better
> The scorn of those ye guard.

The fate of those who take up the White Man's Burden in Conrad's novels is the subject of *Lord Jim* and *Heart of Darkness*.

Marlow's world

Marlow narrates both tales. Though his life has been spent at sea, he is a thoughtful man, at home with history and philosophy. Gazing on the Thames at the close of a London evening in *Heart of Darkness*, he reflects that 'this too has been one of the dark places of the earth'. Here is the theme of Edward Elgar's oratorio *Caractacus* – a theme beloved as well by Kipling, Buchan and Haggard: what would the Romans have thought of ancient Britain? Marlow now conjures up two visions. Casual readers tend to roll them together into a prefiguration of Kurtz. Closer attention shows that Marlow is deliberately contrasting two very different characters. One is a man like himself, a naval commander:

> Imagine the feelings of a commander of a fine – what d'ye call 'em? – trireme in the Mediterranean, ordered suddenly to the north; run overland across the Gauls in a hurry; put in charge of one of these craft the legionaries – a wonderful lot of handy men they must have been, too – used to build, apparently by the hundred, in a month or two, if we may believe what we read. Imagine him here – the very end of the world, a sea the colour of lead, a sky the colour of smoke, a kind of ship about as rigid as a concertina – and going up the river with stores, or orders, or what you like. Sand-banks, marshes, forests, savages, – precious little to eat fit for a civilized man, nothing but Thames water to drink. No Falernian wine here, no going ashore. Here and there a military camp lost in a wilderness, like a needle in a bundle of hay – cold, fog, tempests, disease, exile, and death, – death skulking in the air, in the water, in the bush. They must have been dying like flies here. Oh, yes – he did it. Did it very well, too, no doubt, and without thinking much about it either, except afterwards to brag of what he had gone through in his time, perhaps. They were men enough to face the darkness. And perhaps he was cheered by keeping his eye on a chance of promotion to the fleet at Ravenna by-and-by, if he had good friends in Rome and survived the awful climate. (pp. 139–40)

What kind of a man can face the darkness? Most likely a man like Tom Lingard who doesn't think much about the dangers. Or the stoic Singleton, who had seen men 'die like flies', done his duty and let them get on with their dying. Above all, it is likely to be a man who belongs to a hard-working crew that, in turn, belongs to a fleet held together by the discipline of the seaman's craft and a professional code of conduct.

Next Marlow conjures up an utterly different person in very different circumstances, a man sent ashore with no supports except the platitudinous precepts of official civic morality:

> Think of a decent young citizen in a toga – perhaps too much dice, you know – coming out here in the train of some prefect, or tax-gatherer, or trader even, to mend his fortunes. Land in a swamp, march through the woods, and in some inland post feel the savagery, the utter savagery, had closed round him, – and all that mysterious life of the wilderness that stirs in the forest, in the jungles, in the hearts of wild men. There's no initiation either into such mysteries. He has to live in the midst of the incomprehensible, which is also detestable. And it has a fascination, too, that goes to work upon him. The fascination of the abomination – you know, imagine the growing regrets, the longing to escape, the powerless disgust, the surrender, the hate. (p. 140)

This is a man like Almayer who slowly goes to pieces in the tropics. Or Willems, who finds the demon in himself, makes love to a savage woman and savours the taste of river slime in his mouth.

The contrast brims with possibilities. Conrad had already explored some of its potential in *An Outcast of the Islands* and 'An Outpost of Progress'. But suppose the characters are more complex and the situations less clear-cut. Suppose the naval officer has failed to live up to the code of conduct and is cast ashore 'to mend his fortunes'. Suppose the 'decent young citizen' is not a runaway like Willems, but a rising politician, full of philanthropic projects and liberal sympathies. How would things turn out then, in one of 'the dark places of the earth'?

Lord Jim tells the story of the seaman who fails the test of conduct and gets his second chance on a slimy Eastern river. In all outward appearances Jim resembles Singleton and Lingard. He is powerfully built, square-jawed, blue-eyed – English to the core. Marlow likes Jim's looks: 'I knew his appearance; he came from the right place; he was one of us. He stood there for all the parentage of his kind, for men and women by no means clever or amusing, but whose very existence is based upon honest faith, and upon the instinct of courage' (p. 26). Looking like the hero in an adventure story for boys, he dreams of becoming one.[46] That is his downfall. He fails to see that heroic acts of real life generally arise from 'inglorious toil and by fidelity to a certain standard of conduct' (p. 30). His first test comes on a rust-bucket of a steamer, the *Patna*. 'Owned by a Chinaman, chartered by an Arab' and skippered by a loathsome German, it carries a human cargo of 800 pilgrims bound for Mecca. When a corroded bulkhead threatens to give way, the white officers desert. Miraculously, the ship does not sink and is towed to port by a French naval vessel. Rather than front up to the admiralty court of inquiry, most of the cowardly scum run away. Only Jim stays to face the music. Marlow – fascinated by the contrast between Jim's apparent 'unthinking and blessed stiffness' and the inner flaw that led him to jump with the others – helps him to find work after the revocation of his officer's certificate. No job lasts long because the story of the *Patna* clings to him like a shadow. Eventually Marlow's friend Stein employs Jim as his agent on a remote river convulsed by commercial rivalries. Weak old Rajah Allang has been challenged by a group of ambitious Bugis settlers led by Doramin. A third force is led by Sherif Ali, 'an Arab half-breed, who ... on purely religious grounds, had incited the tribes in the interior' (p. 147). By helping Doramin to prise Sherif Ali from his hilltop fortress, Jim acquires a position of immense power. With Doramin's son, Dain Waris, as his best friend and the step-daughter of a nasty old Malacca Portuguese half-breed as his mistress, Jim establishes peace and acts as de facto magistrate of the district.

Paradise crumbles with the arrival of 'Gentleman' Brown and his truly diabolical crew of pirates. Though Brown's plot to devastate the village fails, he offers to withdraw provided that Jim will guarantee his safe passage down the river. Detecting in Brown's words a reference to his previous disgrace, Jim agrees. On his retreat Brown double-crosses Jim and in an act of gratuitous vengeance kills his friend Dain Waris. Rather than flee with his mistress, Jim gives himself up to be executed by Doramin.

This second part of *Lord Jim* employs much the same cast of characters as *Almayer's Folly* and *Outcast of the Islands*. Rajah Allang takes the role played by Patalolo. Doramin is a wiser, nobler version of Lakamba. Dain Waris resembles the Balinese prince who won Almayer's daughter. Jim's mistress, Jewell, has a white father and echoes all the resentments of Nina (and Kipling's Lispeth) against faithless Europeans who love and leave. Patusan is very much like Sambir in its political and commercial relations. The Dutch claim to sovereignty is an empty boast, because they lack the manpower to put even a single resident on the river. Increased trade with the outside world has drawn adventurers like Doramin, Brown and Sherif Ali, upsetting old power relations. Jim, however, is a very different character from Almayer or Willems. And his situation is different. He comes without much external support, carrying the works of Shakespeare in one hand and Marlow's unloaded pistol in the other. Neither Stein nor Marlow intervenes as Lingard had done in Sambir. Jim cares nothing for money, aiming only to redeem his honour by doing good. But for the fact that he acts on his own authority, he might be taken for a district officer under the system of indirect rule that the British used to rule Malaya,

Fiji and much of tropical Africa. As Lord Lugard put it in a classic policy manual, 'The Resident acts as a sympathetic adviser and counsellor to the native chief, being careful not to interfere so as to lower his prestige ... His advice on matters of general policy must be followed, but the native ruler issues his own instructions to his subordinate chiefs and district heads – not as the orders of the Resident but as his own.'[47]

The power Jim wields is a personal version of the Pax Britannica: 'the power to make peace'. 'It is in this sense alone', Marlow tells us, 'that might so often *is* right' (p. 149). His lordly title, Tuan Jim, expresses the respect he commands, even from those who hate him for interfering with their corrupt scheming. Local gossip credits him with supernatural powers (p. 151). Up to the very eve of his destruction he is full of helpful plans for waterworks and plantations. His powers 'had come to him in a manner like keen scent to a well-bred hound'. Like an English country gentleman, 'he was not eloquent, but there was a dignity in this constitutional reticence, there was a high seriousness in his stammerings'. Not for him the high-blown rhetoric of the liberal do-gooder. Rather, 'he seemed to love that land and the people with a sort of fierce egoism, with a contemptuous tenderness' (p. 142). Like a proper district officer, he preserves the fiction that he is not running the show, merely 'advising' the local rajah. When Jim has finished giving his opinion on a thorny case, 'no one made a sound till the old Rajah sighed faintly, and looking up, with a toss of his head, said quickly, "You hear, my people! No more of these little games"' (p. 143). Jim's account of his approach to cultural complexity verges on a parody of Lord Lugard's approved methods.

> Only the other day an old fool he had never seen in his life came from some village miles away to find out if he should divorce his wife. Fact, solemn word. That's the sort of thing ... He wouldn't have believed it. Would I? Squatted on the verandah chewing betel-nut, sighing and spitting all over the place for more than an hour, and as glum as an undertaker before he came out with that dashed conundrum. That's the kind of thing that isn't so funny as it looks. What was a fellow to say? – Good wife? – Yes. Good wife – old though; started a confounded long story about some brass pots. Been living together for fifteen years – twenty years – could not tell. A long, long time. Good wife. Beat her a little – not much – just a little, when she was young. Had to – for the sake of his honour. Suddenly in her old age she goes and lends three brass pots to her sister's son's wife, and begins to abuse him every day in a loud voice. His enemies jeered at him; his face was utterly blackened. Pots totally lost. Awfully cut up about it. Impossible to fathom a story like that; told him to go home, and promised to come along myself and settle it all. It's all very well to grin, but it was the dashedest nuisance! A day's journey

> through the forest, another day lost in coaxing a lot of silly villagers to get at the rights of the affair. There was the making of a sanguinary shindy in the thing. (p. 153)

There is no hint of Conrad's customary irony in Jim's statement that 'the best' part of his situation is 'the knowledge that had I been wiped out it is this place that would have been the loser' (p. 140). Old Doramin appears to endorse that view when, worrying about 'the future of the country', he confesses his fear that Jim will be like other 'white men who come to us and in a little while they go'. When Marlow insists that Jim will stay, Doramin is puzzled but pleased. 'This was good news indeed' (p. 156). Marlow acknowledges the unbelievable perfection of this vision of one man's private empire.

> And there I was with him, high in the sunshine on the top of that historic hill of his. He dominated the forest, the secular gloom, the old mankind. He was like a figure set up on a pedestal, to represent in his persistent youth the power, and perhaps the virtues, of races that never grow old, that have emerged from the gloom. I don't know why he should always have appeared to me symbolic. Perhaps this is the real cause of my interest in his fate. (p. 142)

Doubtless it is this portrait of indirect rule, uncontaminated by greed or exploitation, that explains Conrad's enormous popularity with real indirect rulers such as Hugh Clifford, who helped construct the constitutional fabric of British Malaya.[48] The trouble is that Jim is not allowed to rest on his pedestal. He must die for Gentleman Brown's sin. Working out the meaning of Jim's destruction is fundamental to understanding Conrad's verdict on the best of all possible private imperialisms.

On one reading, Jim's fatal deal with Brown repeats his desertion from the *Patna*. His feeble excuse for jumping overboard had been the irresistible entreaties of his worthless fellow officers. 'It was their doing as plainly as if they had reached up with a boat-hook and pulled me over' (p. 72). Brown's crew of cut-throats is a thousand times worse, yet Jim, in granting their request for safe conduct, appears to respond to Brown's call for racial solidarity among white men. He has once again abandoned his duty to the brown people entrusted to his care and must pay the penalty. By submitting himself to Doramin's justice, he repeats his appearance before a court of inquiry. As he said before, 'I may have jumped, but I don't run away' (p. 89). And if an imperial moral were to be drawn from his experience, it is that no matter how isolated the situation, self-sacrificing, high-minded attempts at colonial rule will founder on the rocks of racial difference. In the end, white men will stick together.

Alternatively, it can be argued that Jim does redeem himself in Patusan. He had failed the passengers on the *Patna*, not by killing them – for they did not die – but by failing to stick to the code of conduct on which all human safety depends in an uncaring universe. Captain Brierly put it bluntly at the court of inquiry. '"Frankly", he said, "I don't care a snap for all the pilgrims that ever came out of Asia, but a decent man would not have behaved like this to a full cargo of old rags in bales. We aren't an organised body of men, and the only thing that holds us together is just the name for that kind of decency"' (p. 125). Brierly commits suicide soon after the inquiry because he cannot face the idea that his own courage might prove unequal to the unexpected catastrophe. The man who can do his duty even as fear freezes his blood is represented by the stolid French officer who stood watch on the *Patna* while it was being towed to port: one of those 'steady, reliable men who are the raw material of great reputations, one of those uncounted lives that are buried without drums and trumpets under the foundations of monumental successes' (pp. 82–3). It is not Jim's fault that Brown murders Dain Waris. Who could have foreseen such a reckless, wanton act? Yet Jim insists on taking responsibility for the people who depend on him. 'He goes away from a living woman to celebrate his pitiless wedding with a shadowy ideal of conduct' (p. 237). That is to say, this time he goes down with the ship. Fidelity to the idea, 'the only thing that holds us together', 'the name for that kind of decency' makes him worthy of his pedestal.

On this view of *Lord Jim*, the imperial moral is as ambiguous as Kipling's ideal of rule by 'the native born'. Jim has borne the white man's burden under no instructions from home and with no thought of material reward. (We hear nothing of his activities on behalf of the trader, Stein.) The purity of his service is attested by his willingness to lay down his life for 'his people'. His nemesis is the satanic Brown, who invades the river with a 'grim impatience of plunder'. By not destroying the exploiter, he betrays those he guards. Such disinterested service is not of this world. It could only exist, as Hugh Clifford once put it, in an empire where 'no one works for money and no one works for fame'.[49] Lord Lugard called his book on imperial policy *The Dual Mandate* because he saw indirect rule as the solution to the problem of reconciling Britain's need for resources with the duty of promoting the welfare of subject peoples. *Lord Jim* preaches that ultimately there can be no such reconciliation.

Heart of Darkness explores the contrasting fate of that other man, the 'decent young citizen in a toga' who gives up his ideals and succumbs to the darkness. Once again the setting is a realm of private-enterprise colonialism unhindered by the organised power of a state. Conrad did not have to imagine this realm as he had imagined Lingard's river and Jim's Patusan. He had served the Belgian Company for Commerce on the Upper Congo and learned to hate it.[50] By skilfully playing on European commercial and colonial rivalries, King Leopold managed to win international recognition at the Berlin Conference of 1885 for the claims of his company to control a huge swath of the Congo River basin. The Congo Free State was a unique experiment in company rule. It was Belgian in the very limited sense that its progenitor and most of the directors were Belgian, not because Belgium exercised any sort of imperial control. Only after international outrage at company misrule forced Leopold to cede the territory to his nation in 1908 did it become the Belgian Congo. Historians still debate whether Leopold was a humanitarian idealist whose schemes went wrong, or simply a grasping hypocrite.[51] To Conrad, the question was immaterial because he held humanitarian idealists and hypocrites in equal contempt. His own experience working for the company had been miserable. He was actively seeking an excuse to leave without breaking his contract when a life-threatening bout of dysentery made the issue academic. His disease-ravaged body had literally to be carried out of Africa.

There was nothing particularly unusual about Conrad's condemnation of Leopold's chaotic and brutal administration. By the time *Heart of Darkness* was published in 1899, most committed imperialists regarded the Congo Free State as a lesson in what not to do with a conquered territory. Hugh Clifford summed the story up with a colonial administrator's educated eye.

> It is a sombre study of the Congo – the scene is obviously intended for the Congo, though no names are mentioned – in which, while the inefficiency of certain types of European 'administrators' is mercilessly gibbeted, the power of the wilderness, of contact with barbarian and elemental men and facts, to effect the demoralization of the white man is conveyed with marvellous force.[52]

Marlow makes the point about administration in setting the scene for his tale.

> What saves us is efficiency – the devotion to efficiency. But these chaps were not much account, really. They were no colonists; their administration was merely a squeeze, and nothing more, I suspect. They were conquerors, and for that you want only brute force – nothing to boast of, when you have it, since your strength is just an accident arising from the weakness of others. They grabbed what they could get for the sake of what was to be got. It was just robbery with violence, aggravated murder on a great scale, and men going at it blind. (pp. 140–1)

As Conrad had said in *The Nigger of the 'Narcissus'*, good government, whether of ships or territories, depends on efficiency and must be shored up by an unwavering code of conduct. Sordid robbers abound on Leopold's river, but all Marlow's serious attention is concentrated on the mysterious Kurtz, the man 'who had come out equipped with moral ideas of some sort' (p. 178). Kurtz and his situation are most fully understood in the context of Conrad's previous fiction.

Kurtz is manager of a trading station far up a river overhung with decaying tropical vegetation – more like Lingard's river in Borneo than the broad sunny Congo.[53] Marlow's senses are assaulted by 'the smell of mud, of primeval mud' and 'the high stillness of primeval forest' (p. 171). In *An Outcast of the Islands* Willems stooped to drink that mud and was carried back to a poisoned Eden. *Heart of Darkness* abandons the Bible for a Darwinian Genesis. Going up the river 'was like travelling back to the earliest beginnings of the world' (p. 182). The intruders feel like 'wanderers on prehistoric earth, on an earth that wore the aspect of an unknown planet. We could have fancied ourselves the first of men taking possession of an accursed inheritance, to be subdued at the cost of profound anguish and of excessive toil' (pp. 185–6). Subjugating and civilising this wilderness would be work of millennia, not decades. The natives of this land are likewise prehistoric. The steamer slowly makes its way past villagers who greet the mechanical apparition with 'a burst of yells, a whirl of black limbs, a mass of hands clapping, of feet stamping, of bodies swaying, of eyes rolling … The prehistoric man was cursing us, praying to us, welcoming us – who could tell?' (p. 186).

Thus far this appraisal of the African interior is a fairly conventional rehearsal of advanced European opinion at the turn of the twentieth century. Africa is the land that time forgot, its inhabitants stuck in an early stage of human evolution. Conrad goes farther, however, and posits a correspondence between the evolution of life on earth and the construction of the human psyche. Buried deep within even the most apparently civilised person is a remnant of prehistoric uncivilised origins. Under the right, or rather the wrong, circumstances, it may awake. Something within Marlow stirs as he penetrates the darkness:

> The earth seemed unearthly. We are accustomed to look upon the shackled form of a conquered monster, but there – you could look at a thing monstrous and free. It was unearthly, and the men were – No, they were not inhuman. Well, you know, that was the worst of it – this suspicion of their not being inhuman. It would come slowly to one. They howled and leaped, and spun, and made horrid faces; but what thrilled you was just the thought of their humanity – like yours – the thought of your

> remote kinship with this wild and passionate uproar. Ugly. Yes, it was ugly enough; but if you were man enough you would admit to yourself that there was in you just the faintest trace of a response to the terrible frankness of that noise, a dim suspicion of there being a meaning in it which you – you so remote from the night of first ages – could comprehend. And why not? The mind of man is capable of anything – because everything is in it, all the past as well as all the future. (p. 186)

Capable of anything! As far as Marlow is concerned, all the Africans around him are cannibals – not just the 'prehistoric men' on the shore but also his own grinning crew who, in gleeful anticipation, say 'Catch 'im ... eat 'im' (p. 193). Marlow begins to picture himself at a cannibal feast, perhaps as the main course. 'I hoped, yes, I positively hoped, that my aspect was not so – what shall I say – so unappetizing' (pp. 194–5). What holds him back is work and a habit of restraint. 'You wonder I didn't go ashore for a howl and a dance? Well, no – I didn't. Fine sentiments, you say? Fine sentiments be hanged! I had no time. I had to mess about with white-lead and strips of woollen blanket helping to put bandages on those leaky steam-pipes' (p. 187).

Marlow here expounds in rough terms the biological theory that 'ontogeny recapitulates phylogeny': that the development of the individual recapitulates the history of the race to which it belongs. Upholders of this theory viewed the physical development of the human foetus from conception to birth as a recapitulation of the various stages of development undergone by the remote ancestors of the species. Translated into psychology, the theory implied that each person carries deep within himself the inherited drives and instincts that served the human race during the long course of its development. Thus Marlow says the mind is capable of anything 'because everything is in it, all the past'. In the decades preceding Darwin's publication of *The Origin of Species*, scientific racists had been attracted by the idea of polygenesis: the theory that the varieties of mankind were the product of several quite separate 'creations'. Darwin restored faith in descent from a single pair, but there were unsettling undertones in his theory that Conrad exploited to the utmost in *Heart of Darkness*. Polygenesists could despise, flog and exterminate savages, confident in the assumption that those creatures were quite different sorts of beings. Darwinians had to live with the idea that the apparently unrestrained behaviour of the savages they encountered in the dark places of the earth reflected primitive instincts and desires that lurked somewhere within even the most civilised Europeans. The old Biblical view of human nature posited that sin could be redeemed through Christ and godly living. From a Darwinian perspective, primitive instincts could only be suppressed, never eliminated. Extending that line of thought, civilised men were exposing themselves to great personal danger when they went among savages. The wilderness might 'find them out'. As it found out Kurtz.

Much energy has been expended trying to pin down the identity of Kurtz. As with Almayer, there were real people that Conrad might have used as models, but none quite fits the bill.[54] Most of the scholars engaged in this detective work assume that Kurtz is to be found among the imperialists; if not among trading company agents, then among such men as Cecil Rhodes, H. M. Stanley or even King Leopold himself. There are unmistakable indications in the text, however, that Kurtz is a purely fictional embodiment of that old enemy, the self-deluding, pious, benevolent do-gooder whom Conrad, Carlyle and Kipling joined in hating. 'Fine sentiments', Marlow has said, are as useless as fine clothes in this primeval environment.[55] Kurtz is pre-eminently the man of fine sentiments. 'He is an emissary of pity, and science, and progress' (p. 169). He is also evidently close to organised Victorian benevolence. The International Society for the Suppression of Savage Customs – whose name recalls the Aborigines Protection Society and the Anti-Slavery Society – commissioned him to write a report for them. Kurtz arrived in the Congo spouting missionary cant. His talk of chains of station leading to the interior recalls the Wesleyan Methodist strategy for the conversion of heathen South Africa.[56] His description of what might happen on those stations is pure David Livingstone. 'Each station should be like a beacon on the road towards better things, a centre for trade of course, but also for humanizing, improving, instructing' (p. 181). Words, words, words. Marlow remarks with heavy irony that 'the peroration was magnificent, though difficult to remember, you know. It gave me the notion of an exotic Immensity ruled by an august Benevolence' (p. 208).

There is a hint, however, that Kurtz may have been more than just a woolly minded liberal or ranting missionary when he came to the Congo. Marlow finds it strange that he 'never imagined him as doing, you know, but as discoursing' (p. 203). Like Donkin who made his living by 'discoursing with filthy eloquence upon the right of labour to live', Kurtz seems inclined to extreme left-wing politics. Marlow is not exactly sure what Kurtz's profession had been before he left for Africa. He had links to the arty set back home, though it is doubtful that he mastered any craft. He was said to have had the potential to be a fine organist, but as for getting a living he was either 'a painter who wrote for the papers, or else ... a journalist who could paint' (p. 244). Someone, perhaps, like the artists William Morris and Walter Crane who put their talents to work on behalf of the Marxist Social Democratic Federation in England. A journalist who had known

Kurtz in Europe informs Marlow that his 'proper sphere ought to have been politics "on the popular side"'. And not just any leftist group. 'He would have been a splendid leader of an extreme party' (p. 244). That description begins to approach the sinister Professor who manipulates the destinies of the hopeless gang of anarchist revolutionaries in *The Secret Agent*. On the other hand, when the same man is asked what party Kurtz might have led, the answer is 'any party'. One man who could 'electrify large meetings' and whose party affiliation underwent a dramatic shift was Joseph Chamberlain – a radical reformer in Gladstone's cabinet but who changed horses on the issue of Home Rule for Ireland and led the Unionist rebels into coalition with the Conservatives. At the time *Heart of Darkness* was conceived, he was Colonial Secretary in Lord Salisbury's cabinet, renowned for his arguments that imperialism would promote social reform in Britain.

There is nothing to be gained by settling definitively on any of these candidates. As Marlow says, 'all Europe contributed to the making of Kurtz'. It is important, however, to recognise that Conrad managed to cram into this single figment of his imagination almost everything he personally loathed: abstract ideas about social justice, organised philanthropy, radicalism, liberalism, artistic dilettantism and religious cant. At the same time Kurtz lacks every quality Conrad prized: craftsmanship, efficiency, discipline, a fixed code of conduct. Having all of the dangerous ideas and none of the right stuff, it is no wonder that 'the wilderness had found him out early'. His downfall in 'going native' resembles Willems' fate in *An Outcast of the Islands*, but it is infinitely more satisfying for Conrad because of everything Kurtz represents. Willems was a nobody, a shiftless, good-for nothing loafer with no allegiance to any cause other than his own aggrandisement. Why should anyone care that he was destroyed by his passion for 'a completely savage woman' and ended up hating her whole race? Kurtz, in contrast, is a well-connected, well-educated man, famous for his support of good causes. Who better to illustrate the fragile pretences of benevolent sentimentalists?

No definite moment is specified as the moment of Kurtz's 'surrender', but readers of *An Outcast of the Islands* would suspect that the proximate cause is the African woman whom Marlow finds at his side. Like Willems' Aïssa, she is dazzlingly beautiful, 'savage and superb, wild-eyed and magnificent' (pp. 225–6); like Aïssa too, her beauty is linked to the overripe tropical vegetation around her. 'The immense wilderness, the colossal body of the fecund and mysterious life seemed to look at her, pensive, as though it had been looking at the image of its own tenebrous and passionate soul' (p. 226). Just as Aïssa had seemed to offer 'all grace of colour and form, all brilliance, all smiles, but is only the blossoming of the dead', there is a distinctly sinister aspect to this unnamed black woman. Willems complained that Aïssa 'found out something in me. She found it out, and I was lost' (p. 269). Whether it was the African beauty that 'found out something' in Kurtz or the wilderness itself hardly matters, for one mirrors the other. Willems comes to hate all Aïssa's countrymen. In his lucid moments, Kurtz wants to 'exterminate all the brutes', as if to punish the whole race for the disaster of his own seduction.

Kurtz is truly awful. Conrad obviously relished recounting the destruction of this incarnation of all his pet hates. On the other hand, he will not allow Marlow to connive at exposing the way in which Kurtz's Jekyll succumbed so completely to his Hyde.[57] Marlow elects to be 'loyal to the nightmare of my choice'. This may mean that it is better for Europeans to cling to fragile ideals, sentimental religion, fine words, music, poetry and painting than to face dark truths about their inner selves. After all, Conrad's magnificent story 'Karain' is built on the premise that everything that is best and safe in modern civilisation depends on belief in illusions. Alternatively, it may be that Marlow – and Conrad – are owning up to a deeper feeling of kinship with Kurtz than they would wish openly to acknowledge.

Heart of Darkness is a profoundly psychological novel that inevitably invites questions about Conrad's own psychological make-up. He spent much of his life vainly attempting to lay the ghost of a remarkable father. Apollo Korzeniowski had been a man of prodigious talents.[58] After studying Oriental languages, law and literature at the University of St Petersburg, he wrote plays, songs and poetry. He translated Victor Hugo into Polish and tried to launch a Polish journalistic equivalent to the French *Revue des Deux Mondes*. His speciality was writing 'romantic passages of lofty exaltation'. Apollo's cause was Polish nationalism, for which he was first imprisoned and later exiled by the czar. His wife died when Conrad was seven. For much of the next four years, Apollo was his son's sole teacher and companion. Then he too succumbed to tuberculosis. Conrad was deeply affected by the last terrible days when his father appeared not so much a 'man desperately ill, as mortally weary – a vanquished man'.[59]

If the character of Kurtz recalls Apollo Korzeniowski, then the strange young Russian who appears in the latter pages of *Heart of Darkness* seems a cartoon version of Conrad himself. His abandoned hut and a stack of firewood provides the first clue that Kurtz is alive. A message has been scrawled in pencil: '"Wood for you. Hurry up. Approach cautiously." There was a signature, but it was illegible – not Kurtz – a much longer word' (p. 188). Inside the hut Marlow is pleased to find an extensively annotated copy of an ancient manual for seamen: *An Inquiry into Some Points of Seamanship*. The old book, with its 'honest concern for the right way of going to work' (p. 189), gives Marlow the temporary sensation of 'having come upon something unmistakably real'. His first impression is that the annotations have been made in some kind of code or cipher. Later he learns they were made in Russian by a man who has become Kurtz's only white companion at the isolated inland station.

Dressed in multi-coloured rags, resembling nothing so much as a Harlequin, this young man greets Marlow like a long-lost brother.

> 'Brother sailor ... honour ... pleasure ... delight ... introduce myself ... Russian ... son of an arch-priest ... Government of Tambov ... What? Tobacco! English tobacco; the excellent English tobacco! Now that's brotherly. Smoke? Where's a sailor that does not smoke?'
>
> The pipe soothed him, and gradually I made out he had run away from school, had gone to sea in a Russian ship; ran away again; served some time in English ships; was now reconciled with the arch-priest. He made a point of that. (p. 213)

Marlow looks at him, 'lost in astonishment'.

> His very existence was improbable, inexplicable, and altogether bewildering. He was an insoluble problem. It was inconceivable how he had existed, how he had succeeded in getting so far, how he had managed to remain – why he did not instantly disappear. 'I went a little farther,' he said, 'then still a little farther – till I had gone so far that I don't know how I'll ever get back.' (p. 216)

Inexplicable, improbable, an insoluble problem – these words suggest that Marlow's first surmise was correct. The young man is, like the annotations in the manual, 'some kind of code or cipher'. He claims to be twenty-five years old but looks like a child. 'A beardless, boyish face, very fair, no features to speak of, nose peeling, little blue eyes, smiles and frowns chasing each other over that open countenance like sunshine and shadow on a wind-swept plain' (p. 212). Why does Marlow think that his existence is 'inconceivable' and that he should 'instantly disappear'? Marlow's journey up the river has been, all critics agree, a journey back into evolutionary time. It may also be a journey backwards into personal psychological time. Through the eyes of his invented narrator, Conrad can almost see his own child-self, on a 'wind-swept plain' of Eastern Europe. However, the boy is difficult to bring into focus, 'no features to speak of', his signature an illegible scrawl that is not Kurtz but a much longer name. We are not told the name but Korzeniowski would not be a wild guess. Kurtz suggests the German word for short, *kurz*. Marlow says it himself: 'Kurtz – Kurtz – that means short in German – don't it?' (p. 224). Another word for short is *klein*, which also means little. A shortened form of the name of a little boy beginning with 'k'.

Things are complicated (they inevitably are in Conrad) by the fact that a real agent named Klein worked at a Congo river station and that a man named Keyaerts accompanied Conrad on board the river-steamer *Roi des Belges*.[60] Kayerts was the name given to one of the idiot traders in 'An Outpost of Progress'. In the draft manuscript of *Heart of Darkness*, Klein was used in place of Kurtz. But Conrad is ever the master of multiple meanings, codes, ciphers, puzzles, shadow selves and secret sharers. The more meanings the better. What does Marlow think about his trip up the river towards Kurtz and his companion, the ethereal brother sailor?

> to understand the effect of it on me you ought to know how I got out there, what I saw, how I went up that river to the place where I first met the poor chap. It was the farthest point of navigation and the culminating point of my experience. It seemed somehow to throw a kind of light on everything about me – and into my thoughts. (p. 141)

At a hazy distance, Marlow sees a parental Kurtz through the harlequin's child eyes. The boy credits Kurtz with his whole education. 'You ought to have heard him recite poetry', he tells Marlow – 'his own, too, it was, he told me ... Oh, he enlarged my mind! I tell you ... this man has enlarged my mind' (pp. 230, 215). Night after night he sat enthralled by Kurz's monologues 'on love, justice, conduct of life' (p. 222). Once he and Kurtz had talked till dawn: '"We talked of everything ... I forgot there was such a thing as sleep. The night did not seem to last an hour. Everything! Everything! ... Of love, too." "Ah, he talked to you of love!" I said, much amused. "It isn't what you think," he cried, almost passionately. "It was in general. He made me see things – things"' (p. 217).

The entire conception is psychologically astounding. In 1897 Sigmund Freud had subjected himself to what he called psychoanalysis, an adventure that turned into a voyage towards the truth about his relationship with his father. Less than two years later Joseph Conrad undertook an equally laborious psychological voyage towards a confrontation with a father in *Heart of Darkness*. Conrad's description of the perils involved comes very close to being Oedipal in precisely Freud's sense.

Marlow in many ways envies the naive boy. 'If the absolutely pure, uncalculating, unpractical spirit of adventure had ever ruled a human being, it ruled this be-patched youth. I almost envied him the possession of this modest and clear flame' (p. 216). What he does not envy is 'his devotion to Kurtz'. It 'appeared about the most dangerous thing in every way he had come upon so far' (p. 217). Once Kurtz threatened to shoot the boy for not giving him some ivory tusks he had acquired by trading with a nearby chief.

> Well he wanted it, and wouldn't hear reason. He declared he would shoot me unless I gave him the ivory and then cleared out of the country, because he could do so, and had a fancy for it, and there was nothing on earth to prevent him killing whom he jolly well pleased. And it was true, too. I gave him the ivory ... But I didn't clear out. No, no. I couldn't leave him. I had to be careful, of course, till we got friendly again for a time. He had his second illness then. (pp. 218–19)

Bernard Meyer in his *Psychoanalytic Biography* traces much of the imaginative inner conflict that runs through Conrad's work to a persistent unresolved Oedipal 'castration complex'. Though Meyer misses this incident in *Heart of Darkness*, he would not have much trouble dealing with a scene in which an all-powerful father-figure threatens to kill a boy unless he gives up his small ivory tusk.

There is this difference, however, between Freud and Conrad. Freud, by discovering his inner rage at the father who stood between him and possession of the loved mother, achieved reconciliation and a kind of peace. He succeeded in reducing the remembered gigantic father to the dimensions of an ordinary man. The Harlequin represents the way of reconciliation. Referring to his Russian father from whom he had run away, he claims he 'was now reconciled with the arch-priest. He made a point of that'. Marlow, appalled at the Harlequin's devotion to his ersatz father, Kurtz, cannot endorse that kind of reconciliation, even though he declares he will be 'loyal to the nightmare of his choice'. We suspect that the same is true of Marlow's creator. Kurtz at the end has not shrunk to ordinary size. He has grown to grotesque proportions and become fossil ivory amid his hoard of tusks.

> He looked at least seven feet long. His covering had fallen off, and his body emerged from it pitiful and appalling as from a winding-sheet. I could see the cage of his ribs all astir, the bones of his arm waving. It was as though an animated image of death carved out of old ivory had been shaking its hand with menaces at a motionless crowd of men made of dark and glittering bronze. (p. 224)

Marlow, with Conrad at his side, has made the dangerous journey to the psyche's heart of the darkness and returned profoundly shaken. He has looked behind all abstract talk of justice, freedom, love, pity and philanthropy and found a rotting corpse of purely animal, savage man. He has seen naked, Napoleonic greed behind talk about the need for romantic genius to be free. He is determined to ward off that vision and that fate by clinging to work, efficiency, duty and an unwavering code of conduct. To face the darkness, 'he must meet that truth with his own true stuff – with his own inborn strength. Principles won't do. Acquisitions, clothes, pretty rags – rags that would fly off at the first good shake. No; you want a deliberate belief.'

Only the fool can do otherwise – 'a fool, what with sheer fright and fine sentiments, is always safe'. So Marlow watches his rag-clad 'brother sailor' disappear into the twilight. 'One of his pockets (bright red) was bulging with cartridges, from the other (dark blue) peeped "Towson's Inquiry," etc., etc. He seemed to think himself excellently well equipped for a renewed encounter with the wilderness' (p. 230). The last touch carries the suggestion that perhaps he may someday be released from his foolishness. After all, young Joseph Konrad Korzeniowski, full of despair at his failure to achieve his grandiose ambitions, had, one night in Marseilles, reached into his pocket of cartridges and tried to put a bullet through his heart. But he recovered, mastered the art of seamanship, became a commander and found his way to some sort of deliberate belief.

That belief was built on suppression, the suppression of the soul, and the suppression of the truth about our inner savage nature. When Marlow lies to Kurtz's fiancée in Belgium, telling her that her beloved died with her name on his lips, he is helping to preserve some essential fictions that are necessary for the maintenance of civilised life.[61] She may be full of the missionary cant and misplaced pity Conrad despised, but nothing would be gained by telling her that his real words were 'The horror! The horror!' Civilisation, however, depends on more than allowing tender consciences their belief in pious platitudes. It depends on men and governments who will carry out the necessary suppression of savage customs at home and abroad. King Leopold and his private-enterprise colonial hell do nothing for civilisation. They open whole boxes of horrors. In a letter to his publisher Conrad described his work as a fable about 'the criminality of inefficiency and pure selfishness when tackling the civilising work in Africa'.[62] Companies would not do. All Europe came to share his idea. Leopold's experiment was attracting outraged comment (from the usual philanthropic societies) even before Conrad's story appeared. The British East Africa Company, the Royal Niger Company and the various companies set up by the Germans in the hope of conquering territory on the cheap, all collapsed under the weight of administrative costs and were succeeded by direct imperial rule carried on by salaried professional public servants. Only Cecil Rhodes' British South Africa Company managed to struggle on as the government of Rhodesia for the full period of its charter. The men to rule colonies were, in the view of Conrad and most of his imperialist contemporaries in Britain, efficient, incorruptible men. Even the fiercest critics of tropical annexations and company rule agreed with that.[63] 'What saves us', says Marlow, 'is efficiency – the devotion to efficiency.'

That is all very well, but Conrad leaves his readers wondering whether any European is up to the task. Lord Jim did not succumb to Kurtz's temptation, but his accomplishments died with him. Why would he not return to his own people, asked his half-caste mistress? 'Because he's not good enough', Marlow replied, and hastily added, 'Nobody is good enough.' Kurtz possessed every advantage except moral fibre and failed spectacularly. Who was really 'man enough to face the darkness'? Especially in Africa where the civilised man stood face to face with the black, prehistoric savage. Other imperialists insisted that the maintenance of 'standards' – dressing for dinner, avoiding sexual temptation, keeping your hand out of the till – would be good enough. Conrad, with his fixation on race, has doubts. Fearing, even while he pretended to despise the black man, the suspicion of his 'remote kinship', Conrad issued dire warnings. Keep your distance. Do not pity. Do not try to help. Stay on the ship. That was either an admission that colonialism was too dangerous an experiment for poor weak white men to attempt, or it was the plea of the white settler – the foundation of apartheid – to build a firewall of segregation against the threat of the colonial subject. That made Conrad's books unsettling reading in the twentieth century.

Notes

1 Zdzislaw Najder, *Joseph Conrad: A Chronicle* (New Brunswick, NJ: Rutgers University Press, 1983), pp. 109–10.

2 C. T. Watts (ed.), *Joseph Conrad's Letters to R. B. Cunninghame Graham* (Cambridge: Cambridge University Press, 1969), pp. 20–1. Garnett's emphasis in a comment made in a letter to the Scottish radical, Cunninghame Graham.

3 Ibid., p. 45. Critical reluctance to couple Conrad and Kipling is beautifully illustrated by Frederick Karl's laboured attempt to read the same letter as a gleeful attack on 'Kipling, whose success he both envied and deplored'; *Joseph Conrad: The Three Lives* (New York: Farrar, Straus and Giroux, 1979), p. 395.

4 Najder, *Joseph Conrad*, p. 226.

5 Conrad complained of plagiarism in a letter to William Blackwood, whose *Blackwood's Magazine* had published Buchan's story in 1899. See Najder, *Joseph Conrad*, p. 205.

6 Paul Kirschner, *Conrad: The Psychologist as Artist* (Edinburgh: Oliver & Boyd, 1968), pp. 199–221; Ian Watt, *Conrad in the Nineteenth Century* (Berkeley: University of California Press, 1979), pp. 49–50.

7 Rudyard Kipling, *Something of Myself* (Harmondsworth: Penguin, 1992 [1936]), p. 158.

8 Najder, *Joseph Conrad*, p. 324.

9 Rudyard Kipling, *Collected Stories* (London: Everyman, 1994), p. 429.

10 Joseph Conrad, *Almayer's Folly: A Story of an Eastern River* (Oxford: Oxford University Press, 1992). Compare with the poem at the head of Kipling's 'Lispeth':

> Look, you have cast out Love! What Gods are these
> You bid me please?
> The Three in One, the One in Three? Not so!
> To my own Gods I go.

In Rudyard Kipling, *Plain Tales from the Hills* (London: Macmillan, 1891), p. 1. The political point made in Kipling's story is not that missionaries should go about their work in better ways, but that they should give up and leave. Conrad's view seems to have been the same.

11 *Lord Jim*, in Joseph Conrad, *Three Great Works* (Oxford: Oxford University Press, 1994), p. 219; subsequent quotations from this edition.

12 Ibid.

13 F. Karl and L. Davies, *The Collected Letters of Joseph Conrad, Vol. I: 1861–97* (Cambridge: Cambridge University Press, 1982), pp. 16–17. 'Socialism must inevitably end in Caesarism', he concluded, oddly echoing Frederic Seebohm's article 'Socialism and imperialism', in *The Nineteenth Century* 7 (April 1880), 726.

14 Kipling, *Collected Stories*, pp. 173–4.

15 Joseph Conrad, *The Nigger of the 'Narcissus': A Tale of the Sea* (London: Heinemann, 1961), p. 158; subsequent quotations from this edition.

16 Kipling, *Something of Myself*, pp. 87–8.

17 Watts (ed.), *Conrad's Letters to Cunninghame Graham*, p. 116. Conrad's friendship with the Scottish radical Cunninghame Graham is often cited as evidence of some personal sympathy for Graham's socialist sympathies. The letters show clearly that Conrad openly disagreed with most of his friend's political ideals.

18 Kipling, *Something of Myself*, pp. 103–5, 109, 111, 151.

19 See the discussion of Conrad's anti-Americanism in Eloise Knapp Hay, *The Political Novels of Joseph Conrad: A Critical Study* (Chicago: University of Chicago Press, 1963), pp. 167, 199.

20 Avrom Fleishman, *Conrad's Politics: Community and Anarchy in the Fiction of Joseph Conrad* (Baltimore, MD: Johns Hopkins University Press, 1967), p. 170; Watts (ed.), *Conrad's Letters to Cunninghame Graham*, p. 95.

21 Watts (ed.), *Conrad's Letters to Cunninghame Graham*, p. 126.

22 Quoted in Najder, *Joseph Conrad*, p. 261.

23 Ibid., p. 53. In scorning the French Republic, Conrad marked himself out from virtually all politically aware Poles; see Hay, *Political Novels of Joseph Conrad*, p. 49. His lifelong fascination with Napoleon and Bonapartism may owe something to an uncle who rose to the rank of general in the first Napoleon's army; Bernard C. Meyer, *Joseph Conrad: A Psychoanalytic Biography* (Princeton, NJ: Princeton University Press, 1967), p. 25.

24 Watts (ed.), *Conrad's Letters to Cunninghame Grahame*, p. 95. Whether or not Conrad had, as he sometimes claimed, once been a gunrunner for the Spanish royalists, his sympathy for their cause indicates that his pro-Spanish sentiments in 1898 reflected more than a revulsion against American aggression. He stuck to his old opinions even when his young friend Stephen Crane rushed off to enlist in the American army; see Najder, *Joseph Conrad*, p. 226.

25 Hay, *Political Novels of Joseph Conrad*, p. 25; see also Robert Hampson, *Joseph Conrad: Betrayal and Identity* (London: Macmillan, 1992), p. 196. The novel *Chance* includes an extremely unflattering portrait of a feminist governess in Mrs Fyne.

26 Henry Steele Commager, Jr, cited in Hay, *Political Novels of Joseph Conrad*, p. 25.

27 Albert Guerard, Jr, *Joseph Conrad* (New York: New Directions, 1947; published as Vol. I of the quarterly journal *Direction*, which succeeded *Pharos*), p. 52.

28 In a lecture originally presented in 1974 at the University of Massachusetts, Amherst, and largely reprinted in Chinua Achebe, *Hopes and Impediments: Selected Essays, 1965–87* (Oxford: Heinemann, 1987), pp. 1–13. Achebe himself does not deny

Conrad or *Heart of Darkness* places in the firmament of literary greatness. He merely observes that to find such strident racism in so widely read a text says something important about European culture.

29 This is most elegantly accomplished by Benita Parry in *Conrad and Imperialism, Ideological Boundaries and Visionary Frontiers* (London: Macmillan, 1983).

30 Kipling, *Collected Stories*, p. 220. Caliph Harun-al-Rashid appears in *Tales of the Arabian Nights.* Its Victorian translator, Richard Burton, was as celebrated for his African explorations as for his literary accomplishments. See Watt, *Conrad in the Nineteenth Century*, p. 146.

31 Joseph Conrad, *Almayer's Folly, A Story of an Eastern River*, ed. and introduced by Jacques Berthoud (Oxford: Oxford University Press, 1992); subsequent quotations from this edition.

32 The nineteenth-century creation of the 'half-breed' as unnatural and sinister is concisely explored by H. L. Malchow in 'The half-breed as gothic unnatural', in S. West (ed.), *The Victorians and Race* (London: Scolar Press, 1997), pp. 101–11.

33 Prodigious scholarship has identified the place and many of the names that gave Conrad his 'Sambir'. See Norman Sherry, *Conrad's Eastern World* (Cambridge: Cambridge University Press, 1966), pp. 37–138. There was a real Ohlmeijer, though he was a Eurasian with many children; also a Lingard and an Abdulla. None of these characters bears more than a superficial resemblance to the Conrad creations that bear the same names. See also Watts, *Conrad in the Nineteenth Century*, pp. 37–9; Jacques Berthoud, 'Introduction' to *Almayer's Folly*, pp. xlv–xlvi, lix.

34 John Flint has emphasised the importance of Leopold's projects and the North Borneo Company in reviving the popularity of chartered companies that had been widely used in earlier centuries to rule overseas territories. Through the use of chartered companies European powers could forestall rivals in Africa without the burden to their own taxpayers that direct rule would have entailed; 'Chartered companies and the transition from informal sway to colonial rule in Africa', in S. Förster, W. J. Mommsen and R. Robinson (eds), *Bismarck, Europe, and Africa: The Berlin Africa Conference 1884–1885 and the Onset of Partition* (Oxford: Oxford University Press, 1988), pp. 69–84.

35 Joseph Conrad, *An Outcast of the Islands*, ed. J. H. Stape and H. van Marle (Oxford: Oxford University Press, 1992), p. 45; subsequent quotations from this edition.

36 The image of the blow is repeated even more forcefully in a later passage when he feels himself collapse as from 'a deadly gun-shot wound'. Bernard Meyer has called attention to the psychoanalytic implications of Conrad's repeated use of such images. Young men in love are said to have been pierced, shot or impaled by the force of the female. Meyer hypothesises that an unresolved longing for the mother produced in Conrad a typical form of the castration complex, marked by repulsion for all the overt anatomical characteristics of female sexuality. See *Joseph Conrad: A Psychoanalytic Biography*, pp. 46–51, 83, 292–9.

37 N. J. Ryan, *The Making of Modern Malaysia and Singapore* (Oxford: Oxford University Press, 1969), pp. 89–95.

38 'An outpost of progress', in Joseph Conrad, *Heart of Darkness and Other Tales*, ed. by Cedric Watts (Oxford: Oxford University Press, 1990), p. 11; subsequent quotations from this edition.

39 Christopher Fyfe, *A History of Sierra Leone* (Oxford: Oxford University Press, 1962), pp. 13–87. Fyfe also gives a brief account on pp. 546–7 of the scandal created by the mistreatment of Sierra Leone labour recruited for Congo service in 1896.

40 Najder, *Joseph Conrad*, p. 130.

41 Joseph Conrad, *Heart of Darkness*, in *Heart of Darkness and Other Tales*, ed. Cedric Watts (Oxford: Oxford University Press, 1990), pp. 158, 144, 170, 177; subsequent quotations from this edition.

42 Carlyle's 'Occasional discourse on the nigger question' (London: T. Bosworth, 1853) was a hostile response to a strike by West Indian plantation workers. The title was intended to be provocative, as the original version of the essay, published in

Fraser's Magazine in 1849, had been 'Occasional discourse on the Negro question'. Conrad knew Carlyle's work very well. See Watt, *Conrad in the Nineteenth Century*, pp. 149–51, 153, 168, 188. In *Youth*, the young Marlow is shown preparing for his first voyage as an officer by reading Carlyle's *Sartor Resartus*. See Andrea White, *Joseph Conrad and the Adventure Tradition: Constructing and Deconstructing the Imperial Subject* (Cambridge: Cambridge University Press, 1993), pp. 168–9.

43 The political ideas of the book have been much discussed, but its imperial dimensions have generally escaped notice. Norman Sherry, for example, mentions the book only once, as though it belonged neither to Conrad's Western nor Eastern worlds.

44 Donkin's manipulation of Wait also recalls the scene in Shakespeare's *Tempest*, when boorish Stefano and Trinculo recruit Caliban in a scheme to seize Prospero's island for themselves.

45 A political subtext on the Irish question runs through both Conrad's novel and Carlyle's essay.

46 Andrea White has shown how Conrad situated his work in relation to the literature of adventure for boys in *Joseph Conrad and the Adventure Tradition*.

47 Frederick Lugard, *The Dual Mandate in British Tropical Africa*, 5th edn (London: Frank Cass, 1965), p. 201.

48 In an early review, published before he had met the author, Clifford complained that Conrad misread aspects of the 'Malay character'; see Sherry, *Conrad's Eastern World*, pp. 139–40. He was entirely won over, however, by *Lord Jim* and *Heart of Darkness*. Clifford went on to write many works of fiction of his own about the dark places of the earth. Recalling Kipling's passage in 'The man who would be king', he described the thrill of 'an expedition into the Benighted Lands' and the 'tales without number of the States beyond the border – fragmentary echoes of deeds that have their counterparts only in the "Arabian Nights"'. Hugh Clifford, *Bush-Whacking and Other Asiatic Tales and Memories* (London: Heinemann, 1929), p. 85. In *Malayan Monochromes* (New York: Dutton, 1915), pp. 64–5, Clifford describes a situation very like Jim's account of the man and the pots:

> The petition was obviously ridiculous, and no sensible man, of course, would led an ear to it. How can educated Englishmen, who know so many things, and are withal so thoroughly enlightened, take a serious view of such an absurdity? But the State in question had then but recently come under British protection, and the wise man who was at that time its Resident cared far less for the opinions of educated and enlightened Englishmen than for the peace and happiness of the people over whom he ruled.

49 Hugh Clifford, 'At the heels of the white man', in *Studies in Brown Humanity* (London: Grant Richards, 1898), p. 137.

50 La Societé Anonyme Belge pour le Commerce du Haut-Congo was incorporated in 1888; Conrad entered its service in 1890.

51 Jean Stengers, the pre-eminent Belgian historian of the Congo enterprise, argues that the king's idealism represented a genuine conviction; 'Leopold II and the *Association Internationale du Congo*', in Förster *et al.* (eds), *Bismarck, Europe, and Africa*, pp. 229–44.

52 Hugh Clifford, 'The art of Mr Joseph Conrad', *The Spectator* 89 (29 November 1902), 827–8.

53 Norman Sherry has shown how Conrad deliberately darkened and narrowed the river to suit his narrative purposes; pp. 48–51, 70.

54 These are capably summarised in Watt, *Conrad in the Nineteenth Century*, pp. 142–6.

55 Ibid., pp. 149–50. Watt perceptively associates the metaphor of useless clothes with the principle trope of Carlyle's *Sartor Resartus*.

56 J. Whiteside, *History of the Wesleyan Methodist Church of South Africa* (London: Epworth, 1906), p. 357.

57 The death of Kurtz is a moment very like the death of Gagool or Ayesha in Haggard's work, or the unveiling of old Dorian Gray's picture in Oscar Wilde's novel, as well as like Jekyll's transition into Hyde: 'Anything approaching the change that came over his features I have never seen before, and hope never to see again. Oh, I wasn't touched. I was fascinated. It was as though a veil had been rent. I saw on that ivory face the expression of sombre pride, of ruthless power, of craven terror – of an intense and hopeless despair.' Conrad, *Heart of Darkness*, p. 239.

58 See Najder, *Joseph Conrad*, pp. 5–21.

59 Joseph Conrad, *A Personal Record: Some Reminiscences* (London: Dent, 1946 [1906]), p. viii.

60 A staggering amount of detective work on the words Klein, Keyaerts, *kurz* and *klein* has been done by Norman Sherry in *Conrad's Western World* (Cambridge: Cambridge University Press, 1971), pp. 48–118.

61 A careful reading of Marlow's encounter with the 'Intended' will reveal that this is the only lie he tells.

62 Karl, *Joseph Conrad: The Three Lives*, p. 440.

63 John A. Hobson, *Imperialism: A Study* (London: George Allen & Unwin, 1938), pp. 244–6.

CHAPTER FIVE

Elgar and the Gordon Symphony

Best-loved of all English composers, Edward Elgar occupies a higher position in the world of classical music than anyone imagined even at the zenith of his popularity in the Edwardian era. The Elgar Society's webpage catalogues regular concert performances taking place right round the world – not just of the *Enigma Variations*, the concertos and symphonies, but also his huge oratorios: *The Dream of Gerontius*, *The Apostles* and *The Kingdom*.[1] However, at many points in the twentieth century his reputation seemed far from assured. Musical trends were partly to blame. Set beside Stravinsky and the avant-garde of the Second Viennese School, the man Richard Strauss had hailed as the 'first English progressivist' appeared doughty and old-fashioned. Elgar was even more out of touch with prevailing politics in the 1930s, which called into question his deepest attachments to the Monarchy, the Conservative Party, Defence and the Empire. Admirers fought a rear-guard action over subsequent decades, attempting to distance the composer from the political causes he consistently championed. By the 1970s the 'two Elgars' theory had become the entrenched wisdom. Public Elgar pandered to metropolitan jingoes with the *Imperial March*, *Crown of India*, *Pomp and Circumstance* marches, *Coronation Ode* and *Caractacus*. Private Elgar – by implication the real man – cared more for the countryside than the Empire, laying bare his sensitive, tortured soul in the cello and violin concertos, the oratorios, *Enigma* and the symphonies. Thanks to Michael Kennedy and to Ken Russell's influential documentary film, the two Elgars theory long held undisputed sway at the Elgar Birthplace museum. On my first visit in pursuit of Elgar and imperialism, an attendant remarked that 'you'd be wanting the brass band Elgar'.

In the lead-up to the 150th anniversary of his birth, a tide of new scholarship exposed the shaky biographical and musical foundations of the two Elgars theory. The composer's commitment to conservatism and Empire is largely accepted on all sides, even though some maintain it only went 'tweed deep'.[2] More would now incline to agree with Jeffrey Richards' robust observation that 'the first thing is that Elgar was a patriot, a monarchist and a Conservative, and his imperialism was a logical extension of these values'. The 'very fact that some of his most profound work is autobiographical means that he is constantly mingling the personal and the ideological, the public and the private. After all Symphony No. 2 was by Elgar's own admission intended as a tribute to Edward VII.'[3] The end of denial over his imperialism should have rekindled interest in his most ambitious project for a politically charged composition – the symphony he proposed to write in 1898 on the subject of General Charles Gordon, who perished at the hands of Islamist fanatics in Sudan in 1885.[4] That it did not eventuate is due to three factors. First, having promised to produce the symphony for the Three Choirs Festival in September 1899, Elgar informed the Worcester organising committee in May of that year that he could not fulfil the obligation.[5] Some have taken this to imply there is no Gordon symphony to study. Second, Elgar did go on to write a major work on a related theme. His *Dream of Gerontius* was a setting of John Henry Newman's poem, an annotated copy of which had been found among the dead general's papers in Khartoum. Reproducing 'the Gordon markings' became something of a craze among late Victorians.[6] The priest of his local Catholic church presented Elgar with one of the marked volumes on the occasion of his marriage in 1889.[7] Thus it was widely assumed that his ideas about Gordon found eventual expression in the religious oratorio. Third, when Elgar did manage to complete his first symphony in 1908, he quite explicitly denied the work had any non-musical subject. The symphony had 'no programme beyond a wide experience of human life with a great charity (love) and a massive hope in the future'.[8]

While these are weighty considerations, none poses an insuperable obstacle to speculation about what a Gordon symphony might have become in Elgar's hands. Just because he failed to deliver in 1899 does not mean he stopped thinking about the project. When *Gerontius* premiered in 1900, he claimed that 'the poem has been soaking in my mind for at least eight years. All that time I have been gradually assimilating the thoughts of the author into my own musical promptings.'[9] Months after he told the Worcester committee that he could not finish the symphony, August Jaeger, his champion at Novello's music publishing firm, wrote to ask, 'How is that Gordon Symphony getting on! you Sphinx!!'[10] It therefore seems more than probable that the oratorio and symphony were entirely separate projects.

The remainder of this chapter argues that everything Elgar might have had to say about Gordon and Empire went into his Symphony No. 1. Attentive listeners recognised from its first performance the dramatic impact of pitting a grand imperial theme in the tradition of 'Pomp and Circumstance No. 1' against insurgent musical forces marshalled at the opposite end of tonal possibilities. Those who knew the man could cast the drama in more personal terms. The tortured, sensitive soul he hid from the world was asserting itself in vaulting chromatic challenges to conventional musical order. A psychological struggle between the outer man and the turbulent id ran in tandem with the theme of Empire hero Gordon warding off the Sudanese Mahdists. Because his medium was music, any parallels he may have drawn between the business of empire and his own divided self must be guessed at from scattered hints in letters and from comments reported second hand by his intimate friends.

A symphony with no programme?

Elgar's assertion that the work had no programme deserves no more credence than a host of other doubtful assertions made throughout a career marked by deliberately misleading public statements, cryptic asides, puzzles and downright lies. His hypersensitivity and penchant for self-concealment were notorious. Mark Elder of the Hallé Orchestra observed there was 'so much neurosis in Elgar ... he is the British Mahler'.[11] Music critic Ernest Newman, who thought him 'an exceptionally nervous, self-divided and secretly unhappy man', visited the composer as he lay dying. 'After a brief silence, he made a single short remark about himself which I have never disclosed to anyone and have no intention of ever disclosing, for it would lend itself too easily to the crudest of misinterpretations at the hands of thick-fingered psychologists.'[12] So we are denied even that rare glimpse of the inner man. Elgar carried to the grave the secret of the theme 'that goes but is not heard' in his *Enigma Variations* – if indeed there was such a theme. He affected the faintly ridiculous persona of a philistine country squire to fend off intruders. When a young violinist, thrilled by a Promenade concert rehearsal in 1902, asked 'whether he gave lessons in harmony, counterpoint, etc.', his withering and totally false reply was 'My dear boy, I don't know anything about those things.'[13] His denial of a programme for the first symphony may have stemmed from a statement in his published lectures as Peyton Professor of Music at Birmingham University (1905–08). Music, he said, 'which existed without any poetic or literary basis ... was the highest development of the art'.[14] These were precisely the years in which the first symphony was coming together; any suggestion of a programme would have undercut his own argument. That has not stopped others from suspecting that an undisclosed programme lurks within.

Even his friends did not believe him. Newman 'questioned the integrity' of his expressed opinion. Jaeger clearly discerned a programme in the first symphony.[15] Later musical critics agree. Diana McVeagh writes that 'for all his denial ... some kind of inner drama works itself out in this Symphony'.[16] Matthew Riley notes that passages throughout his compositions 'seem to demand interpretation in terms of a personal story or relationship'.[17] David Cox carried speculation further by naming a specific source for the first symphony: 'it is just possible that the life and death of General Gordon had been to some extent responsible in the first place for its inspiration – in the same way that Beethoven's "Eroica" was conceived "in memory of a great man".'[18] Jeffrey Richards reads the opening passage marked *nobilmente* in the symphony as 'so clearly an affirmation of the greatness of Britain that it would seem wilful perversity to disregard its inspiration'.[19]

Other associations link the theme of Empire to Symphony No. 1. The opening motto seems to have come to him while in Rome. After the first performance he despatched an exuberant picture postcard to his friend W. G. McNaught at Novello's.[20] Scrawled across a photograph of the Appian Way are the first three bars of the symphony. While composing in Rome, he told Frank Schuster, 'Here is my Mecca & I love it all.'[21] In 1908, while he was in the final stages of composition, the British press revived memories of Lady Elgar's father, General Roberts, on the fiftieth anniversary of the collapse of the Indian Mutiny in which he had taken a leading role.[22] *Caractacus* had played with parallels between the ancient Roman Empire and modern Britain shortly before Elgar first proposed a Gordon symphony. They were evidently still on his mind. The symphony commences with a drum roll and marches recur throughout the work – which should not come as a surprise as he had set two military marching songs to music while in the final stages of composition.[23] One summoned

> Thousands, thousands of marching feet,
> All through the land, all through the land,
> Gunners and Sappers, Horse and Foot,
> A mighty band, a mighty band

Another, more melancholy and reflective, asked:

> Who shall stay and reap the harvest
> When the autumn days shall come?
> But the drum
> Echoed, 'Come!

Death shall reap the braver harvest,' said the solemn-sounding drum.

A more direct connection to the life and death of Gordon is suggested by Elgar's unmistakeable allusion to *Parsifal* in the stately motto theme that opens and closes the symphony.[24] Though not his favourite Wagner opera, he knew it well, having made a point of seeing it twice at Bayreuth in 1892.[25] Understanding all that might have been implied by the *Parsifal* allusion in Symphony No. 1 means recollecting the character of Wagner's hero and what General Gordon stood for in the minds of late-Victorian Britons.

A Victorian Parsifal

Parsifal's mission is to restore sanctity and tranquillity to Monsalvat, sanctuary of the knights who guard the Holy Grail. Through his own moral failings, their king Amfortas has suffered a grievous wound that will only be healed through the ministrations of a 'pure fool, enlightened by compassion'. Parsifal – pure, fearless, athletic, chivalrous and clueless – eventually emerges as the hoped-for fool. No figure in the annals of the British Empire so resembles Parsifal as Charles George Gordon, CB.

He first attracted notoriety in the 1860s as an officer seconded to the service of the emperor of China in the later stages of the war to suppress the Taiping Rebellion. Put in command of a ragtag body of irregular soldiery improbably named the Ever Victorious Army, Gordon fought a brilliant though highly unorthodox campaign in which he was the star attraction. Casually uniformed, smoking a cigar and armed with nothing more than a light cane, he personally led assaults on the most formidable garrisons. After taking 700 Taiping rebels prisoner at Taitsan, he immediately recruited them to his Ever Victorious legion, where they proved his most fanatically loyal foot soldiers.[26] On the other hand, he summarily executed a man suspected of insubordination. Hailed as 'Chinese Gordon', the hero who had single-handedly put down the Taipings, he took no notice of his adoring English public and went quietly about his work as newly appointed military engineer erecting defences for the lower Thames. About the same time his religious peculiarities began to attract attention. Not only did he fill his free time with feverish Bible study, he published tracts at his own expense and handed them out door-to-door. He ran a charitable enterprise on behalf of the poor boys of his neighbourhood, tending the sick at the workhouse infirmary and taking several into his own home. They were his 'Gravesend laddies', his 'kings', his 'doves', his 'angels', whom he delighted in bathing and dressing. His Victorian contemporaries were far from blind to the implications, though no evidence suggests that he maintained anything but the most ruthless sublimation of his homoerotic inclinations. He confessed to his sister that as early as age fourteen he had wished himself a eunuch.[27] Needless to say, he was as impervious as Parsifal to female seduction.

In 1873 Gordon accepted another secondment to the service of a foreign government, this time as the Khedive of Egypt's governor of Equatorial Province on the upper Nile. His difficult, well nigh impossible task, was suppression of the slave trade that foreign pressure had forced on a reluctant Egypt. Characteristically, he began by appointing to his staff an ex-slave trader whom his predecessor had jailed for treachery. Like the Taiping prisoners recruited to his cause in China, he hoped Abou Saoud would show the zeal of 'the sinner who repenteth'. Gordon continued to display the wild inconstancy of policy and judgement that marked all his positions of command. Having first tried to slash the profits of slave-dealers by nationalising the ivory trade, he confidentially proposed in 1874 to let the slave trade continue as a government monopoly under humanitarian supervision.[28] Fortunately the news did not get out and he finished his governorship with a reputation as a guru on Sudan. By his own appraisal he 'cut off the slave-dealers in their strongholds' and 'made all my people love me'. *Vanity Fair* accorded him a cartoon in 1881 along with this character sketch of 'the grandest Englishman now alive':

> Colonel Gordon is the most conscientious, simple-minded and honest of men. He has a complete contempt for money, and after having again and again rejected opportunities of becoming rich beyond the dreams of avarice, he remains a poor man with nothing in the world but his sword and his honour. The official mind regards it as a sign of madness ... He is set down by officials as being 'cracky' and unsafe to employ ... He is very modest and very gentle, yet full of enthusiasm for what he holds to be right. This enthusiasm often leads him to interfere in matters which he does not understand, and to make in haste statements he has to correct at leisure. But he is a fine, noble, knightly gentleman, such as is found but once in many generations.[29]

Whatever further quests God held in store for this peripatetic imperial freelance Gordon would accept as His Divine Will. It might be solving the problem of Irish poverty by proposing a government buyout of all the landholders. It could be command of Royal Engineers in Mauritius, where earnest study led him to pinpoint an island near the Seychelles as the primal Garden of Eden. It might mean accepting an invitation from King Leopold of the Belgians in 1880 to join in the mighty work of bringing commerce and civilisation to the Congo. Or going as private secretary to the Viceroy of India, where after a few weeks he resigned, having privately concluded that the sooner Britain rid itself of this tarnished jewel in the crown the better. 'It is only the upper ten thousand of England who benefit by it.' Not long after, Gordon answered the call of the prime minister of the Cape Colony, who needed help in settling a tricky situation in Basutoland. Casting his famous piercing blue eyes over Southern Africa, he backed the plucky, pious Transvaal Boers who had just regained their independence from British rule, declared the recently defeated Zulu king Cetshwayo to be 'a fine savage' and formed an immediate bond with fellow bachelor Cecil Rhodes, then in the process of consolidating the De Beers diamond syndicate. As for the Basuto chief Masupha, the decent, manly thing to do was to enter into personal negotiations, even though he had been expressly forbidden to do so. Called to account, he resigned in September 1882, rueing that 'we are a pig-headed race, we Gordons ... What a queer life mine has been, with these fearful rows continually occurring'.[30]

Perhaps his most endearing trait was his frank acknowledgement of the flaws and contradictions in his make-up. Mostly this stemmed from his religious conviction that all mortals had two natures, one spiritual, the other fleshly. 'The world contains the people of two kingdoms, acknowledging two separate kings and two separate systems of government. The one is an everlasting, undefiled, and incorruptible kingdom; the other is mortal, defiled, and corrupt. Christ is the King of the Kingdom of God, and the Devil, anti-Christ, is the king of the kingdom of the earth.'[31] He told his sister, 'Some of my letters are written by one nature, others by another nature.' And there were more than two. 'Talk of two natures in one, I have a hundred and they none think alike, and will all rule.' He could never 'know my own mind for two days consecutively'.[32]

Freed from his earthly commission in South Africa, he travelled to Palestine in 1883 on something like a Grail quest. He would use his reading of the Bible to solve such vexing questions as the resting place of the Ark, the exact location of the Crucifixion and the ancient frontier between the tribes of Benjamin and Judah. Meanwhile a fresh crisis for the British Empire unfolded in Sudan. Believing that a military coup against the ruler of Egypt threatened Britain's strategic interests in the Eastern Mediterranean, Prime Minister William Gladstone despatched an occupying force in 1882 to restore the Khedive and put state finances on a sound footing. Complicating the situation, a revolt had broken out in Sudan, led by a charismatic holy man calling himself the Mahdi: the man who, according to Islamic eschatology, would rid the world of sin and corruption – paving the way for the Last Judgement and the end of time. Because Gladstone maintained the fiction that British forces stayed in Egypt merely to stabilise the Khedive's regime, he was powerless to countermand their plan to send an expeditionary force to crush the Mahdist rebels. When 10,000 men under retired British general William Hicks were wiped out at Omdurman in November 1884, Gladstone was in a pickle.[33] His own inclination was to let Sudan go (he had not long before pronounced the Mahdists to be a people 'rightly struggling to be free'). However, following the annihilation of much of its army, Egypt now lay at the mercy of the Mahdi, while the ruling elite refused to countenance surrender of Sudan. Worse, an improbable coalition of evangelicals and determined imperialists bayed that abandoning Sudan to the slavers would stain the honour of Britain and sin against God. Leading the charge, crusading journalist W. T. Stead of the *Pall Mall Gazette* cried 'Chinese Gordon for the Soudan'.

In an interview with the editor published in January 1884, Gordon delivered a withering judgement on the consequences of a premature abandonment of Sudan. Even to announce a date would embolden the Mahdi to extend his operations to Egypt, arouse Islamic fanaticism throughout the Middle East and gravely imperil Britain's position on the lower Nile. What was needed was a commander to hold Khartoum until 'disunion and tribal jealousies have worked their natural results in the camp of the Mahdi'. Then the beleaguered Egyptian garrisons could be safely withdrawn and British honour vindicated. The Sudanese, who were 'a very nice people', deserved no less than 'the sincere compassion and sympathy of all civilized men'.[34] Within a few weeks Gladstone's cabinet determined to exert more direct control over the Khedive through their resident adviser in Cairo, Evelyn Baring, and to send Gordon to Khartoum with instructions to investigate the measures required for the evacuation of the garrisons. Those who knew the man were apprehensive. Baring thought him 'a queer fellow' with 'a very feminine side to his character'. Robert Hart, who had known him since his China days, confessed that 'Much as I like and respect him, I must say he is *"not all there"*. Whether it is religion, or vanity, or softening of the brain – I don't know; but he seems to be alternately arrogant and slavish, vain and humble, in his senses and out of them.' Sir Hercules Robinson, who had seen him at close quarters at the Cape swore there was 'no one so undecided in word or so decided in action ... he would telegraph one thing in the morning, another thing in the evening, and a third thing the next day'.[35]

Gordon ensured that every aspect of his strange, gallant, foolish and conflicted character would be henceforth on view for all to see through the journals he kept during his final months in besieged Khartoum. Intended for publication, they provoked Lord Northbrook (First Lord of the Admiralty in Gladstone's government) to say later, 'if he had previously read Gordon's book, nothing would have induced him to consent to his going anywhere. It was the book of a madman!'[36] Arthur Rimbaud, the French poet famed for his own excesses, commented succinctly, 'Their Gordon is an idiot.'[37] His judgements on his own situation and future prospects veered as wildly from one extreme to another as in the incessant telegrams with which he bombarded Baring. One moment he determined to smash the Mahdi, the next, to meet him secretly and appoint him Sultan of Kordofan province.[38] On the basis of a 'mystic feeling' he proposed to recruit as his right-hand man a notorious ex-slaver, whose son had perished by Gordon's own orders during his previous stint as governor.[39] Only the outraged howls of the Anti-Slavery Society intervened to prevent it. To forestall the Mahdists in the south he proposed handing territory over to Leopold's Congo Company, which he continued to regard as his future employer. All these thoughts intermingled with spiritual outpourings on Jesus and scriptures. At almost any point during the early months at Khartoum he might have secured the withdrawal of at least some of the Egyptian garrisons. That he did not was sheer obstinacy. 'I own', he wrote, 'to having been very insubordinate to Her Majesty's Government and its officials, but it is my nature, and I cannot help it ... I know if *I* was chief I would never employ *myself*, for I am incorrigible.'[40] Later, after two separate expeditions designed to keep communications open had been cut up by Mahdist forces, evacuation was not an option. He quite rightly observed that 'no one wishes more to be out of it than myself; the *"reasons"* [I cannot] are those horridly plucky Arabs'. At length cabinet colleagues forced a most reluctant Gladstone to approve a Relief Expedition under the command of one of Gordon's old comrades, Sir Garnet Wolseley. Meanwhile, it must be said, Gordon managed the defence of Khartoum with imagination, good sense and skill. Nonetheless, as Wolseley's troops inched forward, the Mahdi launched the final assault that brought Gordon the martyr's death he had so openly courted.

The news provoked a national outpouring of grief, not just in Britain but throughout the Empire, led from the top by a genuinely distraught and anguished queen. In the aftermath, boys' clubs and charitable foundations were established in his honour. A statue was erected in Trafalgar Square[41] and countless lesser commemorations observed around the globe. Even Gladstone, who sustained serious political damage in the affair, wrote that 'Gordon was a hero, and a hero of heroes'. As with Parsifal, chivalry was the word used most often to sum up the pure and noble spirit that redeemed his otherwise foolish character.

For Elgar, however, the Gordon story did not finish with the hero's death. In September 1898 General Herbert Kitchener's troops took their first giant step towards reconquest of Sudan with a bloody and crushing defeat of Mahdist forces at Omdurman. As his first mention of the Gordon Symphony occurs a few weeks after the battle, Elgar must have planned to include some evocation of Kitchener's victory.[42]

With much of Gordon's writings in the public domain, Elgar must also have been aware of his Parsifal's contradictory character and the internal war he felt raging between opposing forces within his psyche. It would be no great stretch to suggest parallels between the external and internal dramas.

Elgar's politics

The realised symphony might also have been expected to marry the story of Gordon and Sudan to the larger theme of British imperialism, which had been at the forefront of the composer's mind since Victoria's Diamond Jubilee of 1897. Two of his most explicit treatments of Empire had just appeared: the *Imperial March*, composed expressly for the Jubilee, and *Caractacus*, which premiered in Leeds a fortnight before his first mention of a Gordon symphony. Before considering the clues to Elgar's musical thinking about Empire embodied in these and other compositions, the non-musical expressions of his political creed deserve attention, if only to dispel the contention that his commitment to imperialism was shallow.

When J. B. Priestley reiterated the common complaint that too much had been made of Elgar 'as a complacent Edwardian Imperialist', he revealed how much his generation had forgotten about British imperialists.[43] Far from complacent, they worried incessantly about Britain's decline, the rise of rival powers and military weakness. In Bernard Porter's classic assessment, 'beneath the display there was fear, behind the self-assertion a feeling of vulnerability which could not be entirely hidden, either from herself or the rivals she was seeking to impress'.[44] Imperialism meant much more than 'dominion over palm and pine'. It encompassed a total programme for shoring up Britain's faltering pre-eminence in the world. Idealists like Curzon, Balfour and Milner shaped it into something very like a religious faith in the early 1890s.[45] Elgar's imperialism typically mixed bellicose patriotic pride with fretfulness about foreign threats and internal complacency. The contention that Elgar simply adopted his wife's conservative and imperialist convictions makes little sense. If, as Harper-Scott contends, 'there is no documentary evidence in his music or his letters to suggest that he was at all interested in it until he married Alice', it is equally true that there is no documentary evidence of her political commitment to imperialism before the marriage.[46] That a woman who devoted her life to serving his greatness and converted to Roman Catholicism to please him would nonetheless impose her politics on him beggars belief.[47] They moved easily as a couple in imperialist circles, conversing with Lutyens about the planning of Delhi, hearing 'a terrible tale of naval unpreparedness' from Admiral Beresford at dinner with the Stuart-Wortleys, corresponding with a colonial governor about African songs.[48] Moreover, Elgar publicly paraded his political enthusiasms in a way Alice never did. He exulted in the Tory victory at the general election of 1895 when imperialism came to the fore as never before.[49] He dreamt of standing for parliament as a Conservative.[50] On the eve of the Great War, he went far out on a limb by lending his name to Lord Milner's manifesto of '20 distinguished men' who pledged to defy the law if necessary to defend Protestant Ulster against inclusion in a united Ireland.[51] And when the war came, regretting that he could not go to the front, he volunteered for Home Guard duty and joined the clamour for conscription in a 'Manifesto on National Service'.[52] After Alice's death his attachment to the cause of Conservatism and Empire remained undimmed. Socialist Ramsay MacDonald's election to the Athenaeum Club prompted Elgar's resignation in 1925.[53] He gladly endorsed the use of 'Land of Hope and Glory' as a Conservative anthem, but warned his music publisher not to 'let any blasted labour rogues or liberals use the tune'.[54]

We may take the word of his contemporaries that above all other composers Elgar expressed imperialism in music. Well before his *Pomp and Circumstance* marches the *Court Journal* noted that 'Mr Elgar has not inaptly been dubbed "the Rudyard Kipling of the musicians."'[55] Charles Villiers Stanford, Professor of Music at Cambridge, enthused that he had 'translated Master Rudyard Kipling into Music' and 'said "blooming beggar" in quite his style'.[56] At the outbreak of the Boer War he sought, unsuccessfully, a commission to set Kipling's *Recessional*.[57] In the midst of the First World War, his setting of Kipling's poems, *Fringes of the Fleet*, elicited from one reviewer the comment that he was unsurprised 'to find the composer entering fully into the patriotic spirit of one who has long stood for a new Imperialism in poetry. Elgar, to some degree, has stood for the same in music.'[58] Elgar did not resist the comparison, having expressed his admiration for Kipling's *Plain Tales* from India as early as 1892.[59] He boasted that he had 'some of the soldier instinct in me'.[60] Alice agreed and cheered him on. At the premiere of 'Pomp and Circumstance No. 3', she exulted, 'the new March is *thrilling* – the most pacific friends were ready to fight!'[61] What contemporaries do not tell us is precisely *how* Elgar translated imperialism into his compositions. There was more to the creed than marching and fighting. There was the awareness that even the greatest of empires was doomed to pass away. There was the articulation of contradictory impulses towards domination and liberation. There was the complex business of confronting and governing subject peoples. A Gordon symphony would have to encompass all these themes and more.

Caractacus

Hints as to how Elgar might have handled the material in 1899 are to be found in his *Imperial March* for the Jubilee of 1897 and *Caractacus*, a large choral work completed the following year. The march is short (less than five minutes), but it strikes attitudes characteristic of all his subsequent marches. An opening drum roll announces a stately military theme marked *pomposo*, which soon gives way a brassy *animato* call to arms. The two military themes gradually intermingle and reach a stirring climax. Suddenly the key shifts to E♭ minor and a delicate trio section unfolds dolce in the strings, suggesting some place of calm far removed from the battlefield – home perhaps, where people know little or nothing of the sacrifices endured by their distant armies. As its strains die away the opening themes return, to be joined near the end by a reminiscence of the trio section – this time fully integrated into the dominant key of B♭. With all tensions resolved, the music strides *molto maestoso* towards an exuberant *stringendo* finish. Transcending the limitations of the slow march format, Elgar imbues his piece with a complexity unknown to composers for marching band of his time, such as John Philip Sousa. The reflective lyrical trio amply illustrates Jeffrey Richards' objection to the two Elgars theory. The man in full inhabits the marches as much as the oratorios and symphonic works. Imperialism as realised in this particular march displays as many facets as the concept possessed in contemporary reality. Elgar's markings tell a tale by turns pompous, aggressively animated, sweetly elegiac and majestic. Any Gordon symphony might be expected to include plenty of march music, not only because of the military context of the last stand, but because the hero sent a brass brand of youngsters out on the palace roof every Thursday to blare defiance at the Mahdist enemy.[62]

Caractacus reveals a great deal about Elgar's attitudes to Empire because he collaborated on its original text with his neighbour, H. A. Acworth, a retired Indian official. Had he simply wished to borrow his wife's politics, he might have asked her for a libretto. (Alice, born in India and daughter of a major general, was a published author of verses and a novel.) There is no question here of working with material imposed from outside. We may take for granted that the finished work expresses Elgar's own deeply held beliefs. He proposed the theme and commissioned the text. He had full power to cut or amend any lines that jarred. While not intended for an operatic performance, the choral cantata includes roles for several individual characters who interact. He chose the theme that Joseph Conrad would ponder the following year in *Heart of Darkness*: Rome's encounter with barbarism in the conquest of Britain. As twilight deepens on the Thames, Conrad's Marlow muses that 'this also has been one of the dark places of the earth'. Imagine 'a decent young citizen in a toga ... coming out here ... and in some inland post feel the savagery, the utter savagery had closed round him'. Elgar knew such dark material lurked in his story, for he confessed to Jaeger that 'Caractacus frightens me in places'.[63]

Evidently it frightened him too much, for he drew back from any portrayal of 'utter savagery' in his musical realisation of the text, even when it dealt with Druidical rites and sacrifices. With words to alert listeners to the meaning of his music, Elgar adopted his customary buttoned-up country squire approach to any threatened psychological revelation. Rather than plunge into the darkness, Elgar explored the paradox involved in simultaneously celebrating Britons' defence of their homeland and identifying with the civilising mission of Roman conquest. Britain must be conquered by Rome so that in another era she may build an even greater empire. His musical solution of the paradox is to gradually transform Britons and Romans from enemies into long-term partners.

As the curtain rises Britain is already under siege and King Caractacus reels from massive defeats. While his watchmen cry 'Alert' along his shrunken battle lines, his daughter Eigen and her lover, the bard Orbin, bring welcome news: a Druid maiden foretells that if Caractacus avoids giving battle on the plain and retreats to the mountain forests, he will wear down the Roman legions and gain the victory. A sceptical king nonetheless calls on the Arch-Druid for a further reading of the omens. Orbin is called to the place of sacrifice in a Sacred Grove to see what may be revealed in the war god's silver shield. When he sees the Roman eagle flying with talons red, the Arch-Druid chooses not to warn the king, but instead prophesies a British triumph. Appalled, Orbin casts aside his bardic cloak and runs with Eigen to join Caractacus. After the inevitable defeat, they are led away in chains to endure the jeers of the populace in a triumphal procession through the streets of Rome. Brought before Emperor Claudius, Caractacus asks what crime he committed in defending his people's liberty and pleads for the lives of the young lovers. Disregarding the crowd baying for British blood, the emperor grants them the right to live out their lives under his protection in Rome. Caractacus in turn asks that Rome teach his people 'order, and law, and liberty with Rome'. Now the chorus leaps two millennia ahead and celebrates Britain's succession as master of a worldwide empire. This, they remind us, is no cause for complacency, for 'opposing cohorts gather' and 'jealous tyrants lower'. 'Britons, alert! And fear not, but gird your loins for fight.' Provided she stands firm a glorious future beckons.

And ever your dominion
    From age to age shall grow
O'er peoples undiscover'd,
    In lands we cannot know
And where the flag of Britain
    Its triple crosses rears,
No slave shall be for subject,
    No trophy wet with tears;
But folk shall bless the banner,
    And bless the crosses twin'd
That bear the gift of freedom
    On every blowing wind;
Nor shall her might diminish
    While firm she holds the faith
Of equal law to all men –
    And holds it to the death;
For all the world shall learn it –
    Though long the task shall be –
The text of Britain's teaching,
    The message of the free;
And when at last they find it,
    The nations all shall stand
And hymn the praise of Britain,
    Like brothers, hand in hand.

Nothing in the Elgar canon, not even the most extravagant verses of 'Land of Hope and Glory', approaches this encomium to Empire. Twenty-first-century American neo-conservatives would be hard pressed to better the programme of endless liberation – of captured hearts and minds. And there is no one to blame but Elgar and his neighbour. Like it or not, this is where Elgar stood politically when he contemplated writing his Gordon symphony.

That said, there is much to admire in the shrewdness with which Acworth and Elgar handle their material. The Druid maiden's suggestion that the Roman legions be lured into guerrilla warfare in the mountain forests recalls not only many British setbacks on India's north-west frontier, but also the massive defeat inflicted on the Romans in the Teutoburg Forest of Germania in 9 AD. In order to achieve his objective of convergence between Rome and Britain, Elgar could not situate Britain and Rome as polar opposites. Both are set in major keys, Britain in E♭ and Rome in C.

Figure 49 Britain theme

Figure 50 Rome theme

In the finale the two themes approach each other and intermingle. When the battle is lost, Caractacus is made to sing a lament in 7/4 time (i.e. a combined time) that alternates elements of 'Rome' and 'Britain'. In defeat he is literally singing Rome's song.

Figure 51 Caractacus lament

The triumphal procession, often played as an independent piece, displays more subtlety than most critics acknowledge. First comes the Rome theme in full military dress played *forte* at a pushy tempo, *allegro maestoso*. After some busy semi-quavers suggesting a bustling metropole, the opening theme returns full blast, only to be displaced at figure 4 by a broad melody associated later (at figure 18) with the beauty of Roman architecture and the costumes of the nobility. Just as abruptly the tone turns nasty as the crowd lift their voices at figure 6 – the same crowd that will shortly shout 'slay the Britons'. The music now departs from its former measured pace and sways off the beat, conjuring barbaric swagger rather than imperial glory.

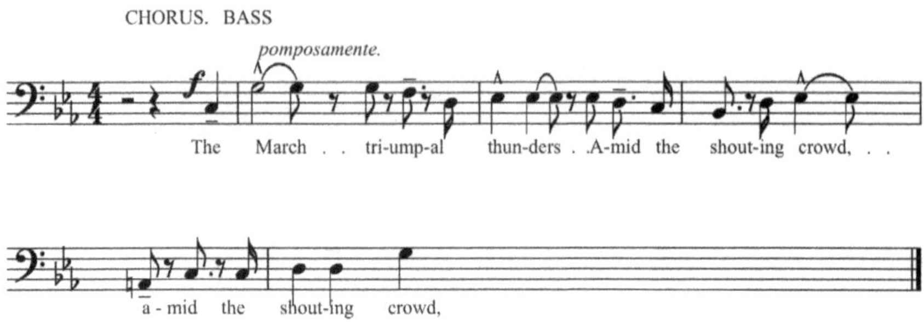

Figure 52 Enter Roman barbarism

Elgar manages simultaneously to depict the Romans as pre-Christian pagans and to reinforce Tory suspicions of the mob, whose passions would always need to be curbed by a wise monarch and nobility – as much in modern Britain as ancient Rome. A dozen years later he would employ similar musical means to depict the former Mughal emperors of India in his *Crown of India* masque.[64]

Set alongside this splendid evocation of a Roman triumph, Elgar's treatment of the Druids and their blood sacrifices sounds timid and anodyne. The libretto promises savage thrills:

Thread the measure left and right,
Druid maidens, clad in white,
Loose your locks, your bosoms bare
Breathe the god-head brooding there
Hov'ring round your floating hair.

A dozen years later Igor Stravinsky would take up this topical theme of our pagan ancestors engaged in human sacrifice and weave it into the driving rhythms of the *Rite of Spring*. The best Elgar can offer is something like a schoolgirls' maypole dance, marked *dolce* and sung *pianissimo*.

As keenly aware as any of his contemporaries of the savage within, who is also our savage past, he will not let it be made explicit. In this case he compounds his evasion by assigning a counterpoint accompaniment to the strings that virtually replicates the delicate trio section of his *Imperial March*. 'Loose your locks, your bosoms bare', lie back and think of England.

Figure 53 Accompaniment to Druid Maidens' 'Thread the measure'

Figure 54 *Imperial March* trio

Here we come very close to the central conundrum of Elgar and his work. The music brims with passion that the man conceals in every other way. Words that brought him too close to self-revelation had to be ignored or downplayed. Whatever wonders (and horrors) lay hidden in the depths of his own psyche could not be brought to the surface in any recognisable form. The superego controlling his musical consciousness insisted that in the end the forces of control, order and nobility must triumph. This is the link between Elgar's public personality, his politics and his music. Dark passionate forces and a multitude of emotions seethe below. Their rebellious insurgency cannot be denied, but it must, at all costs, be subjugated. The subjugators are identified with majesty, purity and nobility. That is why Elgar, the outsider, the shopkeeper's son, the Catholic, the musical autodidact, could never side with revolutionaries or bohemians – why he revered Edward VII as that 'dear kind man'.

Incidentally, the use of something very like the trio melody of *Imperial March* in the maidens' dance tends to confirm the hypothesis that it represents thoughts of home and the English countryside. The composer makes much of woodland themes in *Caractacus*. As the captives trudge wearily forward on the cobbled Roman way, woodland music from their homeland wells up in the hearts. Earlier in the cantata there is a 'Woodland Interlude' Elgar so treasured as to call for its playing when he lay dying. Critics long remarked on the nostalgia evoked by his music; lately skilled musicologists have emerged to explain the techniques he used to achieve this effect.[65] Sometimes – the 'Woodland Interlude' is a prime example – the flow is deliberately interrupted for a reflection on distant times or places. At other times, a fragment of an earlier melody appears before quickly fading in an enactment of the mind's process of recollection. More subtly, muted violins are used to set up what Michael Allis aptly terms a haze, whose appearance invariably signals a withdrawal to an imagined realm of inner peace and contentment – often associated with childhood or nature.

Symphony No. 1

Drawing on what we know about Charles Gordon's life, Elgar's handling of imperial subjects and the composer's complex psychology, it is not impossible to imagine how a Gordon symphony might have been constructed. So voluminous was the outpouring of literature by and about Gordon in the 1880s and 1890s that just about everything known to later biographers would have been readily available, especially his extraordinary journal and letters to confidants like his sister. We might expect that at the overt political level the simple nobility of the hero's aspirations would be set against the fanaticism of the insurgent Mahdist dervishes. This would echo the conflicts and contradictions within the hero's psyche – and the composer's. There would also be moments of withdrawal into nostalgic reveries of childhood and home, or pious introspection. Like the Empire that exercised domination in the name of liberating subject peoples, there would be episodes of reconciliation or even love between the conqueror and the insurgent: moments such as those that motivated Gordon to embrace Taiping prisoners, commend the defeated Zulu king, employ ex-slavers and pine for face-to-face negotiations with the Mahdi. Gordon would perish, but vindication would eventually come in Kitchener's victory at Omdurman and the establishment of humane British rule in Sudan. In psychological terms the struggle against insurgent forces would be a close-run thing, with the superego scoring a narrow last-minute win over the wild forces welling up from the id.

Although all the elements that might have gone into a Gordon symphony appear in the Symphony No. 1, it is impossible to say that it was *the* Gordon symphony, and no such claim will be made. On the other hand, the ideas that caused Elgar to promise the symphony in 1898 persisted in his musical thinking. Pursuing this line of argument helps to show how the composer could express imperialism in purely musical terms without requiring either a giveaway title or text. It also enables us to see more clearly the creative interplay between Elgar's political creed and his ideas about the human psyche – ideas similar to those of Freud and the other subjects of this study. Significantly, the two short statements he did make about the content of Symphony No. 1 point to parallel political and psychological scenarios.

His declaration that there was 'no programme beyond a wide experience of human life with a great charity (love) and a massive hope in the future' suggests concerns for the nation and perhaps all mankind. The other comment, made in a letter to Ernest Newman, refers directly to an interior emotional drama: 'As to the phases of pride, despair, anger, peace & the thousand & one things that occur between the first page & the last, as I said before, I prefer the listener to draw what he can from the sounds he hears.'[66] Emotional vacillations notoriously afflicted both Elgar and Gordon, so it is no surprise to find them explicitly linked to the symphony.

Pianissimo drum rolls in the tympani open the piece, striking a sombre and faintly martial tone. Then a stately motto theme unrolls softly in the winds and viola – in the composer's words, 'noble & elevating … the sort of *ideal* call – in the sense of persuasion, not coercion or command – & something above the everyday & sordid things'.[67] Elgar made copious use of the marking *nobilmente* in his compositions but here, uniquely, he adds the qualification *e semplice*. This not only reinforces the allusion to Parsifal ('pure fool enlightened by compassion') but could equally apply to the best qualities of Charles Gordon. A noted agnostic, Thomas Huxley, remarked that 'of all the people I have met in my life, he and Darwin are the two in whom I have found something bigger than ordinary humanity – an unequalled simplicity and directness of purpose – a sublime unselfishness'.[68]

Figure 55 The Ideal Call

Most likely this represents the aspirations of ideal humanity rather than the hero of the drama. The same can be said of the imperialism espoused by Elgar, Milner and the rest. The ideal could never be realised amid the messy realities of war, diplomacy and colonial administration. Conrad's Marlow famously states the creed:

> The conquest of the earth, which mostly means the taking it away from those who have a different complexion or slightly flatter noses than ourselves, is not a pretty thing when you look into it too much. What redeems it is the idea only. An idea at the back of it; not a sentimental pretence but an idea; and an unselfish belief in the idea – something you can set up, and bow down before, and offer a sacrifice to.[69]

Elgar treats his Ideal Call in similar fashion. It does not appear as a musical subject to be expounded, developed and recapitulated according to the conventions of symphonic form. It is simply stated and allowed to fade into inaudibility. Now the battle begins.

An insurgent challenge rises stridently and *appassionato* in the strings and woodwinds, shortly to be joined by blaring horns. There is also an abrupt change of key, whose meaning has been greatly debated by Elgar scholars.

Figure 56 Opposing forces, Allegro *appassionato*

Is this really a change of key, or a change to no key? Jerrold Northrup Moore, ever attentive to dualities and polarities, identifies it as D minor, the most distant point in the circle of tonalities from the opening A♭ major – the so-called 'diabolus in musica' (devil in music).[70] Others make the case for A minor.[71] Diana McVeagh sensibly asks, 'does it matter? Both keys are distant from A flat, either sets up an imbalance, and the drama lies in the ambiguity. The tonality of the Andante is stable, that of the Allegro, thick with accidentals, unstable.'[72] Agreeing, Julian Rushton writes, 'which key Elgar is proposing matters less than recognition that the jump from the "nobilmente" motto into the Allegro, with no hint of Wagnerian transition, makes a rent in the musical fabric which takes a whole symphony to repair'.[73] Elgar's own judgement in a letter to Jaeger was that in the first symphony he had 'thrown over all key relationships as formerly practised'. The signature of one flat in the Allegro *appassionato* 'means nothing – it is convenient for the players'.[74] Whatever the technicalities, the psychological effect of this rupture is, as James Hepokoski perceptively remarks, to set up a 'Neo-Lisztian battle between the forces of light and dark'.[75]

In a Gordon symphony we would surely identify an insurgent theme with the forces of the Mahdi. We might at the same time think of Gordon's self-admitted multiple natures and hear it as the 'incorrigible' element in his make-up. Or in Elgar's. The composer's friend Billy Reed pointed out that the Ideal Call echoes almost note for the note the final bars of the *Enigma Variations*, the one he named for himself ('E.D.U.'). On another occasion, however, Elgar confessed 'that the only quotation I can find to fit my life comes from the Demons' chorus! [in *Dream of Gerontius*]'.[76] The demon theme itself was but a misshapen version of the E.D.U. motif from *Enigma*.[77] It is difficult to imagine a more direct musical expression of Elgar's conviction of the dual natures at war within his psyche. The insurgent challenge posed by the Allegro *appassionato* is musically as modern as the works Arnold Schoenburg was writing in Vienna or Charles Ives in Connecticut. But Elgar would never present such writing as a stand-alone composition. Throughout his life he used chromaticism and tonal instability to represent exotic or demonic subjects. However powerfully expressed, the tonal centre would invariably hold. So it will be with this symphony, though the struggle rages for fifty minutes.

The Allegro *appassionato* grows ever more furious. The shape of the upper violin line on the page is literally insurgent, repeatedly sweeping from below to far above the staff. A menacing syncopation appears in the tympani and brass that recalls the swaggering climax of the Triumphal March from *Caractacus*, until at length the tempest subsides as if from sheer exhaustion. Suddenly at figure 11 the music retreats to some haven of peace. A lyrical new subject appears in violins and clarinets accompanied by something very like the 'haze' of tremulous passages in the winds, violins and harp that Elgar characteristically employed to evoke memory or nature.[78] As the melody winds on, bird calls flutter forth from the high winds. This is evidently an imagined or recollected refuge, for the key signature remains the same and the opening melodic line goes nowhere in particular – as though time were standing still.[79] Violins sound a broad new melody *piano dolce* at figure 12, repeated *forte cantabile* by the horns and bassoon. Any hope that this new idea will assert its authority over the powers of darkness is soon crushed by an anguished cry emanating from the bassoon and violins (figure 14). Reality stridently reasserts itself and the insurgent forces rampage on for nearly a minute-and-a-half before exhausting themselves once more. What are we to make of this alternation of storm and tranquility, when the same melodic material crops up in both the turbulent and peaceful passages? It might be argued that, far from seeking refuge in nostalgia, Elgar brutally exposes the illusion that woodlands or the haunts of childhood offer genuine escape from the challenges of determined foes. Cast in terms of contemporary political debates, Little Englandism was no answer to Kaiser Wilhelm's naval build-up, the Russian push towards the Eastern Mediterranean or the Mahdi's threat to Suez. Or, as Freud would have argued, your dream of escape from adult trauma into the innocence of childhood is built on a lie. The forces you most fear to confront are precisely the elemental conflicts grounded in a childhood that was far from innocent. They can never be annihilated, only repressed; never destroyed, at best understood.

The abatement of the tempest signals the end of the exposition. Elgar now moves towards the development of his material. The Ideal Call recurs *pianissimo* in muted horns, in a very slow, almost spectral procession counterpointed by a mournful bassoon (figure 18). This acts as a recollection rather than an assertion, for only twelve bars later the violins move off in a new direction (figure 19) towards a version of the woodland refuge (with more birdlike calls from the upper winds five bars before figure 22). This long passage of peace ends at figure 24 with four bars of rising and falling lines in the strings. This Elgar described as a 'restless exploring idea'. Spurred on by the lower strings louder and louder, the brass enter four bars before figure 26. As the tempo races ahead *stringendo* they once more swing off the beat into another syncopated and highly chromatic passage. On and on, until the orchestra collapses *tutti* in another spasm of exhaustion at figure 29. With the entry of a delicate solo violin we return to haunts of peace, despite occasional ominous muttering from forces below, until the horns and violas invoke a shadow of the Ideal Call just before figure 31. Much too far away to offer succour, its appearance only acts as a summons to the original insurgent theme Allegro *appassionato* (figure 32). The recapitulation differs from the initial statement, however, by shifting to the dominant key of A♭ at figure 35, even though the synchopated brass section sounds much as before. By figure 37, the woodland retreat has taken over, still in A♭. Four bars before figure 41, menacing horns and a huge crescendo roll in the tympani plunge us back into the storm that gathers in intensity with long *marcato* downward runs in the brass. This time there is no woodland retreat and calm is not restored for nearly two minutes, when the Ideal Call returns *sotto voce* in the last desks of the violins, violas and celli. For a time it seems as though it will snatch an unexpected victory. With the entry of the horns the melody swells to a solid *forte*. In the background, snatches of lyrical themes from former 'woodland' sections gradually mingle with the motto, as though all the forces of good have united. The great surprise of the movement is that instead the Ideal Call drops away, leaving the quieter lyrical themes to drift on alone until, eleven bars from the end, a solo clarinet plays the faintest far-off echo of the Call. Even that is not allowed to finish, as all sound fades to nothingness.

Elgar commented pointedly that 'the theme does not become triumphant in the 1st movemnt. but emerges in the end as the conquering (subduing) idea'.[80] Reinforcing the quintessentially imperial idea of conquest, Lady Elgar put forward her interpretation of the symphony thus far: 'The great tune so majestic and beautiful. Then the wild underspirits and vain things conquered by it.'[81] Though vastly simplifying the complexity of what has gone on, Edward and Alice direct us towards a plausible imperial/Gordon interpretation. The Empire calls Gordon to Khartoum and then leaves him alone to cope with the ineffectual efforts of the Egyptian government to shore up his position. As the Mahdists tighten the noose his hopes of rescue grow increasingly faint. Meanwhile he draws what comfort he can from religious devotions, nostalgic recollections of lost happiness and the vituperation he directed in his diary against Gladstone's government. At length the announcement of a Relief Expedition raises hope to fever pitch, only to be followed by disappointment at the snail's pace of preparations. Gordon is left alone to contemplate his coming confrontation with the Mahdi. Not much effort is required to imagine this as a possible programme for the movement. First comes the Imperial Call, not in its convoluted party political guise, but as Conrad envisaged it: 'something you can set up and bow down before.' Next comes the Mahdi's insurgent challenge that rises again and again, interspersed with references to Gordon's inner resources of faith and nostalgic recollection. Expectations of imperial action fade like the successively faint echoes of the Call until the announcement of the Relief Expedition raises the volume to *fortissimo*. As the reality of the slow preparations sinks in, Gordon is left alone with his thoughts.

The movement works just as well as a psychological programme. In Freudian language the Ideal Call corresponds to the superego's insistence that the noble conscience should be your guide. The insurgent challenge of the id is represented by the repeated assaults of chromaticism in no readily identifiable key.[82] The endeavours of the besieged ego to repel the 'wild underspirits' by retreating to an imagined world of woodland childhood innocence fail because they are founded on fantasy. Hope resides in the effort to ally the noble calls of conscience to a chancy project of repression. How far that may be feasible still remains to be seen at the movement's end.

Musicologists point out that structurally the second and third movements function as a thematically linked pair, bookended by the similarly related first and final movements.[83] A direct connection is established between the middle movements by the opening passage of scurrying notes in the first violins. That same sequence of notes recurs at half speed at figure 86 and is further slowed at 87. When the third movement commences without a pause, the sequence reappears *adagio* as a magnificent lyrical melody in the strings.

Figure 57 Second movement scurrying semi-quavers

Figure 58 Third movement adagio opening in violins

At the end of that movement all sound dies away at the place Elgar originally annotated with a quotation from the final scene of *Hamlet*: 'the rest is silence.' The clear implication is that we have been witnessing a two-act drama ending in death. Contemporary reviewers heard it as a hero's struggle. The *Birmingham Post* detected an earthly version of *Gerontius*, while *The Star* made a comparison with the hero's life in Richard Strauss's *Heldenleben*. 'The Symphony is more spiritual than the tone-poem. We seem to see the conflicts and the final higher development from within in Elgar's work; from without in the other ... Both seem to speak of love: but in "Heldenleben" it is a human love, in the Symphony it suggests the amor intellectualis Dei.'[84] Pursuing this line of thought, the middle movements might be viewed as a tone poem within a Gordon symphony. Rather than a linear historical narrative, it suggests the hero's path towards a state of internal peace as death approaches. Musicologist James Hepokoski, noting that Elgar's earliest sketches of the symphony in 1904 featured the concluding passages of the third movement, argues persuasively that this is the 'centre point of the work'.[85]

Three militaristic pulses from the percussion and bassoons announce the high-speed second movement; then the scurrying semi-quavers are launched in the upper strings. Elgar had used a similar passage to suggest the bustle of a Roman street throng in *Caractacus*. The effect here is of frantic preparation for some imminent threat, which arrives soon enough when the clarinets and violas break into a brisk sinister march at figure 59. Violins and brass join in and by figure 61 the whole orchestra is bellowing the fascist ditty. At length the strings resume their scurrying business of shoring up the defences, until an entirely new idea breaks in at figure 66. Against a background 'haze' of tremulous sounds from the harp, the flutes play a lilting melody immediately recognisable in the composer's vocabulary as nature or memory. Elgar said as much when, at an orchestral rehearsal, he told the musicians to play it 'like something we hear down by the river'.[86] Characteristically, he wrote this section diatonically in a major key (B♭ major), contrasting it to the tonal uncertainty and chromaticism of the preceding section. The remainder of this short movement explores the interplay of these three elements: the busy scurrying, the sinister march and the river music. As in the first movement, the river music seems to be trying to effect an escape from the real-world conflict between evil forces on the move and feverish efforts to fend them off. About halfway through the movement, at figure 75, the opposing forces join battle. Upper winds, brass and first violins play the march, while bassoons and lower strings go about their scurrying busyness – all at top volume. Another battle is staged at figure 77 as the marching assailants are countered by the river music blared out *fortissimo* in the brass and bassoons. This time the nature music stages an unlooked-for victory and plays on unchallenged, eventually to be joined by the scurrying semi-quavers that then commence their gradual slowing. Faint rumblings of opposition are briefly heard from the contrabassoon at figure 84, but that is all until, just at the end, the last remnants of the march slink away in horns and bassoons – utterly defeated, while the former semi-quaver sequence crawls unchallenged towards its apotheosis in the third movement.

With its magical transition into lush romantic melody in the key of D major, the composer shows his hand. His symphony will be more than the straightforward neo-Lisztian 'battle between the forces of light and dark' suggested in the first movement. It will deal in totally unexpected transformations. Elements that seem diametrically opposed will be shown to be closely related. As Elgar wrote to Jaeger, 'You will find [in the symphony] many subtle *enharmonic* relationships & the widest *looking* divergencies are often closest relationships.'[87] The *adagio* third movement differentiates itself from the others by the absence of a disturbing element. No challenge arises from a distant uncertain key or creepy march. Here and there warnings sound – in the horns at figure 95, two bars before 96 and during the lead-up to 104. Something similar happens at 99 in the oboes. However, in each case, the threat is dissipated by a return to one of the main subjects. Woodland passages are, as in the previous movements, interspersed among the main subjects, generally introduced by a tremulous haze or birdlike calls from the upper winds. The difference is that in the *adagio* they act to reinforce rather than to retreat from the main themes. A lovely intermingling occurs, for example, after figure 97, where the passionate outpouring of a new melody in the lower strings runs alongside tremulous violins and woodland flourishes in the upper winds. Less perceptible but unmistakable references to the Ideal Call recur throughout the movement – most notably four bars before 102, where the whole orchestra appears about to reprise the *fortissimo* passage at figure 3 of the first movement. What we are witnessing here is not a triumphant conclusion but a comingling of elements that earlier had to contend independently with powerful assailants. Those elements continue to interact delightfully until all sound dies away with the final notes from the solo clarinet. No wonder Jaeger discerned 'the most beautiful, and perfect message of peace, chaste feeling, aloofness from all things mundane and common'.[88]

Taken together, the paired inner movements would have fulfilled a transparent function in a Gordon symphony, tracing the hero's inner journey towards death in Khartoum. The flying semi-quavers at the outset of the second movement suggest frantic preparations to meet the Mahdist challenge as hopes of rescue recede. This is very much the picture painted by Colonel Stewart in a letter to Baring: 'Gordon is so full of energy and action that he cannot get along without doing something, and at present he revenges himself for his enforced inactivity by writing letters, despatches, etc., and sending telegrams', messages Baring found increasingly 'bewildering and contradictory'.[89] This is the moment too that Gordon flirts with audacious transformations. On the basis 'of the mystic feeling I felt I had for him', he proposed to make Zobeir Pasha his deputy – even though he had indirectly caused the death of this notorious ex-slave trader's son. He warned Baring that he might disappear for a couple of months to engage in direct negotiations with the Mahdi.[90] He never lost confidence in his ability to make 'all my people love me'. Could there be a more powerful musical evocation of Gordon's vacillation between defence against the enemy and the power of love than the transformation of the busy semi-quaver passage into the spacious love theme at the beginning of the third movement? He was entirely capable of simultaneously pronouncing the Madhi's cause to be just and the man honourable, even as he dreamt of smashing him on the battlefield. Such contradictions pervade the culture and practice of British imperialism.

Enemies might be demonised one minute and lionised the next. The defeated Zulu king Cetshwayo was cheered by London crowds on his way to meet Victoria in 1882.[91] Kipling paid tribute to the Madhi's troops in his 1890 poem, 'Fuzzy Wuzzy'.

> We've fought with many men acrost the seas,
> An' some of 'em was brave an' some was not:
> The Paythan an' the Zulu an' Burmese;
> But the Fuzzy was the finest o' the lot.
> So 'ere's *to* you, Fuzzy-Wuzzy, at your 'ome in the Soudan;
> You're a pore benighted 'eathen but a first-class fightin' man.[92]

John Buchan fantasised in his novel *Greenmantle* that a Scotsman in disguise could so win the affection of Islamist Arabs that he would be accepted as their leader in war against the Turks. Likewise, as Matthew Riley points out, 'in Elgar's historical displacements of the colonial relationship, the distinction between self and other is blurred ... a late-Victorian audience could quite easily have identified now with one side, now with the other'.[93]

As a psychological drama the second and third movements suggest something akin to wish-fulfilment. Disruptive forces represented by the march upset the busyness of quotidian life, provoking a crisis that is eventually resolved by the consolations of tranquillity achieved through a retreat to the world of nature and childhood innocence. Were this the ultimate message of the symphony, it might finish there with this forceful rebuke to the unsettling Freudian doctrine of endless struggle against forbidden desires and destructive impulses. From the very first bars of the final movement it is clear that this is not to be the case. The music plunges back into the storms of the first movement.

Muffled beats in the bass drum recall those that initiated the first two movements. We return to a field of battle. Within quick succession we hear a menacing march played in the key of D minor by lower winds and strings, a flurry of bird calls in the upper winds, a faint recollection of the Ideal Call and an arresting new motif announced by the clarinet. By now the dramatis personae are familiar; it only remains to be seen how the Ideal Call will fulfil its mission as the 'conquering (subduing) idea'. After a good deal of busy work the germ of the clarinet motif emerges as the fully developed second subject of the movement – a rousing melody suggesting horsemen at the gallop.

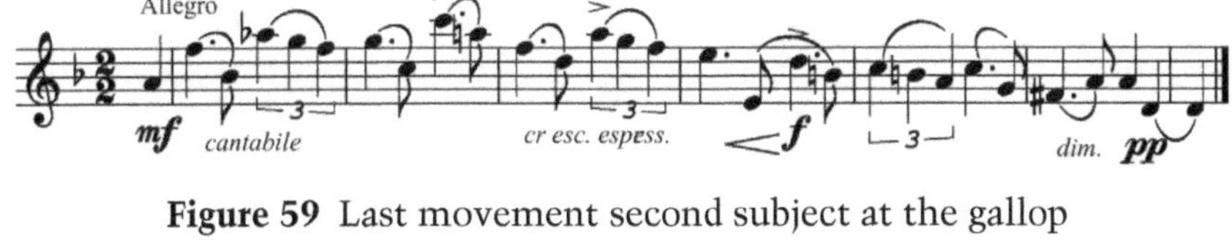

Figure 59 Last movement second subject at the gallop

The menacing march replies to the challenge at 118, reinforced by a thundering descending passage in the tuba. Soon the whole orchestra has swung into the goose step. Lady Elgar in 1918 pronounced this 'pagan tune absolutely a picture of the Huns'.[94] By figure 122 the march has turned into a canon, passed around from section to section. A whole minute passes before the uplifting gallop takes charge, only to be met by an immediate riposte from the march in the low winds and brass.

Figure 60 Last movement sinister march

Now something extraordinary occurs. The violins and violas take up the Ideal Call. Elgar assigns this passage *piano* to the back rows of players, causing listeners to wonder where the sound might be coming from. The effect of the unexpected intervention is to cause the winds and brass to recast the march as a broadly flowing *cantabile*. If ever there was a love theme, this is it.

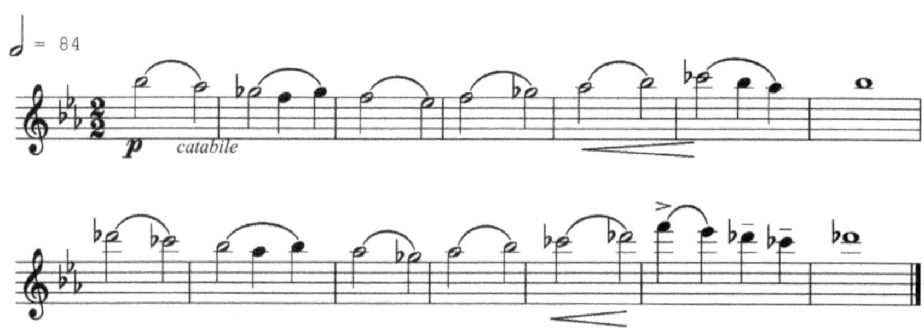

Figure 61 March transformed into love theme

The transformation parallels the transition from the scurrying semi-quavers of the second movement to flowing theme of the *adagio*. However, here it is the menace itself that is transfigured. The faintest enunciation of the Ideal Call has won the enemy over. But not for long. An anguished cry from the violins, marked *con passione*, recalls the insurgent Allegro *appassionato* of the first movement and threatens a new assault. Earlier in the symphony this might have provoked a retreat to the woodlands. Instead the galloping second subject rides to the rescue, with the four horsemen of the horn section in the van. At this point the movement begins to resemble a movie soundtrack, as the march returns in full force at 141. However, its fate in musical terms seems already cast by the four flats of the key signature. We are heading pell-mell towards the home key of A♭. At 146, with only a couple of minutes to go, the Ideal Call returns triumphantly in the horns, punctuated by offbeat blasts from the brass and percussion. Anyone in doubt that we are in the presence of imperial majesty has only to compare the similar treatment of the coronation procession for Henry V at the climax of Elgar's *Falstaff* of 1913.[95] The effect in both cases is not merely conquering but utterly crushing. Insurgency's last charge at figure 149 is quelled by the return of the 'ride to the rescue' music in league with the Ideal Call and all ends in victory. Or does it?

Musicologists marvel that the return to the original key (the tonic) makes such a late appearance. A convention of symphonic composition since the eighteenth century demanded that the key established in the first movement make a decisive return in the last – as illustrated, for example, by the repeated crashing chords that conclude the big Beethoven symphonies. Elgar's Symphony in A♭ is different. Diana McVeagh remarks that 'few symphonies spend so little time in their tonic key'.[96] Still, it does end there. Many contemporaries had already abandoned the convention. 'Elgar', as Harper-Scott observes, 'was almost alone amongst early modernist composers in insisting on a return to a work's opening tonic *regardless of the cost*.'[97] Throughout the first symphony Elgar demonstrates his ability to employ signature techniques of modernism with a dexterity equal to that of the most advanced composers of his time. But he parts company with them by siding with orthodoxy at the end. He thus arrives at a position similar to Haggard, Buchan and the other conservative subjects of this book. Forces of disorder, unreason and rebellion are explored to the fullest extent, but authority must ultimately triumph. Success is achieved at the last possible minute in the face of determined and strangely attractive foes. The effect is to suggest that another fight looms just round the corner – that there can never be a tranquil assurance of effortless superiority. That was precisely the hallmark of Edwardian imperialism.

Conceived as psychological drama, the last movement reiterates the contests of the previous three. The evil march slinks softly into being like a vampire rising from the grave – unkillable, implacable, remorseless. Because it lives within the psyche, its existence is coterminous with the living ego. As section after section of the orchestra falls into step, its seductive, savage power appears overwhelming. This time there will be no escape to the imaginary groves of childhood innocence. Battle is joined directly, with the fortunes swinging now one way, now the other. Psychologically, the climactic moment when the march transforms into a love theme is marvellously ambiguous. Are the insurgents momentarily won over by the love embodied in the Ideal Call? Matthew Riley thinks so:

> In the E♭ minor passage the march reappears transformed – might even say transfigured. The orchestration is luminous and the mood impassioned yet elevated ... If the motto and the march tune can be regarded as 'antagonists' in some kind of drama [!] – an interpretation that the symphony almost irresistibly invites – then the E♭ minor music mediates between them.[98]

Or is this an episode like John Buchan's Davie Crawfurd in Prester John's cave or Haggard's Allan Quatermain doing battle in Kukuanaland, when the temptation to take up the barbarian cause seems utterly irresistible? Freudians would see the contest as ultimately incapable of resolution. Elgar comes close to saying the same thing with his nick-of-time triumph of the conjoined forces of Ideal Call and galloping rescuers – superego and ego engaged in their endless work of id suppression.

How might the movement be interpreted as the final act in a Gordon symphony? It is quite unthinkable that Elgar in 1899 would have concluded such a work with the hero's death. The finale would build a drama around Kitchener's triumph at Omdurman and the clemency of the conquerors. It would make perfect sense to begin with the opposition in charge, as the Mahdists had been in Sudan since 1886, and to have them personified by a malevolent march. The challenge from the Ideal Call sounds, at a distance, like the conscience of Empire awakened to unfinished business. Next we might expect a confident new tune representing Kitchener's regiments, something related but not identical to Gordon's defeated forces. The 'ride to the rescue' music would fit the bill. We might also expect some version of the imperialist's unshakeable fantasy that the hearts and minds of the foes can be truly won – as Caractacus is won over by the Romans in Elgar's cantata. It is hard to imagine a more effective musical rendering of the concept than the transformation of the strutting march into a *cantabile* love theme at the emotional climax of the last movement. The fragility of the moment is exposed by the subsequent reiteration of the march in all its original menace. This must, of course, be answered by a massive surge from the legions of imperial order careering towards their destined victory.

In the end all that can be said is that Symphony No. 1 does everything that might have been expected of a Gordon symphony. If the idea had lived on in Elgar's musical thinking there are good reasons why it would not appear on the title page. A decade had passed since the reconquest of Sudan and Gordon had slipped from the public consciousness. The publication of Lord Cromer's *Modern Egypt* a few months before the symphony's premier in 1908 had turned a cruel new spotlight on the hero's flaws.[99] There was, moreover, the composer's insistence that the symphony without a programme represented the pinnacle of his art. Set against this, we have Jaeger's certainty that there was an undisclosed programme and McVeagh's insight that 'some kind of inner drama works itself out in this Symphony'. With or without Gordon, the symphony realises imperialism in music, as its devotees understood imperialism in the Edwardian era. The Ideal Call existed as an aspiration apart from the sordid politics and grubby warfare that dominated the business of the real-life British Empire. Its triumph was by no means assured, for its enemies were many and formidable. These included not just recalcitrant subject peoples but also the European rivals who had been engaged for the last thirty years in an accelerating arms race. Then there were the internal doubters – pacifists, Little Englanders, Pro-Boers, philanthropic societies and the rest – clamouring for a retreat to the safety of their sceptred isle's green and pleasant land. The discordant insurgencies and menacing marches of the symphony can easily be imagined – as Lady Elgar imagined them – to be any or all of the Empire's enemies. Retreat to a woodland refuge is an ever-present though ultimately futile temptation. Fulfilling the lofty promise of the Ideal Call means rising above the temptation to demonise enemies, to see their common humanity, even to love them, while not losing sight of the distant goal of an empire delivering liberty and justice for all. Or, as Elgar phrased it, 'a wide experience of human life with a great charity (love) and a massive hope in the future'.

Notes

1 www.elgar.org/welcome.htm.

2 J. P. E. Harper-Scott, *Edward Elgar, Modernist* (Cambridge: Cambridge University Press, 2006), p. 18.

3 Jeffrey Richards, *Imperialism and Music: Britain 1876–1953* (Manchester: Manchester University Press, 2001), pp. 44–6. This a judgement echoed by Charles McGuire; 'Functional music: imperialism, the great war, and Elgar as popular composer', in Daniel M. Grimley and Julian Rushton (eds), *The Cambridge Companion to Elgar* (Cambridge: Cambridge University Press, 2004), p. 214.

4 Jerrold Northrup Moore, *Edward Elgar: A Creative Life* (Oxford: Oxford University Press, 1984), p. 246.

5 Robert Anderson, *Elgar* (London: J. M. Dent, 1993), p. 39.

6 Moore, *Edward Elgar*, p. 120.
7 Percy Young, *Elgar O.M.: A Study of a Musician*, 2nd edn (London: White Lion, 1973), p. 61.
8 Percy Young (ed.), *Letters of E. Elgar and Other Writings* (London: Geoffrey Bles, 1956), p. xvii.
9 Anderson, *Elgar*, p. 46.
10 Jaeger to Elgar, 7 November 1899, Elgar Manuscripts 705: 445, Box 23, Worcester Record Office, UK.
11 Richard Morrison, 'Conducting Elgar', in N. Kenyon (intro.), *Elgar: An Anniversary Portrait* (London: Continuum Books, 2007), p. 133.
12 Moore, *Edward Elgar*, p. 358; Ian Parrott, *Elgar* (London: Dent, 1971), p. 31.
13 William H. Reed, *Elgar as I Knew Him* (London: Victor Gollancz, 1936), p. 21.
14 Edward Elgar, *A Future for English Music and Other Lectures*, ed. by Percy Young (London: Dennis Dobson, 1968); Young, *Elgar O.M.*, p. 129; Moore, *Edward Elgar*, p. 480.
15 Young, *Elgar O.M.*, p. 129; H. W. Davies to Elgar, 12 November 1908, Elgar Manuscripts 705: 445, Box 6, parcel xi, Worcester Record Office: 'Jaeger thinks the 1st symphony has a programme. Does it?'
16 Diana McVeagh, *Elgar the Music Maker* (Woodbridge, Suffolk: Boydell, 2007), pp. 120–1.
17 Matthew Riley, *Edward Elgar and the Nostalgic Imagination* (Cambridge: Cambridge University Press, 2007), p. 20.
18 David Cox, 'Edward Elgar', in Robert Simpson (ed.), *The Symphony, Vol. II: Mahler to the Present Day* (New York: Drake Publishers Inc., 1972), p. 20.
19 Richards, *Imperialism and Music*, p. 67.
20 McVeagh, *Elgar the Music Maker*, p. 120.
21 Moore, *Edward Elgar*, pp. 519–20; McVeagh, *Elgar the Music Maker*, p. 120.
22 Anderson, *Elgar*, p. 84.
23 Moore, *Edward Elgar*, p. 523.
24 Parrott, *Elgar*, p. 69. Aidan Thompson spotted another quotation from *Parsifal* in 'Elgar and chivalry', *19th-Century Music* 28 (2005), 262. See also Harper-Scott, *Edward Elgar, Modernist*, pp. 70, 188–9.
25 Young, *Elgar O.M.*, p. 68.
26 Charles Chenevix Trench, *The Road to Khartoum: A Life of General Charles Gordon* (New York: Carroll & Graf, 1989), pp. 36–42.
27 Richard Davenport-Hines, 'Gordon, Charles George (1833–1885)', *Oxford Dictionary of National Biography*, Oxford University Press, 2004; online edn, January 2008 (www.oxforddnb.com/view/article/11029, accessed 14 January 2011).
28 Trench, *Road to Khartoum*, pp. 72–83.
29 Quoted in ibid., p. 166.
30 Ibid., pp. 163, 165–8, 172–8.
31 C. G. Gordon, *Letters of General C. G. Gordon to His Sister M. A. Gordon* (London: Macmillan, 1902), p. 50.
32 Ibid., p. 103.
33 Analysed with unparalleled clarity in R. Robinson, J. Gallagher and A. Denny, *Africa and the Victorians* (London: Macmillan, 1961), chapter 5.
34 *Pall Mall Gazette* (9 January 1884).
35 Davenport-Hines, 'Gordon'.
36 Lord Cromer, *Modern Egypt*, 2 vols (London: Macmillan, 1908), 1:429n.
37 'Leur Gordon est un idiot', quoted in Lytton Strachey, *Eminent Victorians* (London: Echo Library, 2006), p. 171.
38 John Buchan, 'Gordon at Khartoum', in *Men and Deeds* (London: Peter Davies, 1935), p. 219.
39 Cromer, *Modern Egypt*, 1:457.
40 A. Egmont Hake (ed.), *The Journals of Major-Gen. C. G. Gordon, C. B., at Kartoum* (London: Kegan Paul, Trench, & Co., 1885), p. 40.
41 Removed to Victoria Embankment in the 1940s.

42 20 October 1898; Anderson, *Elgar*, p. 39.
43 Quoted in Riley, *Elgar and the Nostalgic Imagination*, p. 149; see also p. 144. Harper-Scott shows the same misunderstanding of the anxious character of *fin-de-siècle* British imperialism when he cites as evidence of Elgar's shaky commitment to the cause the composer's colouring of his most imperial moments 'by a flighty kind of ambiguity that is not always possible to resolve'; *Edward Elgar, Modernist*, p. 17. The same ambiguity will be found in the most resolute imperialists of the time because they shared a keen awareness of the fragility of the enterprise.
44 Bernard Porter, *The Lion's Share: A Short History of British Imperialism, 1850–1970* (London: Longman, 1975), p. 119.
45 Richards, *Imperialism and Music*, p. 53.
46 Harper-Scott, *Edward Elgar, Modernist*, p. 18.
47 On Alice Elgar's conversion, see Charles Edward McGuire, 'Measure of a man: catechizing Elgar's Catholic avatars', in Byron Adams (ed.), *Edward Elgar and his World* (Princeton, NJ: Princeton University Press, 2007), p. 22.
48 Correspondence with Governor L. Robyn of Sierra Leone, Nov. 1907, Box 6, Elgar Manuscripts 705: 445, Worcester Record Office; Young, *Elgar O.M.*, p. 171; Moore, *Edward Elgar*, pp. 550.
49 Young, *Elgar O.M.*, p. 73.
50 Moore, *Edward Elgar*, p. 518.
51 Ibid., p. 664.
52 Ibid., pp. 668–9, 682, 687.
53 Anderson, *Elgar*, p. 157.
54 Ibid., p. 163.
55 Moore, *Edward Elgar*, p. 244.
56 Young, *Elgar O.M.*, p. 94. For the most nuanced and insightful comparison with Kipling, see Richards, *Imperialism and Music*, pp. 51–2.
57 Moore, *Edward Elgar*, p. 338.
58 Quoted in McGuire, 'Functional music', p. 221.
59 Young (ed.), *Letters of E. Elgar*, p. 55.
60 Moore, *Edward Elgar*, p. 339.
61 Ibid., p. 457.
62 Buchan, 'Gordon at Khartoum', p. 235.
63 Elgar to Jaeger, 1 March 1898, quoted in Moore, *Edward Elgar*, p. 233.
64 For a most insightful analysis of *Crown of India*, see Nalini Ghuman, 'Elgar and the British Raj: can the Mughals march?' in Adams (ed.), *Edward Elgar and His World*, pp. 249–85; also McGuire, 'Functional music', p. 217. This contrasts with an older view of Elgar set in opposition to musical orientalism; see J. M. MacKenzie, *Orientalism: History, Theory and the Arts* (Manchester: Manchester University Press, 1995), p. 138.
65 Michael Allis, 'Elgar and the art of retrospective narrative', *Journal of Musicological Research* 19 (2000), 289–328; Riley, *Elgar and the Nostalgic Imagination*, chs 1, 2 and 5.
66 Anderson, *Elgar*, p. 331.
67 Letter to Ernest Newman quoted in Anderson, *Elgar*, p. 321.
68 Quoted in Davenport-Hines, 'Gordon'.
69 Joseph Conrad, *Heart of Darkness and Other Tales*, ed. by Cedric Watts (Oxford: Oxford University Press, 1990), pp. 140–1.
70 Moore, *Edward Elgar*, p. 520.
71 Harper-Scott, *Edward Elgar, Modernist*, pp. 67–8, 88.
72 McVeagh, *Elgar the Music Maker*, pp. 121–2.
73 Julian Rushton, 'In search of the symphony: orchestral music to 1908', in Grimley and Rushton (eds), *The Cambridge Companion to Elgar*, p. 150.
74 Anderson, *Elgar*, p. 322.
75 James Hepokoski, 'Elgar', in D. Kern Holoman (ed.), *The Nineteenth-Century Symphony* (New York: Shirmer Books, 1997), p. 334.
76 Moore, *Edward Elgar*, p. 643.

77 Ibid., p. 308.
78 Riley, *Elgar and the Nostalgic Imagination*, pp. 111–12.
79 See ibid., p. 18: 'Elgar's characteristic manner of preparing and leaving his reminiscences suggests a split between inner and outer spheres of consciousness, a split that is usually not healed in the course of a work.' Again, on p. 20 Riley notes that 'although his idyllic memories are treated fondly, in many cases they are exposed as either unreal or unattainable, and the final impression they leave is not comforting but disturbing or uncanny [in the Freudian sense]'.
80 Anderson, *Elgar*, p. 321.
81 Young, *Elgar O.M.*, p. 191.
82 Parallels with Freudian thought of the era are briefly noted in Moore, *Edward Elgar*, p. 596.
83 Rushton, 'In search of the symphony', p. 151.
84 Moore, *Edward Elgar*, p. 546.
85 Hepokoski, 'Elgar', p. 332.
86 Riley, *Elgar and the Nostalgic Imagination*, pp. 90–1.
87 Quoted in Anderson, *Elgar*, p. 326.
88 Quoted in ibid., p. 328.
89 Cromer, *Modern Egypt*, 1:461.
90 Ibid., 463–4.
91 Jeff Guy, *the Destruction of the Zulu Kingdom* (London: Longman, 1979), p. 151.
92 From *Barrack Room Ballads*, in Rudyard Kipling, *Rudyard Kipling's Verse: Definitive Edition* (London: Hodder & Stoughton, 1940), pp. 400–1.
93 Speaking of *Caractacus* and *King Olaf* in *Elgar and the Nostalgic Imagination*, p. 155.
94 Quoted in Young, *Elgar O.M.*, p. 191.
95 *Falstaff*, at figure 127.
96 McVeagh, *Elgar the Music Maker*, p. 122.
97 J. P. E. Harper-Scott, 'Elgar's invention of the human: *Falstaff*, opus 68', *19th-Century Music* 28 (2005), 249–50.
98 Riley, *Elgar and the Nostalgic Imagination*, p. 44.
99 Earl Cromer had been plain Evelyn Baring during his dealings with Gordon. His memoir, *Modern Egypt*, appeared in March; Elgar's symphony, in December of 1908.

CHAPTER SIX

John Buchan and the loathly opposite

John Buchan mixed art and politics to a greater extent than any British writer between Disraeli and Jeffrey Archer. As he rose in public life from Lord Milner's staff in South Africa (1901–03) to become Britain's wartime Director of Information (1916–18), a Tory MP and eventually Lord Tweedsmuir of Elsfield, governor-general of Canada (1935–40), he produced a stream of best-selling novels with explicit political content. His life and work provide a rare opportunity for studying the eternally vexing problem of locating ideas in the hierarchy of historical causes. Buchan's detractors attack the novels for actively propagating unsavoury and outmoded creeds: the capitalist cult of success, the Empire, patriotism, racism, fresh air, cold baths and Playing the Game.[1] His admirers insist he was by no means a simple-minded reactionary, that he reflected rather than moulded the prejudices of his era, and that in any case his politics are irrelevant to his literary achievement.[2] Neither position is sustainable. John Buchan's political novels are too complex to be fairly described as either the propaganda or the mirror of the generation of British Tories who witnessed both the Scramble for Africa and the Battle of Britain. On the other hand, he lacked the genius of the romance writers whose success he sought to emulate, especially Haggard, Kipling and Conrad.

In the twenty-first century Buchan's work has been perceptively studied for its exposition of 'whiteness', both in the concept of the 'white man' as a type of imperial masculinity and of 'white man's country' as a project in African colonialism.[3] His principal interest for me lies in the test case his novels supply for the hypothesis that the project of Empire reverberated sympathetically with psychoanalytic concepts of the divided self. Nearly twenty years younger than Elgar and Haggard, he first encountered the ideas of Freud when his views on life and politics were still evolving. Soon he was writing them into his novels and relating them to what he saw as a psycho-social crisis in Western civilisation.

Buchan's novels deserve serious attention not only for their demonstration of the impact of fashionable psychological concepts upon modern political discourse but also for the political linkages they disclose between the late-Victorian novel of imperial adventure and the twentieth-century spy thriller. In a literary way they illustrate Rosa Luxemburg's diagnostic comment on imperialism as a stage of economic development.

> What distinguishes imperialism as the last struggle for capitalist world domination is ... the return of the decisive struggle for expansion from those areas which are being fought over back to its home countries. In this way imperialism brings catastrophe as a mode of existence back from the periphery of capitalist development to its point of departure.[4]

Buchan frankly acknowledged his intention to imitate the previous generation of imperial romancers. A young innkeeper who shelters the fleeing hero Richard Hannay in *The Thirty-Nine Steps* (1915) confesses his ambition to 'see life, to travel the world, and write things like Kipling and Conrad'. His reaction to Hannay's tale of his own recent perils is, 'By Gods ... it is all pure Rider Haggard and Conan Doyle'.[5] After an exploration of the imperial adventure yarn in *Prester John*, Buchan specialised in spy thrillers, taking up the idea propounded by Kipling in *Kim* that when a man becomes aware of the alternative personalities hidden in his own bosom, he acquires a permanent identity problem. At the same time, his ability to assume many masks makes him the ideal spy to send into the polyglot underworld of a potentially rebellious empire. Conrad also pointed the way towards Buchan's spies. Recoiling from practical imperialism because of its perpetual tendency to wake up the horrors lurking in the dark corners of European souls, he brought Kipling's spy home in *The Secret Agent* to confront anarchists and diplomats working to awaken those same horrors in ostensibly civilised countries.

In a fictional symposium on imperialism written in 1906 Buchan explicitly set out the theory that linked him to Conrad, Kipling and Haggard, and which would be the foundation of his own fiction for many years to come. A Cecil Rhodes-like multi-millionaire invites a select group of opinion-makers to his East African lodge. A passage wonderfully reminiscent of Haggard's bird's-eye views tells how, from the top of a nearby mountain, 'we saw the kingdoms of the earth spread out beneath us'. One of the guests at this exclusive gathering expounds an aesthetic theory he calls 'romanticism', whose 'central doctrine' is that 'truth, virtue, happiness, all the ideals' are 'attained by a clash of opposites'.[6] All human beings are 'a strange compound' who can never reach 'full stature by starving certain parts of ... nature of their due'. Imperialism, with its clash of opposites – civilisation and barbarism, brain and brawn, East and West – is analogous to the human soul in this cloudy neo-Hegelian conception. To make his meaning clearer Buchan offered one of his favourite inventions, the story of the upright Victorian statesman with an extraordinary secret life. In public, Sir Charles Weston was the supporter of missionary societies, peace and liberal reform. In his private fantasies, however, he was Emperor of Byzantium, warlike, cruel and lustful. For every virtue he espoused in the House of Commons there was an equal and opposing dream of vice. On the day on which he wrote in his official diary, 'Every war – I do not care what its pretext – must be a blunder in statesmanship and a sin against the Most High', he wrote in his secret diary: 'It is the evening of the greatest day in my life. The blood is crusted over my eyes, my left arm is crippled, and I am caked in dust. A quarter of my men are slain, but the enemy have been ground between the millstones.'[7]

Buchan called his invention 'an allegory true of us all'. It first appears in a short story published in 1905 ('The Kings of Orion') and is developed in many subsequent variations. Buchan makes several points with his 'allegory' of the alter ego. First, on a superficial level it is both humorous and satisfying for him to imagine that inside every smug, self-righteous anti-imperialist there is a warlike, domineering Tory crying to be unleashed. In the second place, Buchan uses the idea to express his awareness that his own political opinions are based on something other than pure reason. Commenting on the effects of a personality-changing drug in 'A Lucid Interval', he observes that 'the drug did not create new opinions but elicited those which had hitherto lain dormant. Every man has a creed but in his soul he knows that that creed has another side, possibly no less logical, which it does not suit him to produce.'[8]

The third point Buchan makes with his 'allegory' is that popular with social Darwinists who supported imperialism – that the urges to fight, to kill, to dominate are basic human instincts beneficial to progress and in any case impossible to suppress.[9] By identifying this view of the psyche with his 'new conception of empire', Buchan suggests that the real purpose of imperialism is psychological – a release for domineering impulses that happily benefit those who are dominated. By postulating that the most upright and controlled personality has somewhere a written or unwritten secret diary of subversive fantasies, he also makes a comment on himself. Like many other literary imperialists, John Buchan was an incredibly disciplined personality. He was a man who always dressed for dinner, never missed appointments and finished his work ahead of schedule. He invariably wore a tie that he would never loosen, even when encouraged by his wife and daughter to let a little sun fall on his neck for the sake of his health.[10] The disjunction between his reserved public persona and his dashing fiction invites the conclusion that he used fiction as an outlet for the anxieties and risky impulses he suppressed in every other part of his life. But precisely because Buchan knew what he was doing – as his story of the Emperor of Byzantium plainly shows – it is difficult to specify the content of his own secret fantasies. What he does again and again is to emphasise the existence rather than to reveal the character of an inner self. He takes it for granted that this inner self is a Pandora's box of evil or amoral impulses that ought to remain closed.

Buchan's first South African novel, *Prester John*, is a good example of the format he employed to dramatise his psychological theory. The entire story depends for its effect on the audience's willingness to identify the African with the inner self of the European – to picture the black man as all id and no superego.[11] As a lad in Scotland, Davie Crawfurd witnesses the strange, terrifying spectacle of a black seminary student from South Africa secretly performing heathen rites on a secluded beach. A few years later Crawfurd himself moves to South Africa to seek his fortune by running a rural store. By this time the black seminarian has become the Reverend John Laputa, celebrated for Christian piety and oratorical genius. Not a great deal happens for the first two hundred pages of the book, but an atmosphere of menace grows and darkens. Vague rumours of large-scale diamond thefts by African miners circulate in the back country, but a conspiracy of silence prevents even Captain Jim Arcoll, the famous bush detective and master of disguise, from learning anything very useful. A brush with a nasty 'Portugoose' half-breed who deals in 'illicit' diamonds puts young Crawfurd on the scent that leads him eventually to the secret cave in the hidden valley where Laputa has gathered thousands of followers in preparation for a rebellion. 'Naked as when he was born', Laputa harangues a multitude of Africans; they too are 'naked or all but naked'.[12]

In the darkness of the cave Davie miraculously escapes detection and undergoes initiation rites. He is nearly overpowered by an urge to join the magnificently Satanic Laputa in his rebellion.

> My mind was mesmerized by this amazing man. I could not refrain from shouting with the rest. Indeed I was a convert, if there can be conversion when the emotions are dominant and there is no assent from the brain. I had a mad desire to be of Laputa's party. Or rather, I longed for a leader who should master me and make my soul his own, as this man mastered his followers.[13]

Laputa's attraction lies not just in his splendid body and masterful manner. He preaches a seductive political message: 'he told tales of white infamy, lands snatched from their rightful possessors, unjust laws which forced the Ethiopian to the bondage of a despised caste, the finger of scorn everywhere, and the mocking word.' Just in time Davie manages to remember his duty and steals the necklace that Laputa requires to maintain magico-religious authority over his followers. Although Davie is discovered and pursued across difficult terrain, he succeeds in hiding the necklace before falling prey to exhaustion and illness. Rescued and brought back to civilisation, he lies comatose for days. In this condition he dreams of Laputa's lair and, after regaining consciousness, secures his capture.

In skeletal outline, the formula of *Prester John* is as follows. First, the hero is menaced by vague and mysterious forces that threaten not only him but the entire social order. The leader of the menacing forces is eventually revealed as a villain of superhuman cunning who is able to pose as a respectable member of society. In order to triumph the hero must venture into the villain's wild and lawless terrain. There the hero experiences an almost irresistible urge to join his adversary, as well as a period of prolonged unconscious delirium. Only after he has passed through this period of temptation and unconsciousness can he join forces with the agents of law and order to secure a final victory. That victory is not only a victory over the enemies of constituted authority; it is a victory over his own unconscious rebellious impulses. This formula gives a powerful dramatic presentation of the theory of the split personality that Buchan had expounded statically in his 'allegory' of the Emperor of Byzantium.

It is not incidental, but of the utmost significance, that Buchan gives an overtly political content to his allegory. There is hardly a white South African prejudice that *Prester John* does not invoke in one way or another. Laputa's clandestine rites reinforce the common belief that heathen savagery lurks just below the surface of black Christianity. The ability of the Africans to maintain a strict conspiratorial silence about their planned rebellion reinforces the proverb that 'you never know what they're really thinking' and the conviction that an efficient secret police (Captain Jim Arcoll and his staff) is essential to prevent a general rising. The evil 'Portugoose' and the partly white Laputa represent the perils of miscegenation and at the same time explain the presence of intelligence and leadership ability in Negroid skulls. Though Buchan raises Laputa to Miltonic proportions for certain purposes of his own, the picture drawn of him is by no means incompatible with the legendary 'big buck nigger' (a phrase that Buchan, like Conrad, could use without embarrassment). He is huge, cunning, potent, nearly irresistible. The diamonds that make Laputa's rebellion possible are not leftovers from *King Solomon's Mines*; they are stolen by workers in the pits of the De Beers monopoly that Cecil Rhodes built. Jim Arcoll and his secret police stumble upon rumours of rebellion in the course of their ordinary job of tracking down 'illicit diamonds'. After Laputa' s downfall the diamonds are returned to the monopoly and a vocational school is established to ensure that in the future talented Africans will not be over-educated as Laputa had been. Support for white racism goes hand in hand with support for white capitalism.

While Buchan's purpose in writing *Prester John* had been to rework his allegory rather than to promote white domination in southern Africa, the result of his labours was the creation of a metaphor of evident utility to conservative forces. It directly equated the struggle of the conscious outward self to maintain control of inward evil impulses with the struggle of constituted political and economic authority to maintain dominion over rebellious elements in society. This equation was also of tremendous utility to Buchan personally. It explained and justified his iron self-control, his over-developed sense of decorum. It excused his espousal of Tory political positions in controversies where he knew the other side had the better arguments. It reverberated sympathetically with the Calvinist orthodoxy of his father's church, whose other tenets Buchan had mostly abandoned. At the same time it must be recognised as a new idea not attributable to Buchan's early environment or the persistence of Victorian attitudes. Although composed of hoary assumptions – the beast within, the survival of atavistic instincts, the innate emotionalism of black men – it combined them to enunciate a characteristically twentieth-century concept.

When Buchan published his next novel five years later he raised the political stakes in the contest between good and evil by making the peace and freedom of the whole civilised world hang on the strength of a single man. In *The Thirty-Nine Steps* a gang of German spies hopes to precipitate a world war by assassinating the Greek premier on his visit to London. An American journalist who uncovers elements of their plan is found out by them and killed just after taking refuge in the apartment of Richard Hannay, a wealthy mining engineer just returned from South Africa. Hannay manages to retain the journalist's encoded notebook and as a result becomes the object of a double pursuit. The gang want the notebook and the police blame Hannay for the corpse in his apartment. By fleeing to the wilds of Scotland and adopting a bewildering succession of disguises he succeeds in evading capture long enough to decode the notebook and convince a cabinet minister to go after the gang.

Despite the change of venue Buchan had no difficulty in repeating his familiar structure. The hero is pitted against forces of evil who masquerade as respectable members of society. To defeat them he must lose his own status and identity in a savage landscape beyond the reach of the law. He must also pass through a period of sickness and delirium (in this case a spot of the old malaria) and resist a nearly overpowering impulse to join his arch-enemy:

> There was something weird and devilish in those eyes, cold, malignant, unearthly, and most hellishly clever. They fascinated me like the bright eyes of a snake. I had a strong impulse to throw myself on his mercy and offer to join his side, and if you consider the way I felt about the whole thing you will see that that impulse must have been purely physical, the weakness of a brain mesmerized and mastered by a stronger spirit.[14]

This particular villain has been supposed by some to be Jewish because of an important speech made to Hannay by the doomed American:

> I am giving you what he told me as well as I could make it out. Away behind all the Governments and the armies there was a big subterranean movement going on, engineered by very dangerous people … I gathered that most of the people in it were the sort of educated anarchists that make revolutions, but that beside them there were financiers who were playing for money. A clever man can make big profits on a falling market, and it suited the book of both classes to set Europe by the ears.
>
> He told me some queer things that explained a lot that had puzzled me – things that happened in the Balkan War, how one state suddenly came out on top, why certain men disappeared, and where the sinews of war came from. The aim of the whole conspiracy was to get Russia and Germany at logger-heads.
>
> When I asked why, he said that the anarchist lot thought it would give them their chance. Everything would be in the melting-pot, and they looked to see a new world emerge. The capitalists would rake in the shekels, and make fortunes by buying up wreckage. Capital, he said, had no conscience and no fatherland. Besides the Jew was behind it, and the Jew hated Russia worse than hell.
>
> 'Do you wonder?' he cried. 'For three hundred years they have been persecuted, and this is the return match for the pogroms. The Jew is everywhere, but you have to go far down the backstairs to find it … if you're on the biggest kind of job and are bound to get to the real boss, ten to one you are brought up against a little white-faced Jew in a bath chair with an eye like a rattlesnake. Yes sir, he is the man who is ruling the world just now'.[15]

With respect to Buchan's alleged anti-Semitism there are several observations to be made on this passage. First, it is not Buchan nor even his hero, Hannay, who makes the statement. The second observation is that the only resemblance between the villain of the *Thirty-Nine Steps* and the 'Jew in the bath chair' is the snake-like eye; the man is later identified as a German Junker, the Graf von Schwabing. Third, the fiends behind this particular conspiracy are eventually revealed to be neither financiers nor anarchists; they are agents of Kaiser Bill.

Nevertheless, after all this has been said in fairness to Buchan, the fact remains that the idea of the alliance between Jewish high finance and anarchic, destructive elements in society exercised a continuing fascination for him. The fascination is all the more noteworthy because of the steadfast support he gave to Jews in his public and private life. In 1900 Buchan put the idea in the mouth of the villain in *The Half-Hearted* who proposed to cure the 'sickness' in British society by bankrupting the 'whole gang of Jew speculators and vulgarians who would corrupt a great country'.[16] The idea crops up again in *The Three Hostages* (1923). A gang of criminal profiteers (not specifically identified as Jewish) promotes strikes and revolutions in order to reap huge speculative profits: 'These fellows were wreckers on the grand scale, merchants of pessimism, giving society another kick downhill whenever it had a chance of finding its balance, and then pocketing their profits.'[17] In the early 1930s the idea is still at the centre of Buchan's novel *A Prince of the Captivity*: 'the dictation of masters who were thinking only of their bank balances to a poor devil who was responsible for millions of suffering human beings.'[18]

Precisely because the idea of the Jewish-capitalist conspiracy sits oddly in a writer who showed every sign of cordiality to both Jews and capitalists, the place of this idea in Buchan's work needs to be pinned down. Historians of imperialism will recognise in this conspiracy idea a weirdly distorted version of the economic theory of imperialism popularised in England by J. A. Hobson and Buchan's old classmate at Glasgow University, H. N. Brailsford. In fact, the blame put on capital, with 'no conscience and no fatherland', for 'things that happened in the Balkan war, how one state suddenly came out on top' and 'where the sinews of war came from', is strongly reminiscent of Brailsford's *War of Steel and Gold*, which appeared just a year before the *Thirty-Nine Steps*. But the idea that the titans of finance capital might be leagued together with anarchists or Bolsheviks would have impressed Hobson and Brailsford as the wildest of economic absurdities. They regarded capital's interests in armaments and international tensions as obstacles, not aids, to the reformation of society. It is on this point that a simple-minded Marxist case for Buchan as the apologist of capitalism (a case that can otherwise be very plausibly made) will break down. It was no service to big business to spread the belief that powerful financiers made money from destructive, anti-social activities and would wreck civilisation itself if there were profits to be made in the enterprise.[19]

One plausible explanation for Buchan's constant reiteration of this crazy inversion of the theory of economic imperialism is that it followed logically from his psychology rather than his politics. His allegory of the Emperor of Byzantium implied that every civilised being harbours within himself a powerful alter ego desiring nothing less than the inversion of all civilised values. The alter ego, because it is another aspect of the same person, is no howling werewolf, but a being possessed of the same appearance, manners and powers of reasoning as the outward man. Like Stevenson's Hyde, he is accepted as a gentleman in society. The more talented, rich and imaginative the outward man is in his public career, the more talented, resourceful and imaginative the hidden alter ego will be in his schemes for vice. When Buchan translated this theory into political terms, he identified the conservative top stratum of existing society with the decent, well-behaved individual who is suppressing the evil within himself. This metaphor, if pursued with relentless logic, carries the implication that there are elements working for the revolutionary subversion of the status quo who are indistinguishable in manners and appearance from the most respected, honoured national leaders. The imperatives of his literary conceit – not a slavish, snobbish obsession with success – led Buchan to make top people the protagonists of his stories. Laputa is the least typical of his villains, not only because he is black but because his greatest claim to respectability is his position as an African church leader. Almost all the rest are extremely wealthy men who belong to the most exclusive clubs and dine regularly with cabinet ministers. Lunatic though it may be as political economy, it is a perfectly reasonable deduction from Buchan's fundamental premises.

If it is treated seriously as a call for political action, it appears to advocate a permanent police state apparatus to maintain the existing order. In this respect Buchan bears out the turn-of-the-century fears of J. A. Hobson that habits of autocracy learned abroad would subvert freedom and democracy at home. This type of literature makes a powerful appeal to imaginations hoping to be confirmed in their belief that the enemy is within. When a villainous gang is exposed in *The Three Hostages*, its tentacles are shown to have reached into every corner of the establishment on two continents. The final police dragnet, which is beyond parody, catches: a gentleman in Mayfair; the directors of a Spanish copper company; 'a certain French count of royalist proclivities'; a pious Presbyterian accountant in Glasgow; 'decorous bankers in Genoa'; 'more than one pretty dancer' and 'several fashionable actresses'; an American senator; four members of the French

Chamber of Deputies; 'a mining magnate in Westphalia'; and a 'Prince of the Church' from Rome. This ending demonstrates unquestionably that Buchan selected his villains without respect to race, sex, religion or national origin. Their only common characteristic is inordinate success in life. Jews and non-Jews are allowed to figure as villains (or heroes) *only* if they first qualify as very important people.

There was, however, one other commonly alleged characteristic of Jews that Buchan found useful in his fiction. That was their reputation as rootless wanderers endowed with the chameleon's ability to take on a protective local colouring. In *Greenmantle* (1916) Hannay contrasts the German's abysmal insensitivity with the talents of the adaptable Jew. 'In Germany', he observes, 'only the Jew can get outside himself, and that is why, if you look into the matter, you will find, that a Jew is at the back of most German enterprises.'[20] To the ordinary anti-Semitic nationalist of Buchan's day the notion of the mutable man was an abomination because such a man lacked the supposedly fixed national characteristics that constituted the sole legitimate claim to citizenship. But Buchan needed the notion of the mutable man to make his literary format work. Moreover, as a Scot who had succeeded in reaching the stratospheric reaches of the English upper class, he personally identified with the man who could adapt himself at will to new surroundings. He once gave a speech at a Jewish fund-raising dinner in which he drew numerous parallels between Jews and Scots. The same parallels are often drawn in his novels and laid the basis for the creation of perhaps his most distinctive character, Sandy Arbuthnot, a man spectacularly adept at 'getting outside of himself' and 'into the skin' of other people – the skill Buchan often singles out as particularly found in Jews. 'We call ourselves insular', Hannay muses, 'but the truth is that we are the only race on earth that can produce men capable of getting inside the skin of remote peoples. Perhaps the Scots are better than the English, but we're all a thousand per cent better than anyone else. Sandy was the wandering Scot carried to the pitch of genius.'[21] Though he sometimes talks a silly public school slang ('Oh my sainted aunt'; 'Oh, well done our side'), Sandy is a mysterious, brooding character better known on the Baluchistan frontier than in Mayfair. For information on his doings 'you must consult very different authorities' from *Who's Who*:

> you will hear of him at little forgotten fishing ports where the Albanian mountains dip to the Adriatic. If you struck a Mecca pilgrimage the odds are you would meet a dozen of Sandy's friends in it. In shepherd's huts in the Caucasus you will find bits of his castoff clothing, for he has a knack of shedding garments as he goes. In the caravanserais of Bokhara and Samarkand he is known, and there are shikaris in the Pamirs who still speak of him round their fires.[22]

His ability to adopt different disguises, speak different languages and pretend to espouse alien values exceeds Hannay's and makes him the Empire's most valued secret agent. He alone is able to move into the netherest reaches of the underworld without passing through the obligatory period of sick delirium or drugged unconsciousness that Buchan imposes on all his other heroes.

What is more, Sandy dices with the devil on equal terms. In *The Three Hostages* he uses his knowledge of the arcane works of a fifteenth-century Scottish wizard to expose the villain masquerading as a Tory parliamentarian. When Buchan reworked the ending of Conrad's *Victory* in his novel *The Island of Sheep*, he added Sandy (as an infiltrator) to Conrad's fiendish trio of devil, feline cut-throat and ape-man. Sandy's reply to Hannay's query concerning his whereabouts during the previous few weeks is the reply of Conrad's 'Plain Mr. Jones' to Heist: 'Going to and fro on the earth.'[23] With the invention of Sandy, Buchan had stretched his psychological metaphor to its limits. This wandering Scot, this endlessly mutable man, so resembles the devils of Buchan's thrillers as to be indistinguishable from them for long periods. He points the way to the favourite conceit of mid-twentieth-century spy novels that in the murky world of counter-intelligence work the agents of both sides resemble each other more than they resemble ordinary human beings.

In each of the novels in which he appears, Sandy is a working agent of the enemy whose ultimate allegiance to the right side is only confirmed at the very last minute. His assignment in *Greenmantle* is to infiltrate a German plot aimed at raising an Arab revolt against the Turks. He acts the part of a Near Eastern necromancer so well that the Germans choose him to impersonate the false prophet who is to begin the jihad. He is adept enough at magic to cast a potent spell over Richard Hannay, with the help of wraith-like assistants who call themselves 'The Companions of the Rosy Hours'.

> In an instant I found myself reft away from the present with its dull dangers, and looking at a world all young and fresh and beautiful … I was looking at my first youth. I was feeling the kind of immortal light-heartedness which only a boy knows in the dawning of his days. I had no longer any fear of these magic makers. They were kindly wizards who had brought me into fairyland.
>
> Slowly, very slowly it changed … There was no mistake about its meaning now. All the daintiness and youth had fled, and passion was beating in the air – terrible, savage passion, which belonged neither to day nor night, life nor death, but to the half-world between them. I suddenly felt the dancers as monstrous, inhuman, devilish. The thick scents that floated from the brazier seemed to have the tang of new-shed blood … I now realized that these Companions of the Rosy Hours were the only thing in the world to fear.[24]

This trance is virtually identical to the states of unconsciousness or delirium that Buchan's heroes pass through in other books. First comes a tranquilised passage to early childhood, then a nightmarish compound of savage passion, the scent of fresh blood and other terrors too awful to mention. Any man who can induce it is obviously no ordinary mortal. And although he may ultimately side with the angels it is clear that his power to save the day derives from his ability to turn the devil's own weapons against him. Significantly, the greatest of these weapons is psychological warfare – brainwashing.

The final stage in development of his overarching metaphor was his translation of it into the terminology of psychoanalysis. It was inevitable that a well-read man who could write so graphic an account of a descent via unconsciousness to forgotten childhood joys and terrors would sooner or later stumble across psychoanalytic theory and recognise the similarity between its postulates and his own ideas, first enunciated in the allegory of the Emperor of Byzantium and then developed with increasing complexity in his novels.

Intriguingly, Buchan's first encounter with Freudian theory seems to have been a clinical one. In 1912 he developed a duodenal ulcer that failed to respond to any of the usual treatments and which continued to plague him for the rest of his life. Eventually someone suggested that the illness might have a psychological basis and advised a visit to 'a world-famous Continental psychiatrist, a man noted for tracing such physical ailments as duodenal ulcers to psychic disorders in the patient'. One of Buchan's friends reports that he 'submitted himself to examination and was long closeted with the specialist. The verdict? "Never in my experience have I met anybody less frustrated or less crippled by inhibitions. He is free from neuroses. His trouble must be wholly of physical origin."'[25]

Whether or not this is a fair account of the psychiatrist's report – it has been seized upon by one of Buchan's shriller defenders as definitive proof that he was not a latent homosexual – the visit introduced Buchan to the ideas of Freud, whom he later praised in his autobiography as one of the very few twentieth-century thinkers who had 'opened up new avenues of thought'.[26]

As soon as Buchan grasped the rudiments of psychoanalytic theory he worked them into his fiction. The first of the postwar Richard Hannay novels opens with a Dr Greenslade instructing Hannay in the bearing of the subconscious on the writing of thrillers:

> 'Every doctor nowadays has got to be a bit of a mental pathologist. As I say, you can hardly take anything for granted, and if you want detective stories that are not childish fantasy, you'll have to invent a new kind. Better try your hand, Dick.'

> 'Not I. I'm a lover of sober facts.'
>
> 'But, hang it, man, the facts are no longer sober. Take all this chatter about psycho-analysis. There's nothing very new in the doctrine, but people are beginning to work it out into details, and making considerable asses of themselves in the process. It's an awful thing when a scientific theory becomes the quarry of the half-baked. But as I say, the fact of the subconscious self is as certain as the existence of lungs and arteries.'
>
> 'I don't believe that Dick has any subconscious self,' said Mary.
>
> 'Oh yes he has. Only, people who have led his kind of life have their ordinary self so well managed and disciplined – their wits so much about them, as the phrase goes – that the subconscious rarely gets a show. But I bet if Dick took to thinking about his soul, which he never does, he would find some queer corners.'[27]

Having thus substituted psychoanalysis for the allegory of the Emperor of Byzantium as the theoretical foundation of his fiction, Buchan went on to restructure his political theory accordingly. Dr Greenslade explains to Hannay that in the modern era madness has begun to afflict the world.

> 'The barriers between the conscious and the subconscious have always been pretty stiff in the average man. But now with the general loosening of screws they are growing shaky and the two worlds are getting mixed ... That is why I say that you can't any longer take the clear psychology of most civilized beings for granted. Something is welling up from primeval deeps to muddy it.'
>
> 'I don't object to that', I said. 'We've overdone civilization, and personally I'm all for a little barbarism. I want a simpler world.'
>
> 'Then you won't get it', said Greenslade ... 'The civilized is far simpler than the primeval. All history has been an effort to make definitions, clear rules of thought, clear rules of conduct, solid sanctions by which we can conduct our life. These are the work of the conscious self. The subconscious is an elementary and lawless thing. If it intrudes on life two results must follow. There will be a weakening of the power of reasoning, which, after all, is the thing that brings men nearest to the Almighty. And there will be a failure of nerve.'
>
> I got up to get a light, for I was beginning to feel depressed by the doctor's diagnosis of our times.[28]

When the chief of police operations asks Hannay's assistance in tracking down the perpetrators of a triple kidnapping, he begins 'by saying very much what Dr Greenslade had said the night before. A large part of the world had gone mad, and that involved the growth of inexplicable and unpredictable crime.'[29]

As the result of the weakening of 'all the old sanctities', there had been a proliferation of 'moral imbeciles', a 'hideous untameable breed' found, for example, 'among the young Bolshevik Jews, among the young entry of the wilder Communist sects, and, very notably among the sullen murderous hobbledehoys in Ireland'. All this 'degenerate stuff' was 'being used by a few clever men who are not degenerates or anything of the sort, but only evil'. In other countries brilliant men such as Lenin and Gandhi had organised the 'moral imbeciles' in the cause of revolution; in Western Europe the masterminds were interested in profits rather than proletarians.

> Macgillivray gave me examples of how they used these tools, the fellows who had no thought of profit, and were ready to sacrifice everything, including their lives, for a mad ideal. It was a masterpiece of cold-blooded, devilish ingenuity. Hideous, and yet comic too; for the spectacle of these feverish cranks toiling to create a new heaven and a new earth and thinking themselves the leaders of mankind, when they were dancing like puppets at the will of a few scoundrels engaged in the most ancient of pursuits, was an irony to make the gods laugh.[30]

This analysis of postwar politics is enough to make anybody laugh, except perhaps someone who recollects that the forged 'Protocols of the Elders of Zion' began circulating in England and America about the time Buchan was writing *The Three Hostages*. But Buchan's premise here is quite different from the infamous Protocols that purported to prove that Jewish conspirators were deliberately corrupting the young for revolutionary purposes. Buchan's premise is nothing more than a rehash of his old inversion of the Hobson–Brailsford theory of economic imperialism: capitalist profiteers are promoting disorder, war and degeneracy in order to fill their pockets. His reason for putting things in this way is, again, his psychological metaphor. The villainous mastermind is required to be an alter ego virtually indistinguishable from the leaders of the society he intends to destroy. Buchan needed capitalists, statesmen and Presbyterian 'elders of the kirk' as villains; Lenin and Gandhi and the Elders of Zion would not do.

In *The Three Hostages* the master criminal is Dominick Medina (not a Jew, but of indeterminate, partly Irish descent), a rising star in parliament whose oratorical brilliance, superb marksmanship and impeccable upper-class manners hide the familiar satanic purpose of ruling the world. It is interesting and instructive to see how in this novel Buchan adapted the basic structure of *Prester John* to accord with his new psychoanalytic model. As in *Prester John*, the villain plans to accomplish his ends by mobilising the unreasoning passions of mankind. With John Laputa, Buchan could play upon the average reader's belief in the genetically savage nature of Africans. In *The Three Hostages* the savagery lies in the subconscious minds of Europeans and must be got to the surface with special techniques. Medina uses hypnotism and Eastern mysticism. Under his spell respectable people forsake their normal world of hunts and garden parties. They paint their faces, dress as flappers and dance endlessly to the powerful rhythms of a 'nigger band' in a dancehall attached to Medina's hideout. In *Prester John* the villain is pursued into his own mad terrain, a hidden valley, a secret cave. In *The Three Hostages* the pursuit becomes overtly psychological. The pursuers 'search the subconscious' for clues by playing word association games. Hannay and his friends undergo hypnosis and experience the same return to childhood and the same urge to join the villain that Buchan had conjured up in his earlier novels with dreams, drugs or delirium.[31] Convinced that the partially hypnotised Hannay is truly under his power, Medina treats him 'as an Oriental tyrant might treat a favourite slave'.

> He unbent to me as a relief to his long spiritual tension, and let me see the innermost dreams of his heart. I realized with a shudder that he thought me a part of that hideous world he had created, and – I think for the first time in the business – I knew fear on my own account ... I remember that he talked a good deal of politics, but ye gods!, what a change from the respectable conservative views which he had once treated me to ... By his way of it the War had cracked the veneer [of civilisation] and the real stuff was showing through. He rejoiced in the prospect ... Mad, you will say. Yes, mad beyond doubt, but it was the most convincing kind of madness.[32]

In the end the criminal must be defeated by turning his own uncivilised methods against him. Mutable Sandy Arbuthnot acquires influence over him in the guise of a swami and leads him into a trap where Hannay threatens him with blackmail and mutilation.

Buchan continued to use explicit references to psychoanalysis in subsequent novels and stories.[33] His very clever novel *John Macnab* opens with three eminent Englishmen – a barrister, a financier and a statesman – slinking off secretly and independently to consult a doctor about attacks of debilitating world-weariness. The doctor's advice is to 'steal a horse in some part of the world where a horse-thief is usually hanged'. In other words, live dangerously, go into the underworld, make contact with the underside of your personality. The three conspire to commit offences against property (the game laws), thereby risking loss of status, exposure and disgrace. In a short story on the same theme, a Conservative peer who shows up at a Tory rally looking like a tramp commences his descent into disreputability by being mistaken for a mental patient in a 'Kurhaus', 'supposed to be the last thing in science outside Germany', where a doctor probes for 'the subconscious complexes' that had addled his wits.[34] Another story, 'The Loathly Opposite', features a German cryptographer, code named 'Reinmar', who turns psychiatrist after the war. By chance two British code-breakers who once wrestled with his baffling telegraphic messages turn up as patients at the Alpine sanatorium where he works. The deliberate parallel drawn between the intelligence agent's struggle to decode the enemy's messages and the psychiatrist's probe for the secret springs of madness points up: (1) Buchan's habitual use of the spy as a metaphor for probing the subconscious; and (2) his hostility to the idea of being probed himself. The psychiatrist is the enemy.

In *The Dancing Floor* Buchan made his most sustained and successful use of the psychoanalytic model. Vernon, the central character, is haunted from earliest childhood by a dream that recurs on the same day every spring. In the dream he waits in a bare room for a terrifying, nameless thing that lurks down the corridor of a huge, rambling house. Each year the thing moves one room closer. He rejects a friend's suggestion that he seek help from 'the new Vienna doctrine' in purging the dream; his choice is to meet this threatening destiny with stoic determination.[35] Destiny arrives one spring on a Greek island where a rich young woman is besieged by villagers who believe her to be a witch because her degenerate father had long ago dabbled in obscene mysteries. Blaming her for recent crop failures, they lapse from Christianity and plan a pagan rite of purgation that is to culminate in the burning of her mansion. Vernon arrives to save her at the very time she is engaged in removing incredibly obscene murals from the inner rooms of the house. They manage an escape by dressing up as ancient Greek deities and marching triumphantly out of the burning mansion in shining white robes. The purging of the house and its vile inner chambers is accompanied by the lifting of the fearful despondency that had previously haunted Vernon's life. 'Something fell from him – the elderliness, the preoccupation, the stiff dogma of his recent years. He recaptured the spirit which had open arms for novelty. He felt an eagerness to be up and doing. The vanishing of his dream had left the chambers of his mind swept and garnished, and youth does not tolerate empty rooms.'[36] With this account of sanity regained through a traumatic encounter with the content of a childhood nightmare, Buchan moved from psychoanalytic theory towards psychoanalytic clinical therapy. The obstacle that stood between him and further movement in this direction was his unshakeable conviction that the hidden contents of the subconscious self are irredeemably horrific, as atavistic and vile as the murals in the island mansion. Accepting them as natural and essentially harmless was unthinkable. To linger too long in their presence was to run the risk of madness, a danger that figures prominently in almost every story Buchan ever wrote and which utterly belies his reputation as a writer of healthy, harmless thrillers.

His thrillers are, in fact, anything but harmless. Their danger goes well beyond the casual comments about race, nationality and capitalist success that have caught the attention of his detractors. It is Buchan's direct linkage of derangement in society with derangement in the self that is most fraught with peril. The proximate source of this equation was the fiction Buchan most admired in the previous generation, the imperial adventure stories of Haggard, Kipling and Conrad that had first expressed the idea of a Jekyll–Hyde split in the psyche and given it dramatic expression in encounters between civilisation and savagery beyond imperial frontiers. Conrad saw the great crime of imperialism as the bringing of men dangerously close to their interior darkness. Kipling and Conrad made mutable men into spies and secret agents.

Buchan began by exploring his own 'allegory true of us all' on the Indian frontier and the South African highveld, then transferred it to war-torn Europe. Whereas his predecessors had displayed the savage within us by stripping off the trappings of civilisation in far away places, Buchan dressed the savage as a leader of society, gave him access to cabinet secrets and put him on the board of directors of big companies. To make his point stronger, Buchan inverted the recently devised theory of economic imperialism that singled out little cliques of finance capitalists as the most important force making for national antagonisms and political reaction. In Buchan's version, it was men at the pinnacle of society who were stirring up crime and revolution. Finally, Buchan moved beyond metaphor to postulate a causal connection between discord in society and discord in the psyche. Rebellion against the status quo in the Empire was not merely *like* the emergence of vile forces from the subconscious; it was actually *caused by* the emergence of those forces at the behest of powerful men who occupied important positions in society but whose identities were hidden under clever disguises. The only way of defeating the plotters was to enter into their lawless world and turn their weapons against them.

If the political message in Buchan's best-selling novels is taken seriously, it has vicious implications in any society where large numbers of individuals fear for their status, safety and sanity. One example of such a society was apartheid South Africa, where Buchan's novels enjoyed an ongoing popularity with white readers. Other examples can be found in Western Europe after each of the world wars. The message is that the Enemy is Within, that he uses honest idealists as his unwitting dupes and tools, that he must be countered by spies and secret police and the unrelenting suppression of anything that might open the Pandora's box of the subconscious (drugs, pornography, free thought, etc.). Buchan's ability to write his own anxieties about his status and his subconscious into his books made this message especially pointed. At best, the message gives aid and comfort to paranoid politicians determined to root out the traitors in high places. At worst, it points the way to fascism.

It must be a lasting comfort to admirers of Buchan the man and literary craftsman that he baulked at following that road when it beckoned. His one political novel of the 1930s that concerns fascism is *A Prince of the Captivity*. Although it is full of ominous-sounding warnings about the failings of democracy, the necessity of bosses and workers to abandon the old orthodoxies and the world's crying need for really strong leaders, it is forthright in its condemnation of the Nazis as well as the communists. It is the Maynard Keynes-like character Warren Creevey who rises up at the end of the book to save democratic capitalism, in what must surely rank among the best-ever examples of art prefiguring life. But the fact remains that Buchan played with some very dangerous ideas.

Notes

1 See Graham Greene, *The Lost Childhood* (London: Eyre & Spottiswoode, 1951), pp. 104–5; Richard Usborne, *Clubland Heroes* (London: Constable, 1953); Jonathan Gathorne-Hardy, *The English Public School* (London: Hodder & Stoughton, 1977), pp. 154–6.

2 Gertrude Himmelfarb, 'John Buchan: the last Victorian', in *Victorian Minds* (London: Weidenfeld & Nicolson, 1968); David Daniell, *The Interpreter's House: A Critical Assessment of John Buchan* (London: Thomas Nelson, 1975); Roger Kimball, 'Catching up with John Buchan', *Fortnightly Review* (27 June 2012).

3 Bill Schwarz, *Memories of Empire, Vol. I: The White Man's World* (Oxford: Oxford University Press, 2011), pp. 247–75; Jeremy Foster, *Washed with Sun: Landscape and the Making of White South Africa* (Pittsburgh: University of Pittsburgh Press, 2008), pp. 119–43.

4 R. Luxemburg, 'The accumulation of capital: an anti-critique', in K. J. Tarbuck (ed.), *Imperialism and the Accumulation of Capital* (London: Allen Lane the Penguin Press, 1972), p. 147.

5 John Buchan, *The Four Adventures of Richard Hannay* (London: Hodder & Stoughton, 1933), pp. 33–4.

6 John Buchan, *A Lodge in the Wilderness* (London: William Blackwood, 1906), pp. 269–72.

7 Ibid., p. 278.

8 John Buchan, *The Moon Endureth: Tales and Fancies* (London: Thomas Nelson, 1923), p. 88.

9 Anti-imperialists of the Edwardian era considered this the most difficult of the imperialist fallacies to combat. See John A. Hobson, *Imperialism: A Study*, 3rd edn (London: George Allen & Unwin, 1938), pp. 162–95; Norman Angell, *The Great Illusion* (London: Heinemann, 1910), part 2.

10 Susan Tweedsmuir, *John Buchan by His Wife and Friends* (London: Hodder & Stoughton, 1947), pp. 57, 102–3. J. A. Smith's *John Buchan and His World* (London: Thames & Hudson, 1979) includes twenty-four pictures of Buchan taken between 1891 and 1939; indoors or outdoors, hunting, fishing or mountaineering,

he is always in a tie except when it is superseded by some ceremonial costume. See also Anna Buchan, *Unforgettable, Unforgotten* (London: Hodder & Stoughton, 1945), p. 215, which cites his practice of having the gardener send him one suit in the morning and another in the evening.

11 For a splendid and insightful close reading of the novel, see Craig Smith, 'Every man must kill the thing he loves: empire, homoerotics, and nationalism in John Buchan's *Prester John*', *NOVEL: A Forum on Fiction* 28 (1995), 173–200.

12 The homoerotic attraction and repulsion experienced by Davie Crawfurd in this extraordinary scene are suggested in Calvin Hernton, *Sex and Racism* (London: André Deutsch, 1969), pp. 20–1, in which a Southern racist woman relates a recurring nightmare:

> It happened at least three or four times a week. I was in a cave. I don't know where the cave was located, but it was dark, and I was always alone, and there was no way out. I never knew how I got there; the dream always started with me just there – in the dark cave – naked, and shivering from the cold. I would wander around bumping into the, walls, trying to find a way out. Then I would feel myself falling and tumbling down what seemed like endless stairs, and I always landed in a pit. There was still no light, but I knew that there were people around me; I could feel their presence. When my eyes got used to the dark and I could see who the people were – they were Negroes, a whole lot of them, a hundred or more maybe; they were all around me, and they were naked.
>
> At first, I always thought the naked Negroes wanted to rape me one by one. But then it would come to me that the black Negroes were laughing, were making fun of me, were dancing around, pointing at me, mocking me. And I would soon discover why: it seemed that my hands, both of them, were ingrown, were actually *webbed* to the flesh of my womb. And I had been born that way, and it was terrible, and I would start crying and trying to free my hands ... and the wild laughter of the Negroes and their free, swinging sex would drive me almost crazy. And then it always – in pain and agony, I would tear my hands free from my womb, and I would be crying, and blood and bits of my flesh would be all over the dark cave. Right away, the dark cave would get bright with light, almost blinding with light. A strange thing would always happen then – I would look up and around, and all of those black Negroes – their faces and bodies, I mean – would be white as snow ... and it would be myself who had turned black.

13 John Buchan, *Prester John* (London: Thomas Nelson and Sons, 1957), pp. 119–20.

14 Buchan, *The Four Adventures*, pp. 72–3.

15 Ibid., p. 7.

16 John Buchan, *The Half-Hearted* (London: Ibister & Co., 1900, downloaded as ebook from http://manybooks.net), p. 101.

17 Buchan, *The Four Adventures*, p. 902.

18 John Buchan, *A Prince of the Captivity* (London: Thomas Nelson, 1933), p. 323.

19 It might have been a service if all Buchan's financier villains had been identified as Jews. The failings of capitalism could then be based on these scapegoats. But few, if any, are Jews.

20 Buchan, *The Four Adventures*, p. 211.

21 Ibid., p. 153.

22 Ibid., pp. 152–3.

23 John Buchan, *The Island of Sheep* (London: Thomas Nelson, 1939), p. 29.

24 Buchan, *The Four Adventures*, pp. 286–7.

25 Tweedsmuir, *John Buchan by His Wife*, pp. 164–5; Daniell, *Interpreter's House*, pp. 85, 88.

26 John Buchan, *Memory Hold-the-Door* (London: Hodder & Stoughton, 1941), p. 203.

27 Buchan, *The Four Adventures*, p. 859.

28 Ibid., pp. 860–1.
29 Ibid., pp. 871–3.
30 Ibid., pp. 902–3.
31 See the account of hypnotism given by the Marquis de la Tour du Pin in ibid., p. 1070.
32 Ibid., pp. 1125–6.
33 However, as psychoanalysis became more and more identified with the hated avant-garde, these references become humorous or slighting.
34 Buchan, 'The frying pan and the fire', *The Runagates Club* (A Project Gutenberg of Australia eBook, No.: 0301381h.html).
35 John Buchan, *The Dancing Floor* (London: Thomas Nelson, 1926), p. 43.
36 Ibid., p. 281.

CHAPTER SEVEN

Lawrence of Arabia: great white hope of the Edwardian imperial romancers

Precious few romantic heroes emerged from the hecatombs of the Great War in Europe. American war correspondent Lowell Thomas had the inspired idea of looking for them further east. With credentials supplied by Colonel John Buchan from Britain's Ministry of Information, Thomas joined General Edmund Allenby's Egyptian Expeditionary Force on its Palestine campaign.[1] Soon after the fall of Jerusalem in December 1917, he encountered a hero to rank with the best of them. Thomas E. Lawrence had been seconded as a military attaché to Arabs in revolt against Turkish rule. Formerly an archaeologist in Syria, Lawrence was fluent in Arabic and soon graduated from liaison work to active participation in military operations. Lowell Thomas caught up with him in Jerusalem and instantly grasped his cinematic potential. Mounted on a camel and clad in the full-dress robes of an Arab sherif, Lawrence cut a dashing figure for the cameras. By 1919 Thomas had worked the Lawrence story into a stage show initially titled, 'Freeing Holy Arabia'. A reporter who saw it in Toronto proclaimed in headline print:

STORY OF LAWRENCE LIKE HAGGARD NOVEL

He was the 'British Boy Who United Arabs' – 'AN UNCROWNED KING' who 'Was Largely Responsible for Successful Revolt Against the Turks'. The 'average hearer had to pinch himself to determine whether he were actually hearing a true story and seeing motion pictures of its incidents, or were listening to some new romance by a Sir Rider Haggard or a Kipling.'[2]

Quickly Thomas pushed the Lawrence episode to the centre of his drama. When he turned the show into a book, *With Lawrence in Arabia*, he emphasised aspects sure to resonate with readers of Haggard, Conrad, Kipling and Buchan. Lawrence, 'one of the most picturesque personalities of modern times', would be 'blazoned on the romantic pages of history' with Clive of India and Gordon of Khartoum. When the Arab forces took Aqaba they seized the strategic port 'where the great fleets of King Solomon rode at anchor three thousand years ago'. To safeguard it, Lawrence had to fight a battle at Petra under the shadow of the 'barren volcanic range called King Solomon's Mountains', among 'the immemorial and perfect ruins of a lost civilization', where the

> Crusaders, with their flashing spears and pennants blazoned with the coats-of-arms of half the medieval barons of Europe, were the last warriors to clank in armour ... Lawrence, the archaeologist, garbed in Arab kit, had wandered over this country before the war, and knew every foot of the region from the driest water-hole to the most dilapidated column in Petra.[3]

By the time Thomas took the multi-media spectacle to London's Covent Garden opera house in August 1919, his portrayal of Lawrence's character had struck deep roots in the public imagination. An Oxford graduate, he was, so far as Thomas was aware, 'the only European who was ever accepted by the Arabs as one of themselves'. He could plug a bullseye at thirty paces with his frontier vintage Colt revolver and had set 'a record for fast camel trekking that may stand some years'. He was, moreover, a modest hero with an aversion to honours and medals. His sway over the Arab people made him a sought-after adjudicator of local disputes.[4] More than any man alive,

> Thomas Edward Lawrence drank the cup of Arabian wisdom and absorbed the spirit of the nomad peoples. Few Westerners ever acquired greater influence over an Oriental people. He had united the scattered tribes of Arabia and induced chieftains who had been bitter enemies for generations to forget their feuds and fight side by side for the same cause. From remote parts of Arabia swarthy sons of the desert had swarmed to his standard as if he had been a new prophet.[5]

Lowell Thomas's brief acquaintance with Lawrence launched his lucrative career as a journalist and travel writer. In return he made a formerly obscure subaltern into Lawrence of Arabia.

Like General Gordon in courage and contempt for honours – but free from religious fanaticism, alcoholic over-indulgence and rash pronouncements – Lawrence possessed all the attributes likely to attract the attention of literary, ideological and artistic imperialists. Even before Thomas put his name in lights, Kipling took Lawrence under his wing. They met at a London dinner party shortly before Lawrence went to the Versailles Peace Conference in January 1919 as a technical adviser to the British delegation and unofficial counsellor/translator to Prince Feisal's Arab delegation.[6] Kipling strongly encouraged him to write up his account of the Arab Revolt, which Lawrence commenced towards the end of the Versailles Conference. The same year, through his Oxford connections he fell into the clutches of Lionel Curtis – former member of Lord Milner's South African 'Kindergarten', patron of Herbert Baker and friend of John Buchan. As Beit Lecturer in Imperial History since 1912, Curtis had emerged as the chief ideologist of a new conception of the British Empire, which he rebadged as the Commonwealth and vigorously promoted through the periodical, *The Round Table*. Encouraged by Curtis, Lawrence made a successful application for a fellowship at All Souls College in 1919 with the intention of supporting his projected book. When he found the atmosphere uncongenial, Herbert Baker offered him rooms above his architectural office in Westminster.[7] John Buchan claimed to have heard of Lawrence before the war through mutual friends but did not meet him until 1920. 'Then we found we had much in common ... Similar tastes in literature; the same philosophy of empire.'[8]

What is more, Lawrence spoke and wrote like an artist – their kind of artist. The older men fell for him head over heels. For Herbert Baker, 'it was love at first sight; he radiated some magnetic influence, such as long ago I experienced in the presence of Cecil Rhodes'.[9] Tramping the streets of London on summer evenings, Lawrence shared his critical opinions on architecture like a trained professional:

> In his criticism of architecture he would search for the naked truth regardless of tradition or fame. He saw the faults of St. Paul's – not indeed its faultless dome – as Wren no doubt himself knew them, being bound, as he confesses, by the rigid Palladian standards of his day. He was equally critical of the nihilistic tendencies of the 'Modernist' who, in revolt against the atrophies and pedantries of traditional styles, ignored the eternal verities of his art.[10]

Lionel Curtis watched him enthral a packed common room of Oxford undergraduates, thinking that 'had anyone taken his talk down in shorthand, the uncorrected transcript would have been a literary and historical masterpiece'. Though most were battle-weary veterans, 'at the end of the evening, [if] he had asked them to follow him on some wild adventure into the heart of Asia or Africa, one saw that all of them would have done so unquestioningly'.[11] Baker used practically the same formulation: 'I felt I would have followed him had I been younger, in any adventurous quest; just as we all felt a compelling force to do the tasks Rhodes set us to do.'[12] Buchan likewise: 'I am not a very tractable person or much of a hero-worshipper, but I could have followed Lawrence over the edge of the world. I loved him for himself, and also because there seemed to be reborn in him all the lost friends of my youth.'[13] Joseph Conrad, who met Lawrence through his friend Cunninghame Graham in July 1920, fell immediately into conversation about questions of literary technique, Conrad characteristically 'admitting but little conscious design. Lawrence would say that he himself had over-studied his own craftsmanship'.[14]

Best of all, their love did not go unrequited. Lawrence had read Conrad before the war. His copy of *Lord Jim* was dated 'Paris, 1919', indicating that he was reading it about the time he began his epic *Seven Pillars of Wisdom*. He kept up a correspondence with Buchan and Curtis till the end of his life. Buchan he called 'the great romancer of our blind and undeserving generation'. His books were 'like athletes racing: so clean-lined, speedy, breathless'.[15] Lawrence referred to a three-volume set of Kipling's works presented to him by publisher F. N. Doubleday in 1920 as 'luscious Kipling'.[16] To Lawrence he was the 'giant of the objective', the perfect complement to Conrad, the 'giant of the subjective'.[17] Edward Elgar's Symphony No. 2 hit him 'between wind and water. It is exactly the mode that I most desire, and so it moves me more than anything else – of music – that I have ever heard.'[18] At Elgar's invitation he attended the celebrated recording session when the teenage Yehudi Menuhin performed the *Violin Concerto*. 'Spellbound at the glorious sounds', Lawrence sat 'serious and silent, looking straight ahead with those unforgettable blue eyes which seemed to see into the life of things'.[19] Herbert Baker willingly allowed himself to be instructed by Lawrence in medieval architecture; accompanying him to Cobham parish church near his home, Baker was astonished at the younger man's comprehensive knowledge of the memorial brasses set in the paving stones.[20] When completing a commission on government buildings for Nairobi, Baker took careful note of his advice that tropical sun ought to be treated as an enemy. 'All pavements should be covered over with light vaulting.' Lawrence was delighted to add his name to the list of subscribers for Baker's chapel at Fairbridge Farm School, an institution for poor boys established south of Perth, Western Australia.[21]

The Lawrence with whom the imperialists fell in love in the early 1920s was not Lawrence as we know him in the twenty-first century, a neurotically conflicted individual whose merits and defects have been the subject of more than eighty biographical studies, many documentaries and a blockbuster film. They knew him mainly through his own self-representation, which, if truth be told, was not far removed from Lowell Thomas's sensationalised version. Lawrence must have recounted snatches of his Arabian adventures on numerous occasions like that which Lionel Curtis witnessed at Oxford. When not secluded in his rooms, he happily regaled small gatherings with lively yarns. From the time of his first meeting with Kipling until 1922 he was continually engaged in writing the story of his wartime experiences. This he undertook at a breathless pace that would have amazed even Rider Haggard. He regularly turned out four to five thousand words a day, and on one stupendous dash wrote thirty thousand words in twenty-two hours.[22] The first draft of *The Seven Pillars of Wisdom* was, by his own account, completed in Paris by June of 1919 and then lost on a platform while he was changing trains at Reading. Since the wartime notes on which it was based had been 'destroyed as each section was finished', the second draft scribbled out in Herbert Baker's office garret had to be dredged up from memory alone. With this as a guide, he produced a third and final draft during 1921.[23] Regardless of the veracity of his account, the story of the Arab Revolt as told in *Seven Pillars* must closely approximate the version known to his new circle of acquaintances. The 1922 draft was privately printed in eight copies and circulated to literary friends. Kipling, Curtis and Baker certainly read it. Buchan may have as well. Yet it remained unpublished for four more years. When questioned by friends on his reasons for delaying publication, Lawrence raised vague fears about copyright, possible libel actions and his own judgement that it was 'not good enough'.[24]

In the same breath he perceptively observed that 'I move in its pages like St. Anthony among the devils'.[25] The fourth-century saint had gone to the desert to escape the temptations of ordinary life, only to find himself beset by demons sent to inflict physical and psychological damage. The deep structure of *Seven Pillars* is precisely that of the great imperial romances: a journey into the unknown that tests the psyche and the body of the protagonist on a quest to achieve a noble goal on behalf of an alien race. Readers oscillate between thinking he will emerge like Haggard's and Buchan's heroes – shaken but invigorated – and fearing that, on the contrary, like Conrad's Kurtz, the wilderness 'will find him out'.

The Arab Revolt as imperial romance

His British commanders despatched him with little in the way of positive instructions to make contact with Arab leaders in the Hejaz, who had agreed to spearhead a revolt against the Turks in return for money and arms. Lawrence formed his own opinion that old Hussein, Sherif of Mecca, was not up to the task. Next he tallied the merits of Hussein's sons, rejecting each in turn before deciding that Feisal was the prince born to lead his people to victory. 'In appearance he was tall, graceful and vigorous, with the most beautiful gait, and a royal dignity of head and shoulders.' Here 'was offered to our hand, which had only to be big enough to take it, a prophet who, if veiled, would give cogent form to the idea behind the activity of the Arab Revolt. The aim of my trip was fulfilled.'[26] The episode resembles nothing so much as the adventurers' discovery in *King Solomon's Mines* that the mysterious Ignosi was the rightful king of Kukuanaland. Lawrence's role would be to devise the strategy for the struggle. As he later told Liddell Hart, 'to be "King without the crown" has been his desire. He did not ask for command but that his policy and strategy should be adopted in the Arab theatre of war.' Feisal not only falls in with his plans but insists that Lawrence accompany him dressed as a brother, in the full-dress robes of a Sherif:

> Suddenly Feisal asked me if I would wear Arab clothes like his own while in the camp. I should find it better for my own part, since it was a comfortable dress in which to live Arab-fashion as we must do. Besides, the tribesmen would then understand how to take me. The only wearers of khaki in their experience had been Turkish officers, before whom they took up an instinctive defence. If I wore Meccan clothes, they would behave to me as though I were really one of the leaders; and I might slip in and out of Feisal's tent without making a sensation which he had to explain away each time to strangers.
>
> I agreed at once, very gladly; for army uniform was abominable when camel-riding or when sitting about on the ground; and the Arab things, which I had learned to manage before the war, were cleaner and more decent in the desert. Hejris was pleased, too, and exercised his fancy in fitting me out in splendid white silk and gold-embroidered wedding garments which had been sent to Feisal lately.[27]

Having now entered totally into an alternative racial identity like his fictional predecessors – Henry Curtis in leopard skins, Sandy Arbuthnot in Arab robes and Kim in 'the full protection of the road' – Lawrence was ready to face the physical perils of the quest. Self-control was the key:

> I had learned to eat much one time; then to go two, three, or four days without food; and after to overeat. I made it a rule to avoid rules in food; and by a course of exceptions accustomed myself to no custom at all.
>
> So, organically, I was efficient in the desert, felt neither hunger nor surfeit, and was not distracted by thought of food. On the march I could go dry between wells, and, like the Arabs, could drink greatly to-day for the thirst of yesterday and of to-morrow.
>
> In the same way, though sleep remained for me the richest pleasure in the world, I supplied its place by the uneasy swaying in the saddle of a night march ... Such liberties came from years of control (contempt of use might well be the lesson of our manhood), and they fitted me peculiarly for our work: but, of course, in me they came half by training, half by trying, out of mixed choice and poverty, not effortlessly, as with the Arabs. Yet in compensation stood my energy of motive. Their less taut wills flagged before mine flagged, and by comparison made me seem tough and active.[28]

Corporeal tests follow in quick, hard succession, proving him physically superior to his Bedouin companions. The long circuitous march preparatory to the audacious assault on the port of Aqaba from the desert side meant not just privations of food and water, but a desperate ride to rescue a poor unfortunate who had tumbled from the saddle. There followed a dire bout of dysentery that plunged him in and out of consciousness for days.

In the imperial romances periods of prolonged delirium or unconsciousness often precede moments of revelation and prophetic insight. Haggard's Leo Vincey hovers near to death from fever until Ayesha awakens him to a heightened spiritual existence in the lost city of Kôr. Kipling's Kim lapses into unconsciousness under the nauseating ministrations of Huneefa, prior to his emergence as a secret agent in Indian costume. In *Greenmantle*, the 'Companions of the Rosy Hours' send Buchan's Richard Hannay into a narcotic dream where he alternates between the 'light-heartedness which only a boy knows in the dawning of his days' and 'terrible, savage passion … monstrous'.[29] For eight days Lawrence lay in his tent, 'till my brain, sick of unsupported thinking, had to be dragged to its work by an effort of will, and went off into a doze whenever that effort was relaxed. The fever passed: my dysentery ceased; and with restored strength the present again became actual to me.'[30] In this semi-conscious state the secret of successful guerrilla warfare in the desert comes to him in a bolt of inspiration. With no fixed abode and no fortress, he, Feisal and 'a few zealots' could spread the spirit of revolt over all Arabia. Attacking here and there, they would defy reprisals by melting away into the dunes. With 'sedition putting up her head in every unoccupied one of those hundred thousand square miles', the Turks would 'need six hundred thousand men to meet the ill wills of all the Arab peoples' – a plainly impossible task.[31]

Armed with his new sense of invincibility, Lawrence embarks on a series of exploits like those to be found in any novel of imperial fiction. He accompanies Feisal across desolate wastes in a brilliantly successful attack on Aqaba. He hatches a plan to ambush Turkish forces, which, since it 'sounded in the proper descent from books of adventure', was at once 'agreed enthusiastically'.[32] When his Arab comrades hesitate to attack an enemy outpost under a full moon, Lawrence consults his pocket almanac and promises that 'to-night for a while there should be no moon' due to an eclipse. 'Duly it came and the Arabs forced the post without loss, while the superstitious soldiers were firing rifles and clanging copper pots to rescue the threatened satellite.'[33] He passes through Roman ruins musing on the hubris of the old empire builders who were blind to 'the transience of politics'.[34] Several of his stories challenge credulity, among them this anecdote that comes very close to a passage in *Kim* where Colonel Creighton banters flirtatiously with an old Indian woman. After blowing up a train Lawrence finds that:

> In the end of the wagon sat an ancient and very tremulous Arab dame, who asked me what it was all about. I explained. She said that though an old friend and hostess of Feisal, she was too infirm to travel and must wait her death there. I replied that she would not be harmed. The Turks were almost arrived and would recover what remained of the train ... Months after there came to me secretly from Damascus a letter and a pleasant little Baluchi carpet from the lady Ayesha, daughter of Jellal el Lel, of Medina, in memory of an odd meeting.[35]

In the tradition of Sir Henry Curtis 'giving laws' to the Kukuana, Kipling's Daniel Dravot's rule in Kafiristan and Conrad's Jim settling village disputes up a godforsaken Malayan river, Lawrence falls easily into the role of an irregular British district officer meting out justice:

> The men were a mad lot, sharpened to distraction by hope of success. They would listen to no word but mine, and brought me their troubles for judgement. In the six days' raid there came to a head, and were settled, twelve cases of assault with weapons, four camel-liftings, one marriage, two thefts, a divorce, fourteen feuds, two evil eyes, and a bewitchment.[36]

By the same token, he can fall prey to bloodlust when righteous vengeance demands. Having witnessed atrocities at the village of Tafileh, he rides into battle against a Turkish battalion with the cry of 'no prisoners'. Liddell Hart attributed this to 'a fit of Berserker rage' of the sort Haggard's heroes are prone to suffer.[37]

Lawrence also followed the imperial adventure plotline by portraying himself as a soul divided and torn by conflicting impulses. 'Now', he writes, 'I found myself dividing into parts.' One part 'went on riding wisely', while 'another hovering above and to the right bent down curiously, and asked what the flesh was doing'. The 'night passed in these mutual conversation' between 'the divided selves'.[38]

Lawrence expressed attitudes towards Arabs and their culture that vary as widely as those of Haggard's and Kipling's fictional heroes. He can be richly appreciative of Arab spectacle. In a scene worthy of Elgar's Mughal music from *Crown of India*:

> The march became rather splendid and barbaric. First rode Feisal in white, then Sharraf at his right in red head-cloth and henna-dyed tunic and cloak, myself on his left in white and scarlet, behind us three banners of faded crimson silk with gilt spikes, behind them the drummers playing a march, and behind them again the wild mass of twelve hundred bouncing camels of the bodyguard, packed as closely as they could move,

> the men in every variety of coloured clothes and the camels nearly as brilliant in their trappings.[39]

And, on another musical occasion, he describes how Shakir 'upright and alone in their midst, performed the dance of their song'. As he sang 'he threw back his head, and at the close of each phrase raised his hands, to let the full sleeves run back upon his shoulders, while he waved his bare arms weirdly. The tribe around him beat time with their hands, or bayed out the refrains at this nod.'[40] On the other hand, he could write in Conradian vein of 'the negroes, tom-tom playing themselves to red madness each night under the ridge. Their faces, being clearly different from our own, were tolerable; but it hurt that they should possess exact counterparts of all our bodies.' Later he admitted to being 'tired to death of these Arabs; petty incarnate Semites who attained heights and depths beyond our reach'.[41] He made the conventional distinction between the good, 'unspoiled' denizens of the desert and the intolerable townsmen. The Bedouin were saved by the simplicity and poverty of their lives. 'If forced into civilized life they would have succumbed like any savage race to its diseases, meanness, luxury, cruelty, crooked dealing, artifice; and, like savages, they would have suffered them exaggeratedly for lack of inoculation.'[42] After 'the blunt Beduin, who would thrust in, hailing me, "Ya Auruns", and put their need without compliments, these smooth townspeople were maddening as they crawled for an audience with their Prince and Bey and Lord and Deliverer. So I flung away from them in a rage.'[43]

This real-life imperial romance ought to have concluded with Lawrence riding triumphantly to victory and issuing a declaration along the lines of Haggard's hero, Sir Henry Curtis, who had 'no fancy for handing over this beautiful country to be torn and fought for by speculators, tourists, politicians and teachers'. Nor would he endow it with 'the greed, drunkenness, new diseases, gunpowder, and general demoralization which chiefly mark the progress of civilization amongst unsophisticated peoples'.[44] As we have just seen, those sentiments almost precisely expressed Lawrence's feelings about the Bedouin. However, as Lawrence knew very well, wartime politics precluded any simple outcome. What precisely would count as victory? Britain and her allies aimed to win the war against the Central Powers. Considered in isolation the object of the Arab Revolt was freedom from Turkish rule. But freedom for whom and for what geographical entity? Britain had made an unambiguous commitment to freedom for the lands held by Hussein as Sherif of Mecca and his neighbour Ibn Saud. In addition, Britain's War Cabinet agreed that their Arab allies might keep territory they conquered from Turkey in the war, subject only to the prior claims of the French.[45] But with the British and Arabs operating in tandem in the closing stages of the campaign, who could say what the latter had conquered?

In a geopolitical situation laden with ambiguity Lawrence made up his own mind about what constituted the latent Arab nation. Without authorisation, British or Arab, he decided that Feisal, his prophet prince, should rule the postwar Arab nation. Its territory should stretch from Mecca in the south to Damascus in the north, bounded on the west by Egypt and on the east by Mesopotamia. He declared, moreover, that prior entry of Arab forces into Damascus would constitute the act of conquest specified by the War Cabinet, and thereby secure Feisal's claim to all of Syria. In short, he wrote his own fairytale ending to his desert adventure well ahead of its actual outcome. Having written it, he immediately began to fret that events would conspire to wreck it.

And why, one might ask, shouldn't they? Feisal had no right to usurp the prerogatives of his father, Hussein. Nor did the British high command endorse him as future king. Lawrence alone anointed him. The Arabs who rose against the Turks had not been promised a postwar collective existence as a nation-state by Britain or anyone else. Lawrence decided that ought to be the goal and that Damascus should be their capital. He further specified that the form of government should be monarchical. It was, he declared, the idea of the British Crown that swayed them towards a wartime alliance. 'Ancient and artificial societies like this of the Sherifs and feudal chieftains of Arabia found a sense of honourable security when dealing with us in such proof that the highest place in our state was not a prize for merit or ambition.'[46] Educated townsmen would necessarily occupy influential positions in the future state, but their oleaginous manners and corruption should be curbed by the natural integrity of the Bedouin head of state.[47] There would be no talk of democracy. Arabs craved monarchs and an aristocracy.[48] Needless to say, Lawrence consulted no Arabs on constitutional questions.

Nonetheless, he insisted on treating his self-devised programme of national fulfilment as a 'promise' that British and European realpolitik was bent on undermining from the start. He sounds this leitmotif of duplicity early in *The Seven Pillars of Wisdom*. Even before the advance on Aqaba, Lawrence begins to torture himself with a supposed conflict of loyalties between the Empire he served and his imagined fulfilment of the Arab Revolt. In an effort to resolve internal doubts he undertakes a risky undercover camel ride into Syria, an excursion so vaguely described as to raise doubts as to its reality:

> Clearly, I had no shadow of leave to engage the Arabs, unknowing, in a gamble of life and death. Inevitably and justly we should reap bitterness,

> a sorry fruit of heroic endeavour. So in resentment at my false place (did ever second lieutenant so lie abroad for his betters?) I undertook this long, dangerous ride, in which to see the more important of Feisal's secret friends, and to study key-positions of our future campaigns: but the results were incommensurate with the risks, and the act artistically unjustifiable, like the motive. I had whispered to myself 'Let me chance it, now, before we begin,' seeing that this was the last chance, and that after a successful capture of Akaba I would never again possess myself freely, without association, in the security lurking for the obscure in their protective shadow.[49]

Incredibly, in Lawrence's mind the whole heroic enterprise has already taken shape before its first positive act had been undertaken. He casts his supposed secret reconnaissance as a throw of the dice – 'the last chance' – after which the entire denouement will be reckoned as preordained. And although 'a gamble of life and death', its success will 'inevitably and justly ... reap bitterness'. Strangest of all, he judges his actions like a novelist in terms of their 'artistic' merit.

All this suggests either that he wrote his account with hindsight or that even before his involvement he had written himself into an imagined storybook. There are reasons to think the latter. He told friends that as an adolescent he studied warfare and the Crusades because he 'was filled with the idea of freeing a people'. Not that he admired crusading as a religious enterprise; his sympathies lay more with the Saracen opposition. In secondary school he nourished hopes of 'hustling into form, while I lived, the new Asia which time was inexorably bringing upon us'.[50] About the same time that he began wearing Arab robes on archaeological digs, he had written of his preference for the Arab as opposed to the European; 'that is to say the Arab untouched' for 'the vulgarity of the half-Europeanized Arab is appalling'.[51] At the beginning of the war, fully two years before his involvement with the Arabs, he had 'meant to be a general and knighted, when thirty'.[52] Thus the imperial romance he lived was one he had already dreamed.

Yet with the prizes nearly within his grasp he agonises over his bona fides. 'Not being a perfect fool', he 'could see that if we won the war the promises to the Arabs were dead paper. Had I been an honourable adviser I would have sent my men home, and not let them risk their lives for such stuff. Yet the Arab inspiration was our main tool in winning the Eastern war.' At the same time he claims to have known that Hussein, 'the half-witted old man had obtained from us no concrete or unqualified undertaking of any sort'. On the one hand, he knows the false undertakings that made him ashamed were not undertakings at all; on the other, he treats them as solemn promises. No wonder that his 'mental tug of war between honesty and loyalty, after swaying a while, settled again expediently into deadlock'.[53] Put another way, his interminable internal debates made him 'a standing court martial on myself'.[54]

Lawrence's paralysis and withdrawal from public life

After stepping onto the international stage as the real-life embodiment of the heroes imagined by the imperial romancers, Lawrence fled the limelight for reasons none could grasp. Deserting All Souls College, he enlisted as a private in the Royal Air Force under the assumed name of Ross. When found out and expelled, he sought refuge in the Tank Corps, again as a lowly private. He would accept no position of responsibility, let alone command. His friends were as puzzled as the public. A succession of biographers has looked to psychology and psychiatry for answers. One popular line has been to attribute his behaviour to a paralysis of will precipitated by having been beaten and sodomised during a visit incognito to the Turkish stronghold of Deraa. One problem with this explanation is that we have only Lawrence's word that the incident took place. Historians have plausibly doubted that it did.[55] If the trauma had been great enough to inflict permanent damage, how is it that Lawrence could relate it so clearly in *Seven Pillars*? Another explanation holds that Lawrence could not associate himself with what he considered to be Britain's betrayal of the Arabs. However, several years intervened between the end of the war and his retreat from public life. In the interval Lawrence seemed a model of energy and accomplishment on behalf of the Empire. Something else must account for the strange turn of his life.

From the inception of the Paris peace negotiations Lawrence maintained a very high public profile through letters and articles promoting his vision for the future of the Middle East and Britain's overseas empire. A letter to *The Times* in July 1920 set out his opinions on what had gone wrong in Iraq (Mesopotamia), where Britain's postwar administration faced a rebellion costly in lives and treasure, with no end in sight. The problem, as he saw it, was the direct involvement of British public servants as administrators and British troops as police. Instead, Britain should have moved quickly to establish an Arab government, defence force and police. 'We should then hold of Mesopotamia exactly as much (or as little) as we hold of South Africa or Canada.' Pressing on with the analogy, he anticipated the objection that 'the idea of brown Dominions in the British Empire is grotesque', but 'the only alternative seems to be conquest, which the ordinary Englishman does not want, and cannot afford'.[56] In practical terms the oil of Iraq meant a great deal to Britain; however, it could never be extracted under conditions of war. 'I think if it is so necessary for us, it could be made the subject of a bargain. The Arabs seem willing to shed their blood for freedom; how much more their oil!'

Beneath the sarcasm lurked a serious analysis of imperial policy, parallel to that being propagated by Lionel Curtis in *The Round Table*. The big idea was that the entire Empire should move in the direction of a non-racial association of Dominions known as the Commonwealth. Peoples capable of self-government would exercise self-government through the parliamentary institutions of the Westminster system of responsible government. Others should be governed at the local level by leaders possessing the authority conferred by tradition, subject to the guidance of British advisers and a single metropolitan authority for the conduct of defence and foreign relations. Beyond the colonies of white settlement the implementation of the new model was closely associated with the great imperial 'proconsuls': Milner, Curzon and Lugard. The first important step had been the Montagu–Chelmsford reforms of 1918 in India that greatly extended powers of self-government at the local level. The following year Lord Milner produced a report on the future of Egypt that likewise accorded considerable powers of self-government under the established monarchy while maintaining the imperial connection under the rubric of an 'alliance'.

Lawrence had first raised the idea of a similar arrangement for Iraq in a letter to Lord Curzon in September 1919. Something akin to a 'Milner commission' should 'bring Mesopotamia into line with the new constitution of Egypt'. His own ambition was 'that the Arabs should be our first brown dominion, and not our last brown colony'.[57] A year later he expanded upon his ideas in an unsigned article for *The Round Table* on 'The Changing East'. In his diagnosis Asia was currently suffering 'the civilisation-disease, the inevitable effect of too close contact with the West. The aborigines of Australia got it when they met us, and they died of it ... Asia is tougher, older, more numerous, and will not die of us – but indubitably we have made her very ill.'[58] His prescribed remedy was a 'new Imperialism' marked by less interference with subject peoples' lives:

> This new Imperialism is not just withdrawal and neglect on our part. It involves an active side of imposing responsibility on the local peoples. It is what they clamour for, but an unpopular gift when giving. We have to demand from them provision for their own defence. This is the first stage towards self-respect in peoples. They must find their own troops to replace our armies of occupation which we are going to withdraw.[59]

It could not be enough to put traditional leaders at the head of local government. Britain would:

> find our best helpers not in our former most obedient subjects, but among those now most active in agitating against us, for it will be the intellectual leaders of the people who will serve the purpose, and these are not the philosophers nor the rich, but the demagogues and the politicians. It seems a curious class to which to entrust the carefully begun edifices of our colonial governments – but in essence it will not be dissimilar to the members of our own House of Commons, whom we entrust with our own liberties. They will not wish to take charge, but we can force their hand by preparing to go.

These measures would win the support of the people because they would shield them from the ever-present threat of annexation by less attractive empires:

> We do not risk losing them to another power – for the Englishman is liked by everyone who has not too much to do with him, and the British Empire is so much the largest concern in the world that it offers unrivalled inducements to small peoples to join it. Egypt, Persia and Mesopotamia, if assured of eventual dominion status, and present internal autonomy, would be delighted to affiliate with us, and would then cost us no more in men and money than Canada or Australia.

In practical terms, leadership of Britain's Arab dominion would eventually gravitate from Damascus to Baghdad, which 'must be the ultimate regent, with perhaps five times the population of Syria, and many times its wealth. Mesopotamia will be the master of the Middle East, and the power controlling its destinies will dominate all its neighbours.'[60]

His references to 'the largest concern in the world' and 'the power controlling its destinies' underscore his devotion to the idea of Empire. As E. M. Forster noted, 'T. E. was intensely patriotic, lived for the Empire'.[61] Most of his worry about betraying the Arabs arose from his suspicion that their historic capital would fall to the French Empire. He had seen Feisal installed in Damascus only to see him chased out by French authorities in 1920. When in 1921 Winston Churchill was commissioned to sort out Britain's costly mistakes in the Middle East, he turned to Lawrence for help. Without hesitation he answered Churchill's call. Within a few months of joining the Colonial Office staff he had the satisfaction of seeing Feisal on the throne of Iraq and his brother Abdullah set up as Emir of Transjordan. Although no 'brown Dominion' had emerged, Lawrence judged that his 'part of the Middle East job was done … and on the whole, well done'. Under the watchful eye of the Royal Air Force both states accepted their role as loyal

British allies. Whether the Iraqis would ever be fit for self-government without a king, Lawrence could not say. With the vagueness characteristic of postwar British imperialists he assumed that day would come, 'but whether 7 or 70 or 7000 years hence, God knows'.[62]

A footnote to the first published version of *Seven Pillars* informs readers that Churchill's work in 1921 fulfilled '(I think) our promises in letter and spirit (where humanly possible) without sacrificing any interest of our Empire or any interest of the peoples concerned. So we were quit of the war-time Eastern adventure, with clean hands, but three years too late to earn the gratitude which peoples, if not states, can pay.'[63] Lawrence's friend, the eminent historian Lewis Namier, agreed. To say that he sought obscurity because the 'British Government had "let down the Arabs" ... was nonsense. He never felt that way, and as adviser for Arab affairs to Mr. Churchill had full scope for working further on their behalf.'[64] A grateful Churchill offered him his pick of 'governorships and great commands', all of which he refused. 'As a last resort' he despatched him to 'Trans-Jordania, where sudden difficulties had arisen. He had plenary powers. He used them with his old vigour. He removed officers. He used force. He restored complete tranquillity. Everyone was delighted with the success of his mission; but nothing would persuade him to continue.'[65]

Lawrence's circle of Conservative admirers united in their disappointment that this paragon of the imperial legend should refuse honours and high commands. Lionel Curtis remarked 'with some bitterness that he might be Prime Minister if he would'.[66] Buchan, who smoothed the way for his enlistment in the Royal Air Force, nonetheless regretted the lost possibilities: 'he might have led the nation to a new way of life.'[67] Recognising that 'his character has been a quarry for the [psycho]analysts', Buchan preferred to attribute Lawrence's withdrawal 'from his natural career of action' to the wartime experiences that unbalanced him and damaged his nerves. On reflection Buchan went further, arguing 'there was a fissure in him from the start; the dream and the business did not march together; his will was not always the servant of his intelligence; he was an agonist, a self-tormentor, who ran to meet suffering halfway.'[68] If we take Lawrence as the epitome of the man who set out deliberately to live out the paradigmatic imperial romance, there is considerable force in Buchan's observation that 'the dream and the business did not march together'.

According to the dream, the struggle to win savage peoples to the Empire was analogous to the European individual's struggle to master the tumultuous inner life of the subconscious. The excitement of both enterprises arose from the encounter with barbarism compelling enough to tempt the ruling faculties to surrender through 'the fascination of the abomination'. Conrad's fictional Lord Jim came closest to prefiguring Lawrence's very real paralysis of will. Jim grew up imagining himself the hero of countless future dramas, yet when faced with his first opportunity to save imperilled alien lives, he falters. The cowardly crew of the *Patna* abandon their shipload of Indian Muslim pilgrims when the bulkheads show signs of failing. Although he might have stayed to safeguard the passengers, at the last moment Jim jumps to join the European crew on the lifeboat. The heroic part he might have taken falls to the stoic seaman assigned to stand guard on the bridge when the stricken ship is towed to safety by a French naval vessel. Found out, Jim's fellow crew melt away into the teeming masses of the East. He alone elects to face the music before a maritime commission. The sympathetic Captain Marlow, recognising him as 'one of us', undertakes to find him a path to redemption. Jim, who cares nothing for wages or profits, rejects all mundane employments, electing eventually to become the agent of a trading firm far up a Malayan river. There he finds adventure and romance as confidant and adviser to the local rajah. Living as one of them he settles disputes, defends them against enemies and inaugurates schemes of progress. A local woman becomes his concubine and the rajah's son, his boon companion and blood brother. All goes awry when 'Gentleman Brown' and his gang of European cut-throats arrive, bent on pillage. With the invaders thwarted and at his mercy, Jim grants their request for safe passage out of the country. The consequence is Brown's gratuitous attack on a village during which Jim's 'brother' Dain Waris is killed. Tragically, Jim has re-enacted the betrayal of the *Patna* pilgrims. Leaving his weeping lover he goes willingly to his death at the hands of the Rajah, seeing it as just punishment for his unwitting treachery. He let Brown escape as though he too somehow deserved credit for being 'one of us'. Who could be good enough to be simultaneously one of us and one of them? The judgement of Marlow, Conrad's narrative voice, is categorical: 'Nobody, nobody is good enough.'[69]

The certainty that nobody was good enough, certainly not him, informs *The Seven Pillars of Wisdom* from start to finish. Whether Lawrence truly experienced the feelings of shamming and bad faith expressed again and again in its pages cannot be known. He made certain that we could not know through the calculated destruction of his wartime journals and the dubious story of the manuscript left in the Reading railway waiting room. By the time the penultimate version was printed in 1922 Lawrence had woven the threads of self-doubt and guilt into the text. They were real enough then. The record shows that he broke no fundamental promises to 'the Arabs' because no such promises had been made. His sense of fraud and deceit arose from a different source. He had assumed the role of an Arab when he knew he could be no such thing. When he pronounced the Arabs to be 'petty incarnate Semites who attained heights and depths beyond our reach', he meant precisely that. At the heights of their being, they could trust their souls to a just and merciful God in which he plainly did not believe. The depths were graphically explored. Deprived of the companionship of women apart from harlots of the town whose 'raddled meat' was 'unpalatable to a man of healthy parts', young men revolted. In 'horror of such sordid commerce', some 'youths began indifferently to slake one another's few needs in their own clean bodies'. Others, 'thirsting to punish appetites they could not wholly prevent, took a savage pride in degrading the body, and offered themselves fiercely in any habit which promised physical pain or filth'.[70] Lawrence rubs it in by telling us that 'medical examination of some batches of Turkish prisoners found nearly half of them with unnaturally acquired venereal disease'.[71] Bedouin shepherds 'turned savage, more animal than man, haunting the flocks, and finding the satisfaction of their adult appetites in them, to the exclusion of more licit affections'.[72] He jeered at one of the Arab leaders 'for being so old and yet so foolish like the rest of his race, who regarded our comic reproductive processes, not as an unhygienic pleasure, but as a main business of life'.[73] Men's sexual being plainly revolted him; men's 'possession of bodies was degradation enough'.[74]

In Conrad's terms, the desert had 'found him out', pushing into the foreground his revulsion against his own body and its appetites. Later, while serving in the Royal Air Force, he wrote to Lionel Curtis about the unbridled carnality and lecherous talk of the men in his hut. How different from the world of knowledge and literature. Yet, 'We are all guilty alike, you know. You wouldn't exist, I wouldn't exist, without this carnality ... A filthy business all of it, and yet Hut 12 shows me the truth behind Freud. Sex is an integer in all of us, and the nearer nature we are, the more constantly, the more completely a product of that integer.'[75] The identification of the inner self with the savage other that underpinned the imperial romance was hardly possible under the cold light of Freud's revelations. Lawrence's possibly imagined defilement by the Turks at Deraa might be viewed as a confrontation with this realisation. For three years after the Great War he had continued to act the perfect hybrid, most compellingly when he wore Arab headgear over his British uniform in Paris. In the depths of his soul he knew the falseness of his position. When he entered the Royal Air Force in 1922 he left all pretence behind. Never again did he visit the scenes of his triumphs nor hold on to the old Arab friendships. More than that, he held himself aloof from contact with all exotic peoples and places. When posted against his will to Karachi, he told Herbert Baker he found his camp, 'beyond which he never went, more dreary "than any deserts of Arabia" ... He saw nothing in India but what was sordid and mean.'[76] Bitterly, he drew this moral from his Arab adventure:

> Pray God that men reading the story will not for love of the glamour of strangeness, go out to prostitute themselves and their talents in serving another race.
>
> A man who gives himself to be a possession of aliens leads a Yahoo life, having bartered his soul to a brute-master. He is not of them. He may stand against them, persuade himself of a mission, batter and twist them into something which they, of their own accord, would not have been. Then he is exploiting his old environment to press them out of theirs. Or, after my model, he may imitate them so well that they spuriously imitate him back again. Then he is giving away his own environment: pretending to theirs; and pretences are hollow, worthless things.[77]

So Lawrence put off his Arab garb for the last time and put on the uniform of a private in His Majesty's service, insisting repeatedly that he would accept no position of command, even as a non-commissioned officer. He saw plainly enough that he would always be 'one of us' and could never again risk the experiment of playing at being 'them'. Rather than jump from the threatened ship like Conrad's Jim, he would assume the stance of the French seaman assigned to the *Patna* – doing his duty as his superiors saw that duty, risking death but not self-deception.

Despite the lowly position he sought in the military, Lawrence remained in close contact with the conservative political and literary circles that craved his company. In his last years, while resisting advances from the British Union of Fascists, he was welcomed into Lady Astor's 'Cliveden Set'. But he took no more part in formulating policy for the Empire. His creative output was limited to a translation of Homer's *Odyssey* and his posthumously published account of enlisted men's existence in the Royal Air Force (*The Mint*). His personal odyssey had demonstrated the impossibility of living out the dream embodied in the imperial romance. The identification of the contents of the subconscious with the savage other could not survive the twin blows of contact with real people on the frontiers of Empire and confrontation with the revelations of psychoanalysis.

Notes

1 Lowell Thomas, *With Lawrence in Arabia*, 10th edn (London: Hutchinson & Co., 1926 [1924]), p. vi.

2 Quoted by Jeremy Wilson, T. E. Lawrence Studies, http://telstudies.org/discussion/diplomacy_1918-1922/list_harry_chase_portraits.shtml.

3 Thomas, *With Lawrence in Arabia*, pp. 17, 83, 165, 180–1.
4 Ibid., pp. 121, 123, 144–5, 198.
5 Ibid., p. 281.
6 John Mack, *A Prince of Our Disorder: The Life of T. E. Lawrence* (Oxford: Oxford University Press, 1990), pp. 261, 264.
7 Ibid., p. 283.
8 John Buchan, *Memory Hold-the-Door* (London: Hodder & Stoughton, 1940), p. 212.
9 A. W. Lawrence (ed.), *T. E. Lawrence by His Friends* (London: Jonathan Cape, 1937), p. 248.
10 Ibid., p. 249.
11 Ibid., p. 259.
12 Ibid., p. 197.
13 Buchan, *Memory Hold-the-Door*, p. 218.
14 Ton Hoenselaars and Gene M. Moore, 'Joseph Conrad and T. E. Lawrence', *Conradiana* 27 (1995): 3–20; Lawrence, *T. E. Lawrence by His Friends*, p. 250.
15 David Garnett (ed.), *The Letters of T. E. Lawrence* (London: Jonathan Cape, 1938), p. 773.
16 Ibid., p. 304.
17 Ibid., pp. 301–2.
18 Ibid., pp. 744–5.
19 Violinist Vera Hockman's account quoted in Robert Anderson, *Elgar* (London: J. M. Dent, 1993), p. 170.
20 Lawrence, *T. E. Lawrence by His Friends*, p. 250.
21 The building of the chapel is comprehensively treated in David Dolan with Christine Lewis, *The Fairbridge Chapel: Sir Herbert Baker's Labour of Love* (Perth: API Network, 2004).
22 Mack, *Prince of our Disorder*, p. 284.
23 T. E. Lawrence, *The Seven Pillars of Wisdom* (New York: Dell, 1962 [1926]), pp. 21–2.
24 Mack, *Prince of Our Disorder*, p. 312.
25 Ibid., p. 134.
26 Lawrence, *Seven Pillars*, pp. 99, 100.
27 Ibid., p. 128. Even before the war he had taken to wearing Arab robes while working on Syrian archaeological sites, proving that the wish to identify with the alien other predated his involvement in the Arab Revolt; see Mack, *Prince of Our Disorder*, p. 83.
28 Lawrence, *Seven Pillars*, p. 466.
29 John Buchan, *The Four Adventures of Richard Hannay* (London: Hodder & Stoughton, 1933), pp. 286–7.
30 Lawrence, *Seven Pillars*, p. 199.
31 Ibid., p. 195.
32 Ibid., p. 600.
33 Ibid., p. 311.
34 Ibid., p. 587.
35 Ibid., p. 372.
36 Ibid., p. 378. Alternative versions of the story appear in B. H. Liddell Hart, *'T. E. Lawrence': In Arabia and After* (London: Jonathan Cape, 1935), p. 235 and Thomas, *With Lawrence in Arabia*, p. 123.
37 Liddell Hart, *'T. E. Lawrence'*, p. 271.
38 Lawrence, *Seven Pillars*, p. 451.
39 Ibid., p. 143.
40 Ibid., p. 207. In a prefiguration of this role Lawrence had reportedly arbitrated local disputes during his archaeological work in Syria. See Mack, *Prince of Our Disorder*, p. 91.
41 Lawrence, *Seven Pillars*, p. 586.
42 Ibid., p. 223.
43 Ibid., p. 448.
44 H. Rider Haggard, *Allan Quatermain* (London: Longmans, Green & Co., 1888), p. 276.

45 Lawrence, *Seven Pillars*, p. 553.
46 Ibid., p. 216.
47 Ibid., p. 338.
48 Thomas, *With Lawrence in Arabia*, p. 286.
49 Lawrence, *Seven Pillars*, p. 280.
50 Mack, *Prince of Our Disorder*, pp. 23, 37.
51 Ibid., p. 92.
52 Lawrence, *Seven Pillars*, p. 560.
53 Ibid., p. 216. Later scholars pointed out that the British promise to Hussein was 'limited to the Arabs of the Hijaz region of Arabia'; see Mack, *Prince of Our Disorder*, p. 129.
54 Lawrence, *Seven Pillars*, p. 561.
55 Notably William Langer, the eminent American historian, known later in his career for his interest in the potential of psycho-history; see Mack, *Prince of Our Disorder*, pp. 232, 406n.
56 Letter to the editor, signed T. E. Lawrence, All Souls College, *The Times* (23 July 1920), p. 15.
57 Garnett (ed.), *Letters of T. E. Lawrence*, p. 291.
58 T. E. Lawrence (unsigned), 'The changing East', *The Round Table* 10 (1920), 757.
59 Ibid., 771–2.
60 Ibid., 766.
61 Lawrence (ed.), *Lawrence by His Friends*, p. 233.
62 Mack, *Prince of Our Disorder*, p. 303.
63 Lawrence, *Seven Pillars*, p. 279.
64 Lawrence (ed.), *Lawrence by His Friends*, p. 229.
65 Ibid., p. 16.
66 Ibid., p. 258.
67 Buchan, *Memory-Hold-the-Door*, p. 214.
68 Ibid., pp. 214–15.
69 Joseph Conrad, *Lord Jim* (New York: Holt, Rinehart and Winston, 1957), p. 276.
70 Lawrence, *Seven Pillars*, p. 29.
71 Ibid., p. 55.
72 Ibid., p. 203.
73 Ibid., p. 349.
74 Ibid., p. 565.
75 Garnett (ed.), *Letters of T. E. Lawrence*, p. 414.
76 Lawrence (ed.), *Lawrence by His Friends*, p. 222.
77 Lawrence, *Seven Pillars*, p. 30.

Epilogue: the death-knell of the imperial romance and imperial rule

The analogy some creative individuals drew between a savage inner self held in check by an imperial apparatus of self-control, and the policies required for the governance of Britain's new tropical empire in the years between Gordon's death at Khartoum and Lawrence's adventures in Arabia, had spurred a variety of stimulating endeavours in the arts. Little by little the credos and theories that sustained them wilted and then perished. The paralysis that gripped Lawrence after the war showed that at a personal level the fantasy of the ruler who could enter at will into the life of savage subjects was foredoomed. But that was only one factor among many tearing at the fabric of ideas that linked the Edwardian imperialist artists.

The real-life political counterparts of the imperial romance were Britain's experiments with indirect rule from Fiji and Zululand in the 1880s to Nigeria and Tanganyika in the early twentieth century. These fostered some interesting partnerships between administrators and traditional leaders, before succumbing to the more powerful forces of anti-colonial nationalism led by educated elites. Promotion of 'traditional leaders' as imperial partners foundered first in India – outflanked by the alternative version of tradition presented by Gandhi and the nationalist politics of Nehru. Indirect rule then rapidly gave way to institutions of self-government across the Empire. Kwame Nkrumah displaced the Asantehene in Ghana and the Kabaka of Buganda gave way to Milton Obote. Other traditional leaders fell like ninepins, until at last in South Africa Zulu Chief Mangosuthu Buthelezi was eclipsed by the democratic Zulu traditionalist, Jacob Zuma of the African National Congress.

None of the newly independent nations of Asia and Africa showed much interest in defending old ways of life. Even the self-proclaimed 'African socialist' Julius Nyerere of Tanzania energetically promoted modernisation and economic development of precisely the sort Rider

Haggard's Sir Henry Curtis pledged to oppose at the end of *King Solomon's Mines* and *Allan Quatermain*.

It seemed for a time as though the psycho-social agenda of safeguarding civilisation through repression that the Edwardian conservative artists shared with Freud would succumb to the all-conquering forces of modernism with its counter project of embracing primitivism and lifting the lid on the contents of the subconscious. This was especially so during the brief heyday of surrealism in the 1930s. However, as this book has argued, the modernists and the Edwardian imperialists had more or less identical conceptions of the primitive and the psyche. Both faced fundamental challenges when anthropology questioned the presumption of savage irrationality and the 'savages' spoke up for themselves.

Whether aligned with Franz Boas or Stanislaw Malinowski, the most influential twentieth-century anthropologists tried to show that what Western minds had dismissed as irrationality in savage life made perfect sense when viewed from another perspective. Apparently pointless customary practices, taboos and kinship systems had evolved to suit peculiar environments. Far from acting out the wild impulses of the id, so-called primitive peoples were governed in most aspects of their lives by complex rule systems and patterns of culture that 'functioned' to ensure production and reproduction. That called into question the whole analogy between imperial rule and psychic repression that had proved such a fruitful source of creative energy for the subjects of this book.

During and after decolonisation, the Empire began, in the well-known phrase, to 'write back'. With the expansion of educational opportunities after the Second World War young people encountered the fiction of Haggard, Buchan and Conrad but failed to recognise themselves. African novelist Chinua Achebe comically observed after reading *King Solomon's Mines* and *Prester John* that:

> I did not see myself as an African ... I took sides with the whitemen against the savages. In other words I went through my first level of schooling thinking I was of the party of the white man in his hair-raising adventures and narrow escapes. The whiteman was good and reasonable and intelligent and courageous. The savages arrayed against him were sinister and stupid or, at the most, cunning. I hated their guts.[1]

As they grew up, writers like Achebe and Ngugi wa Thiongo found their youthful readings not so much an inspiration as 'a wonderful preparation for the day we would be old enough to read between the lines and ask questions'.[2] Taking a wider view, Nigerian playwright Wole Soyinka came to see the Edwardian romancers as intellectually linked to Renaissance authors such as Hakluyt and to the ancient Greek traveller Herodotus. The 'notorious' Conrad was simply one in a long procession of writers engaged in the 'fictioning of Africa'.[3]

Even when considered from a purely European point of view, romantic heroes like Allan Quatermain had had their day by the 1930s. Their weird excursions into self-discovery, attained through confrontation with internal and external savagery, disappeared from contemporary popular literature even as they won new generations of readers. Although a direct line of descent can be drawn from Buchan's Richard Hannay to H. C. McNeile's Bulldog Drummond to Ian Fleming's James Bond, Drummond and Bond emerge from war service rather than the far-flung Empire. They also differ from Hannay in their lack of hidden depths. They are tough, strong, ruthless, uncomplicated. Indiana Jones is a cinematic caricature deriving from Allan Quatermain and T. E. Lawrence (a trained archaeologist with a phobia for reptiles) but operates out of the United States. Wilbur Smith's novels owe some debts to Haggard, but differ in their more overt articulation of the gung-ho great white hunter ideology still treasured by the descendants of white settlers in Southern Africa. Like Bond, Smith's hunter Courtney meets plenty of shes but no She-who-must-be-obeyed.

Herbert Baker and Edward Elgar have no counterparts in architecture or music of the post-Second World War era. No architect since Baker has used landscape as he did to project an image of imperial power. And, of course, with decolonisation the market for such buildings dried up. British composers Ralph Vaughan Williams and William Walton tapped a vein of Englishness and monarchical pomp that derives from Elgar, but neither attempted much in the way of music for Empire. Benjamin Britten's generation evinced revulsion for both Elgar's politics and his music. 'Little England' flourished as never before in the arts of the 1950s and 1960s. Contemporary American composer John Williams has shown his ability to whip off an imperial march fit to stand alongside the best of them, but without serious political ideological purpose. For grand British patriotic occasions like the 'Last Night of the Proms' and the 2012 London Olympics, present-day audiences can choose between Elgar and, well, Elgar.

Though the work of the imperial romancers has not lost its power to move and charm, the particular confluence of politics, science and aesthetics that brought it into being is gone, never to return.

Notes

1 Ezenwa-Ohaeto, *Chinua Achebe: A Biography* (Oxford: James Currey, 1997), p. 27.
2 Ibid. See also Carol Sicherman, *Ngugi wa Thiongo: Making of a Rebel* (London: Hans Zell, 1990), p. 21.
3 Wole Soyinka, *Of Africa* (New Haven, CT: Yale University Press, 2012), pp. 38, 40.

INDEX

Note: Literary and other creative works are listed under the creator's name.